ROUTLEDGE LIBRARY EDITIONS: LITERARY THEORY

Volume 21

LITERATURE AS COMMUNICATION AND COGNITION IN BAKHTIN AND LOTMAN

LITERATURE AS COMMUNICATION AND COGNITION IN BAKHTIN AND LOTMAN

ALLAN REID

LONDON AND NEW YORK

First published in 1990 by Garland Publishing

This edition first published in 2017
by Routledge
2 Park Square, Milton Park, Abingdon, Oxon OX14 4RN

and by Routledge
711 Third Avenue, New York, NY 10017

Routledge is an imprint of the Taylor & Francis Group, an informa business

© 1990 Allan Reid

All rights reserved. No part of this book may be reprinted or reproduced or utilised in any form or by any electronic, mechanical, or other means, now known or hereafter invented, including photocopying and recording, or in any information storage or retrieval system, without permission in writing from the publishers.

Trademark notice: Product or corporate names may be trademarks or registered trademarks, and are used only for identification and explanation without intent to infringe.

British Library Cataloguing in Publication Data
A catalogue record for this book is available from the British Library

ISBN: 978-1-138-69377-7 (Set)
ISBN: 978-1-315-52921-9 (Set) (ebk)
ISBN: 978-1-138-69358-6 (Volume 21) (hbk)
ISBN: 978-1-138-69359-3 (Volume 21) (pbk)
ISBN: 978-1-315-53029-1 (Volume 21) (ebk)

Publisher's Note
The publisher has gone to great lengths to ensure the quality of this reprint but points out that some imperfections in the original copies may be apparent.

Disclaimer
The publisher has made every effort to trace copyright holders and would welcome correspondence from those they have been unable to trace.

LITERATURE AS COMMUNICATION AND COGNITION IN BAKHTIN AND LOTMAN

Allan Reid

GARLAND PUBLISHING
New York & London
1990

To Maria, Patryk, Michal and Bernard,

with love and thanks for their patience and support

Copyright © 1990 by Allan Reid
All Rights Reserved

Library of Congress Cataloging-in-Publication Data

Reid, Allan.
 Literature as communication and cognition in Bakhtin and Lotman/ Allan Reid.
 p. cm.—(Garland studies in comparative literature)
 Includes bibliographical references (p.
 ISBN 0-8240-2521-0 (alk. paper)
 1. Bakhtin, M. M. (Mikhail Mikhailovich), 1895–1975.
 2. Lotman, IU. M. (IUrii Mikhailovich), 1922– .
 3. Literature—History and criticism—Theory, etc.
 4. Criticism—History—20th century. I. Title. II. Series.
 PG2947.B3R45   1990
 801'.95'0947—dc20   90-3759

Printed on acid-free, 250-year-life paper.
Manufactured in the United States of America

CONTENTS

Preface	ix
I Introduction	3
I.1 General Statement of the Problem	3
I.2 Methodology and Organization	4
I.3 The Question of Authorship	5
Notes	19
II The State of the Question	31
II.1 The Moscow-Tartu School on Bakhtin	31
II.2 Bakhtin on Soviet Semiotics	37
II.3 The Bakhtin-Lotman Connection in Western Scholarship	45
Notes	51
III LITERATURE, LANGUAGE AND LINGUISTICS	65
III.1 Russian Formalism and the Question of Literariness (Literaturnost')	66
III.2 Czech Structuralism and the Aesthetic Function	70
III.3 Roman Jakobson - Poetry and Linguistics	73
III.4 Bakhtin - Content, Material and Form	76
III.5 Lotman's Definitions of Literature	91
Notes	107
IV BAKHTIN AND LOTMAN LITERATURE AS COMMUNICATION AND COGNITION	131
IV.1 Methodology	132
IV.2 Text	140
IV.3 Communication	144
IV.4 Cognition	153
Notes	162
V CONCLUSION	179
Notes	183
VI BIBLIOGRAPHY	185
VI.1 Works by Bakhtin and the Bakhtin Circle	185
VI.1.1 Works by Bakhtin.	185
VI.1.2. Works by the Bakhtin Circle.	186

VI.2 Works by Lotman and the Moscow-Tartu School	187
VI.2.1 Anthologies, Journals, *Festschriften*, etc.	187
VI.2.2 Works by Lotman.	188
VI.2.3 Works by other members of the Moscow-Tartu School.	192
VI.3 General Works	193
VI.4 Works on Cybernetics, Information Theory, and Philosophy of Science	208
VI.5 Bibliographical Works	209

PREFACE

Since his re-emergence from exile and enforced silence some 30 years ago, Mikhail Mikhailovich Bakhtin has become a dominant figure in diverse areas of the humanities and social sciences. He has been both fiercely embraced and sharply rejected by thinkers from all across the spectrum of ideologies and methodologies. At present, there are indications that a period of revisionism is setting in, and it can be hoped that this will temper and restrain the scope of the debates around Bakhtin's ideas while leading us to an even greater appreciation of the depth of his insights.

Iurii Mikhailovich Lotman, a somewhat younger colleague of Bakhtin's, is probably the only scholar of the Soviet era to have undertaken a project as vast and complex as Bakhtin's. They stand out as giants against a rather mediocre background, almost as barren as the terrible Siberian wasteland which has witnessed the squander of so much human potential in that country. Lotman, though certainly not a stranger to western scholars, is not nearly as well known as Bakhtin outside of the Soviet Union, and certainly not outside the field of literary studies. No doubt, this is partly a reflection of his own peculiar style and the difficulties he presents to his readers whether in the original or in translation.

What is particularly striking, however, is that no serious attempt has been made to bring these two thinkers into confrontation on the central questions of their respective theoretical enterprises. Bakhtin has been compared to nearly everyone and everything; Lotman is almost always considered alone. It became clear to me several years ago that there are strong and important reasons for trying to fill this gap and that is what I set out to do in what follows.

      I was first introduced to Bakhtin and Lotman in a series of lectures by Dr. Lucjan Suchanek of the Institut filologii rosyjskiej of the Jagiellonian University, Cracow, Poland, while I was there studying and doing research in 1980-81. Subsequently, Dr. R.L. Busch of the University of Alberta further stimulated my interest in this direction through his perceptive incorporation of Bakhtin and Lotman into several graduate courses in Russian literature. I am very fortunate that Dr. Busch agreed to be my doctoral supervisor and I owe a great deal to his constant encouragement and support , his constructive criticism and advice. His personal commitment and deep familiarity with Russian literary theory were sources of inspiration and perseverance. Among others who deserve special acknowledgement and thanks, I would like to single out Dr. E. Mozejko, of the University of Alberta, an outstanding scholar and teacher, whose assistance and support has been invaluable.

LITERATURE AS COMMUNICATION AND COGNITION IN BAKHTIN AND LOTMAN

I INTRODUCTION

I.1 General Statement of the Problem

In this dissertation I intend to argue for the existence of a significant connection between the theories of literature and culture of Mikhail Mikhailovich Bakhtin (1895-1975) and Iurii Mikhailovich Lotman (b. 1922). There is general, if largely tacit, agreement in the academic or scholarly community that there is such a connection; however, it is generally held to refer to Bakhtin's influence on Lotman from the late 1960's and/or Bakhtin's critical views of Lotman which he expressed late in his life. The major thrust of this study, meanwhile, is to demonstrate that the critical theories of Lotman and Bakhtin are highly compatible independent of and prior to any direct influence. While they each belong to separate schools and generations, and they actually had little if anything in the way of specific, direct, formative influence on each other,[1] still, in many central respects they share considerably more with each other than they do both with their own contemporaries and with those whose labels they sometimes wear and whose battle trenches they frequently share. This commonality, or compatibility, as I see it, extends:
(a) to their respective notions of what literature is--if not terminologically, then at least by the ramifications of these notions;
(b) to the relationship of literature to other areas of culture, especially the particular manner in which literature and all of culture are related to language; (c) to methodological considerations of how we know, study

and theorize about literature. While Bakhtin and Lotman also have significant points of difference--how could they not?--including terminology, emphasis, and aspects of their methodological orientation, these differences are not nearly as striking or as fundamental as that which separates them from other theorists and schools with nominally similar orientations. And here reference must be made especially to Russian formalism, to Czech structuralism, to separate trends within the Soviet semiotics movement, and less frequently to western variants of structuralism and semiotics.[2]

What Bakhtin and Lotman have most significantly in common is best expressed in terms of the notion of literature as information and communication, and as part of cognition, especially as it involves the referential and broadly contextual semantic orientation which this gives to the study of and theorizing about literature. This manifests itself most obviously in their notions and concepts of language and language use, their critical attitudes to formalist approaches to literature, their strong grounding in and use of history, and their notions of culture and of the relation of literature to the broader system of culture, including the other systems within it.

I.2 Methodology and Organization

In this study I will examine various aspects of the problem at hand in several ways. I will want to establish a historical perspective which locates Bakhtin and Lotman historically within their disciplines. I will present a review of how their relationship has been referred to and described to date. Because the role of history is an important element in the work of both these scholars, history will also merge with analysis. This will especially be true when I turn to the question of how Bakhtin and Lotman reacted to and defined their positions in terms of their predecessors. These historical questions will not all be raised in one section of the study but will arise in various sections as required by the material at hand.

I will also select and analyze certain basic concepts which are central to the works of Bakhtin and Lotman. In particular I will examine their respective notions of what language is, what literature is, how language and literature are related, and how they are located in the field of culture. In examining these areas I will discuss Bakhtin and Lotman each separately and then, in conclusion, point up whatever significant points of interrelationship emerge. The final section of my study will examine those fundamental principles which bring these two literary theoreticians together, primarily in the key areas of methodology, communication and cognition.

The bodies of work of both thinkers are imposingly large and complex and have evolved and changed with time.[3] In this study I will refer to most of their major works and numerous smaller works. Both more strictly theoretical studies and works devoted to applications of theoretical principles will be discussed.[4] Some further bibliographical considerations will be introduced in the discussion of the question of authorship below. Secondary literature has been gathered from a broad range of sources and will be referred to when necessary and useful. The literature on Bakhtin and Lotman appears to be growing very rapidly with predictable variations in quality, yet the combined study of these two scholars is still largely a neglected area: I hope to contribute something to begin the process of filling this lacuna, and establishing, at the very least, that the study of the connection between these two theorists is a valid undertaking and yields worthwhile results.

I.3 The Question of Authorship

While he still remains, in many respects, an enigmatic figure, detailed biographical studies of Bakhtin do exist. The major biographical monograph by Clark and Holquist[5] is to be singled out as the most complete and competent, but one should also mention other studies, including especially the pioneering article by Kozhinov and Konkin,[6] and Todorov's biographical introduction to his study of Bakhtin.[7] Practically all other biographical writings follow or are based on these works, especially on the first two.[8]

Although Lotman the man is no stranger to many of his colleagues inside and outside the Soviet Union, no one as yet has undertaken to present him to the broader public, i.e. to those not fortunate enough to have been his student or colleague, or to have attended one of the famous "summer schools" or other symposia led or attended by him.

A short biographical essay was prepared for the *Festschrift* dedicated to him on the occasion of his 60th birthday,[9] but it is more like an annotated *curriculum vitae* than a biography.[10] The scant biographical references in Ann Shukman's monograph on Lotman and Soviet semiotics also stay within the context of his *curriculum vitae*.[11] The brief bio-article by Victor Terras in Handbook of Russian Literature[12] is even less helpful. Terras is first of all unacceptably terse in treating such a major figure. More importantly, however, in this rather brief paragraph he makes a number of misleading or incomplete statements, for example: "Lotman has expanded his structural-semiotic approach to some areas beyond literature, such as the theater, film, the visual arts, and general culture." Given the crucial importance and abundance of Lotman's general culturological studies, especially after 1970, it is inappropriate to dispose of them in this way or to group them together with his far more limited, if important, studies of film and visual art. Terras refers to a journal he calls Trudy po russkoi i slavyanskim literaturam, which sounds like a mistranslation back into Russian of an English translation of the real title which is Труды по русской и славянской филологии.[13] Similarly he incorrectly cites and annotates a journal he calls *Semeiotike*, which is really the first word in the title of the series usually known as Труды по знаковым системам, to which he refers elsewhere in this brief paragraph. One wonders if Terras has ever actually seen the journals he is writing about. This clearly points up the need for some sort of authoritative scholarly biographical work on Lotman.[14] He has become a major figure in the semiotics movement, known, respected, studied and translated throughout the world; however his biography, except for the terse details of his scholarly career, largely remains to be written. Nevertheless, Lotman the man, while largely unknown, though still alive, seems less enigmatic or problematic than the figure of Bakhtin, recently deceased and quite extensively researched.[15]

Since I have nothing new to contribute, I do not wish to take up strictly biographical concerns except for one key aspect of Bakhtin's biography which any study of his work must confront. This is the question of the authorship of certain works variously attributed to Bakhtin and/or certain of his friends and interlocutors, in particular P.N. Medvedev (1891-1938) and V.N. Voloshinov (1894-1936). Medvedev and Voloshinov were members of the so-called Bakhtin circle or circles, also known as the Bakhtin School. It was not an organized entity, being more like a regular gathering of friends and fellow-spirits. While it has come to be referred to as the Bakhtin circle in recent years, at the time it was meeting it was informal and collegial. It "met" at various times in Vitebsk, Nevel, and Petrograd/Leningrad during the early years of the Soviet period, i.e. until such gatherings became practically impossible due to the threat and/or fact of arrest and similar inconveniences. Its members included at various times a number of outstanding individuals--thinkers, artists, and scholars--such as L.V. Pumpian'skii, M.B. Iudina, B.N. Zubakin, M.I.Kagan, I.I. Sollertinskii, Marc Chagall occasionally, N. Klinev, K.K. Vaginov, M.I. Tubianskii, and I.I. Kanaev. Topics of discussion and study included a wide range of questions in the areas of philosophy, theology, the arts, sciences and politics.

As noted, the first mention of the circle many years after it and most of its members had ceased to exist was by A.A. Leont'ev in a short work on psycholinguistics.[16] Almost in passing he devotes about two pages to the Bakhtin circle and Voloshinov's Marxism and the Philosophy of Language in particular.[17] The circle and its works did not attract a great deal of attention until 1973 when Viach. Vs. Ivanov burst upon the scene with his article "On the Significance of Mikhail Mikhailovich Bakhtin's Ideas on Sign, Utterance, and Dialogue for Modern Semiotics," and his claim therein for attributing the authorship of the disputed texts to Bakhtin.[18] Since that time, it has become a major issue, although it is questionable whether anyone has faced it in its full implications.[19] Irwin Titunik quite aptly summed up the general state of the question in 1976 and again in 1984, when he made the following statement concerning the Bakhtin scholarly legacy:

> In its full dimensions this problem turns out to be so fraught with puzzles, enigmas, contradictions, unanswered--even unasked--questions on so many different levels (including that of straight biographical and bibliographical information) and so charged with hidden (whether real or imagined) political implications (*sub specie sovietica*) as to boggle all but the mind unusually adept at what are usually called 'byzantine intrigues.'[20]

Today, in 1989, the situation remains essentially the same as Titunik described it 5 years ago.

The list of which works are "disputed" forms part of the controversy, and varies significantly.[21] The works with which I am most concerned are those by Voloshinov and Medvedev, and especially--because of their importance--Voloshinov's books on Freudism and on Marxism and the philosophy of language, and Medvedev's book on formalism.[22] It is worth noting that the fluidity of the list is a significant point against accepting the arguments put forward by those who would attribute all or conceivably any of them to Bakhtin, as it points up how questionable and frequently *ad hoc* their arguments are.

While it is obviously crucial to the fullest understanding of Bakhtin to be able to delimit his opus and identify its components, given the *status quo*, I would contend that in the case of Bakhtin, this is, strictly speaking, not possible at present. Although respected scholars have made bold statements, proclaimed possession of incontrovertible evidence, and put forward various arguments in favor of attributing authorship of the texts to Bakhtin, the evidence is essentially missing, and the arguments are specious at best but more often non-existent. On the other hand, those who argue for non-attribution or diminished attribution of these texts to Bakhtin make more plausible, common-sensical, and text-based arguments, and they have the obvious advantage of not having to produce documentation beyond the names of the authors found on the published texts. This latter point is, as I see it, the crucial one, despite its surface banality. I will outline some details of the problem presently, but let me say at the outset that I would strongly contend that if there is no persuasive evidence--hard documentary evidence--to back up a claim for authorship, it should not be made. However, when made, it should be considered a hypothesis or speculation, not a fact.

My position, therefore, is the exact opposite of Clark and Holquist's, when they say " . . . nothing has established that Bakhtin could *not* have written the disputed texts and published them under friends' names."[23] Such a remark flies in the face of the fundamental tradition of Anglo-American jurisprudence established over several hundred years according to which innocence is presumed until guilt is proved. Surely the burden of proof is on those who would revise the apparent "facts". If there is new information contrary to the situation which is held to obtain, then it must be produced and shared. Let me turn to a brief review of the question.

In his seminal and ground-breaking essay of 1973, Viach. Vs. Ivanov, in his closing footnote, claimed the testimony of witnesses and inter-textual corroboration for the then startling assertion that Bakhtin was the author of the disputed texts.[24] He did this in an almost offhand manner, and since that time, i.e. during the last fifteen years or so, although he has frequently repeated his claim,[25] he has not advanced his case materially, logically, or in any other way. The so-called inter-textual corroborations are in need of much support and elaboration, and ultimately, are anything but clear, as he would have it.[26] The witnesses he mentions have never been named[27] and there are no apparent reasons for their remaining secret, as this is not at all a hands-off matter in the Soviet Union.[28] Ivanov once compared the purported publishing by

Bakhtin of his works under other's names with Soren Kierkegaard's use of pseudonyms.[29] This is ludicrous almost beyond belief. First of all, the Dane's pseudonyms were just that, pseudonyms, and secondly, the complex psychological and philosophical reasons for his use of them[30] really bear no analogy to the Bakhtin situation no matter how one assesses it.

Besides Ivanov, a number of commentators and scholars have devised ingenious ways of accounting for or supporting the unusual publication practices posited by Ivanov *et al*. Albert J. Wehrle[31] makes several "contributions" to the discussion. He relates an experiment conducted by a certain V.N. Turbin in 1965 (!).[32] The intent was to try to pin down Bakhtin on the question of who had written <u>The Formal Method</u>. Bakhtin had already apparently provided several responses which were somewhat at variance with each other. Turbin quietly "laid a copy of <u>The Formal Method</u> on the table without a word. Bakhtin said nothing, but his wife exclaimed: 'Oh, how many times I copied that!'"[33] This is apparently taken as evidence in support of Bakhtin's authorship. Of course, it proves nothing, and what is more, it follows a reference to the fact that the Bakhtins and the Medvedevs were living together *communally* at the time the book was being written.[34] This circumstance suggests that even if Mrs. Bakhtin did copy it, it need not have been Bakhtin's. Wehrle also refers to the somewhat authoritative statements by Vadim V. Kozhinov that the disputed texts were written "on the basis of conversations with Mikhail Mikhailovich."[35] Wehrle, it would seem, wants it both ways.[36]

He proceeds to conjure up a scheme according to which Pushkin's <u>Повести Белкина</u>, with its complex relations between levels of speech, forms an analogy with the Bakhtin/Medvedev/Voloshinov situation. Because his argument is totally devoid of logic--he himself calls it speculation--it could only be reproduced word for word, and I will forego that exercise. Independently of his argument, he arrives at the conclusion that "the works of the Bakhtin school can be seen as the realization of a dialogic interaction."[37] This not very astounding conclusion does not speak to the problem of authorship as it could refer to any such interactive endeavor. He then suggests a possible framework for a stylistic analysis of the texts, but it is rather superficial.[38] He refers to correspondence from Kozhinov in which the latter notes "it is a long story."[39] He relates that V.N. Turbin feels that Bakhtin gave the text to Medvedev " . . . as a gift, in the communal spirit. This interpretation keeps alive the ethos of the early days of 'Marxist Romanticism.'"[40] Finally, he likens the Bakhtin school to a

Renaissance studio where the master oversees and plans the whole and assigns parts for realization to his students.[41]

Most scholars seem content to defer to the authority of Ivanov and/or of Clark and Holquist in the matter. Examples include B. Schnaiderman,[42] Clive Thompson,[43] and Thomas Winner,[44] who in addition to the authority of Ivanov, refers to private conversations he had with Bakhtin during which the latter is claimed to have confirmed his own authorship.

Tzvetan Todorov has made a number of statements on the subject but his "final" word would appear to reside in his most elaborate discussion of the question to date.[45] He looks quite thoroughly and evenly at most aspects of the question and arrives at the following conclusion:

> In the absence of truly convincing external evidence, . . . I would prefer to say that these texts were conceived by the same author(s) but that they were written, in part or in whole, by others."[46]

However, that does not work very well for him, and he must perform some "dialogical" acrobatics[47] which permit him to include the disputed texts in Bakhtin's bibliography and therefore in his biography. Accordingly, Todorov is able to devise a scheme for representing Bakhtin's development in terms of six periods, the second of which is described thus:

> 1926-1929: methodological and critical writings, aggressively Marxist, none signed by Bakhtin; this is the 'sociological' period. Working out of the ideas that will be the basis of the texts of the next period.[48]

The following period, the third, dependent as he says on the preceding one, includes the Dostoevsky book (1929). This dependency is on a period characterized by works which Bakhtin did not write--according to Todorov--and includes a book on Dostoevsky which he probably began to conceive--according to just about everyone, including Todorov[49]--as early as 1922, i.e. prior to this second period. If this were not already dubious enough, he then proceeds to the following conclusion:

> The existence of these definite periods in Bakhtin's life is undeniable, even if their exact boundaries are at times subject to uncertainty. And yet one can state, at the same time and with equal validity, that, properly speaking, there is no *development* in Bakhtin's work.[50]

Todorov's picture is rather confusing, since he does in fact say that Bakhtin both did and did not author the disputed texts, and did and did not develop over time, but at the same time, he does present a valuable review of the issues at the heart of the question.

Ann Shukman, in her brief "Introduction" to a collection of writings by members of the Bakhtin school, takes a more restrained approach: "The problem of the authorship of these works has already been fully and frequently aired and is probably ultimately insoluble."[51] She looks at both sides of the debate, and arrives at a position according to which a resolution resides in the realm of context or dialogue,[52] which is to say there is room to discuss the texts within the context of the Bakhtin circle without establishing the *ur-author*.

I would like to turn to Clark and Holquist's treatment of the question, but before doing so I will digress somewhat and take up another controversial aspect of Bakhtin's biography. This is the question of the role and place of religion in Bakhtin's life and thought and, in particular, Clark and Holquist's version of it. The reason for turning to it at this point is that it highlights serious methodological and scholarly deficencies in their monograph.[53] They devote an entire chapter entitled "Religious Activities and the Arrest"[54] plus numerous scattered references throughout the work to the matter of religion in Bakhtin's biography. They have *no* reliable documentation to support anything they say on this subject, other than that he and his associates had an interest in religion and theology, some of his associates and friends were committed to religious beliefs, while others were atheists, and there were a number of religious organizations and movements in the Soviet Union during the first decade after the Revolution with which Bakhtin was in fact not connected, although he may have shared some of their views but for the most part he did not. This chapter abounds in contradiction, circumlocution, speculation, and truly questionable scholarship at the same time as it hypostatizes speculation and possibility.

We read, for example, that "Bakhtin was a religious man. [. . .] He was known in intellectual circles of those days as a *cerkovnik* . . ."[55] Their source for this is a 1978 interview with Viktor Shklovskii, who "may have exaggerated Bakhtin's involvement in the church."[56] As if it had any bearing whatsoever, they believe they can strengthen their case by introducing the following information:

> But as late as April 19, 1925, Bakhtin's mother and sisters opened their Easter letters to Nikolai in Paris with the Russian Orthodox Easter Greeting 'Christ is risen!'[57]

This is obviously totally irrelevant if not tied to Bakhtin somehow, which it is not. Clark and Holquist go on:

> This term [*cerkovnik*] does not mean that he was a churchgoer but implies simply that he was ideologically committed to the church. Although he later became less involved in religion, he remained a believer in the Orthodox tradition all his life. [. . .]
>
> But Bakhtin was never a conventional Russian Orthodox in the sense of conforming to an organized religion. [. . .] His religious views came not so much from traditional Orthodox thinking within the church as from the religious revival in the early twentieth century. [. . .] Indeed he was not interested so much in religion as in the philosophy of religion. He and the other members of his group did not separate religious from other philosophical concerns.[58]

The first statement ("Bakhtin was a religious man.") is seriously contradicted by the last one, and in between there is a strong gradation from one to the other. One wonders how they did not see what they were in fact saying here. None of this is supported by documents of any kind except the reference to the Shklovskii interview which they themselves call into question. And the remainder of the chapter does nothing to improve or clarify the situation.

To the best of my knowledge, there is only one extant document which can be said to affirm Bakhtin's religious views.[59] It is a newspaper report of a debate on the topic of "God and Socialism" in which Bakhtin took part and which was held on Novmeber 27, 1918. In this report we learn only that in the debate Bakhtin stood on the side of religion, but that he was not totally against socialism, his reservations being voiced in terms of the concern that socialism does not have provisions to look after the dead. Clark and Holquist refer to this text but not in their discussion on religion. It is referred to in an earlier context, and no reference is made there to Bakhtin's religious views.[60] Perhaps this is because this unique document does not enlighten us as to Bakhtin's views on religion beyond implying that he had some, and its sarcastic, polemical and not very literate tone does not lend it much authority or credibility.

Further serious contradictions begin to emerge when the claims made in Clark and Holquist's biography are compared with statements made elsewhere by Holquist. In one place, for example, there is a totally different modality in reference to this question: "*If there is something like a God concept in Bakhtin*, it is surely the superaddressee, . . . "[61] In another place Holquist's presentation of the religious dimension is even less probable when he makes the following undocumented and certainly unsupportable assertion: " . . . the theoretical epicenter of his work--[is] how to reconcile modern linguistics with the biblical assurance that the Word became flesh . . . "[62]

This lengthy though not exhaustive excursion into Clark and Holquist's presentation of Bakhtin's religious views and activities was necessary in order to establish that the question of authorship is not the only aspect of Bakhtin's biography to show the effects of inadequate standards of scholarship and hypostatized speculation. Since other scholars rely so extensively on their presentation, together with Ivanov's version of the question, these things have a way of pervading the entire discussion in a manner which is deleterious to any attempt to arrive at a valid or true evaluation of the problem. In order to emphasize the extent to which this unscholarly methodology colors their discussion of the disputed texts, I reproduce the following passage from the chapter entitled "The Disputed Texts."

> After the closing of the Russian Contemporary in 1924, Bakhtin realized that he was not going to be able to publish his work. He thus had no other adequate source of income unless he published under others' names. Medvedev and Voloshinov were sufficiently cynical to see no harm in such a thing. Moreover, Medvedev, who was already helping Bakhtin out financially, was ambitious for his own academic and publishing career and wanted an impressive book to add to his dossier. An attack on the Formalists would be especially timely. He therefore contracted with Bakhtin for Bakhtin to write the Formalism book, in return for which Medvedev undertook to help get Bakhtin's Dostoevsky book published. Bakhtin later declared that the Dostoevsky book would never have been published in 1929 if it had not been for Medvedev's help.* The cynicism was not all on Voloshinov's and Medvedev's side. Bakhtin was himself a great lover of rascals and would have taken delight in pulling off so large-scale a hoax.[63]

The entire passage is, first of all, undocumented, except one reference--which I have marked here with an asterisk (*)--to an interview with Viktor Shklovskii, and he is here identified as a witness of questionable credibility.[64] Secondly, except for the last sentence, or more properly the last clause,[65] the entire passage is written in the indicative mood, which in a serious biography suggests factual narrative. In fact, it is *pure invention* and has no place in a serious scholarly biography. Unfortunately, the discussion of their presentation of the question of religion and the discussion of this passage cast a great shadow of doubt on their entire enterprise, and especially on what they have to say about the question of authorship.

They have a number of arguments for attributing the disputed texts to Bakhtin. They clearly admit--although they do not always take it into account--that there is no documentary evidence to decide the matter once and for all. Bakhtin's own behavior and statements in the 1960's and 1970's were highly ambivalent as they relate it. For example,

> In 1975 Bakhtin assented to the preparation of a document to clarify matters for VAAP, which states that Bakhtin wrote the three disputed books and one of the articles. . . . But when this document was presented to Bakhtin for his signature, he refused to sign it. At the level of legal evidence, this only deepens the mystery.[66]

All of this leaves room for considerable doubt, and not only on the level of legal evidence. Likewise, there are conflicting and unsupported eyewitness reports,[67] many of which are questionable and none of which comes even close to meeting common standards of documentation. Clark and Holquist refer at some length to the communal spirit of the Bakhtin circle and their methods of notetaking and notekeeping as an explanation of how the texts could have come to be published under names other than Bakhtin's,[68] and they even repeat, almost literally, and without the traditional footnote to recognize their source, Wehrle's analogy of the Renaissance studio.[69] They examine at somewhat greater length questions of style and ideology, but their arguments are of a very poor quality, and frequently *ad hoc*.[70] They apply very subjective categories and judgements to the effect that the better the material the more likely it is to have been written by Bakhtin as opposed to Medvedev or Voloshinov.[71] They suggest a text-based strategem for using methodology as a criterion, but it turns out to be extremely shallow. They refer to a feature which they characterize as

> an authorial strategy which was a hallmark of Bakhtin's longer publications, [including non-disputed texts]. This feature is an opening section which sets up two contrasting approaches to the subject at hand, . . . and then advances the author's own position as one that avoids the mistakes of either extreme.[72]

If Clark and Holquist had looked back to their reading of Aristotle, they would likely have recalled that "The Philosopher" used the same technique, which he probably developed by refining certain features of the typical Platonic-Socratic dialogue[73] or *dialectic*, and which has been used in various forms countless times since, and is usually called dialectic, whether in deference to Hegel, Marx, or the Greeks.

In the following section, I will discuss the views of Perlina and Titunik who offer views that take up major questions raised by Clark and Holquist and propose methodologies and solutions which are in sharp contrast to those of the biographers. It is worth noting beforehand that Titunik and Perlina do not arrive at totally compatible conclusions, though they do not actually contradict each other either. This highlights the need for an inclusive and more embracing methodology, but leaving aside that desideratum for the moment, an examination of their approach and arguments shows they are both, first of all, more thorough, secondly, more scrupulous, and finally, more objective than Clark and Holquist in particular, and practically all the other scholars who follow and share the latters' views in this matter.

In Nina Perlina's article, which is to be found in a special edition of the University of Ottawa Quarterly, which is to say it is not easily accessible, she is concerned that Clark and Holquist's assertion that Bakhtin "ventroliquized" his works through his friends undermines the differences among the three, not to mention underrating their respective contributions. In other words, while she will admit the possibility of some ventroliquism on Bakhtin's part, she adamantly refuses to allow Voloshinov and Medvedev to be called "dummies."[74] She puts forth a broadly based argument to the effect that Medvedev's works clearly do belong to him, while leaving room for the possibility or even likelihood of input, common ideas, and advice from Bakhtin, who was, after all, the dominant figure in the circle. She has a three-fold argument based on a broad contextual perspective in which she considers: "1. Medvedev's earlier articles; 2. some works of contemporary critics; 3. the works written by Bakhtin during the same period."[75] I will mention just some of the points she makes.

She notes that Medvedev was the author of over 65 published works, about 35 of which had appeared by the time the Formal Method was published.[76] It should be born in mind that Clark and Holquist had argued that Medvedev's publishing career needed a boost![77] Perlina points to a definite evolution of ideas through his works, not only in the disputed texts, but by referring to a large number of others as well, making at least a reasonable case for continuity of authorship. She shows some of the things that the three writers had in common, but also some things which Medvedev had in common with other contemporaries, e.g. Trotsky, Lunacharsky, and Plekhanov,[78] noting that it was for similarities to Trotsky in particular that he was eventually arrested. The point here is that to look for common ideas, themes, methods, etc., is only valid if it is done on a broader basis than just within the triad of Bakhtin-Medvedev-Voloshinov.

The obverse of this is demonstrated when she argues that Bakhtin's earlier work contra the formalists, i.e. "Проблема содержания, материала и формы,"[79] differs in significant respects--largely irreconcilable respects--from Medvedev's Formal Method.[80] For example, Medvedev uses quotes in his polemic very extensively, while Bakhtin eschews these, as he always does. This makes sense within Bakhtin's theory of discourse, since quotations torn from their context are not able to engage in meaningful dialogue with the text into which they are inserted. Again, why would Bakhtin write the Formal Method, after having completed a "methodological analysis of central concepts and problems of poetics on the basis of general systematic aesthetics."[81] The Formal Method, insofar as it is to a large extent a review and survey, is far less effective, and would seem to be redundant if written by Bakhtin. She notes some significant similarities and differences and concludes that Bakhtin's presence is felt, but not to the extent that he is to be considered the author. There is speculation that he may have written an introduction to his friend's work, but for political reasons it came to be impossible to include it in its original form, and so Medvedev incorporated it into the text along with other possible comments from Bakhtin.[82]

In reference to Voloshinov, she takes a different aproach. She notes that if we go by Ivanov's list of works by Voloshinov imputed to Bakhtin, it follows that the former never published anything. There were such scholars at the time, and no doubt there are some now, but Voloshinov does not appear to have been of their ilk.[83] Perlina uses a rather detailed analysis of terminology to demonstrate that the terminology of Marxism and the Philosophy of Language is far from unique or original.[84] She contends that through Voloshinov, Bakhtin has appropriated the vocabulary of Bogdanov-Malinovsky and empiriomonism. Her point is to show just how complex the problem of attribution is and the necessity of basing a resolution on as large a number of factors as possible. Her final word on Marxism and the Philosophy of Language is that Voloshinov is responsible for Part I and the first chapter of Part II, while the rest of Part II and Part III are Bakhtin's. This is particularly interesting when contrasted with Irwin Titunik's findings.

Writing in 1984,[85] without yet having read the manuscript of Clark and Holquist's biography, nor having read Perlina's article, which he appears not to have known, Titunik begins by presenting a brief but concise review of much of the issue. He pays his respects to those who claim first-hand knowledge of the answer, but reserves the right to remain skeptical in the face of a lack of hard evidence and especially in view of unresolved contradictions and puzzles.[86]

He turns to the question of why Bakhtin would have been motivated to publish under his friends' names. Here he offers samples of answers which have been proposed and notes that as a group they are highly inadequate and "bewilderingly various and at variance."[87] He then raises a number of questions, none of which he feels is critical, but each of which is the sort of itch that insists on being scratched. One of these is the question of quantity: if we take together all the works Bakhtin is imputed to have written during the period 1925-1929, it amounts to somewhere in excess of 1700 pages, most of it having been written in the last two years of that period, and the number of fields of study covered by those pages is also rather remarkable, perhaps improbable, though not impossible.[88]

Next, he takes up the matter of a near total absence of cross-referencing between texts with different signatories. He gives the three (he says two but gives three) cases of cross-referencing he has located. One of these is simply innocuous, while the other two are examples of explicit disagreement of Voloshinov with Medvedev. He poses the question of whether this is a case of Bakhtin disagreeing with Bakhtin![89] It would seem to be appropriate to expect cross-referencing when the subjects being discussed are very close or the same. He then very convincingly analyzes jarring inconsistencies in the usage of *key* terminology by the three scholars.[90] (The inconsistencies are not so jarring if the three authors are, in fact, three different people.)

The major concern of Titunik's article addresses the question of Marxism in the works of all three.[91] He points out major inconsistencies in interpretations by the leading scholars in the field, perhaps the most entertaining of which involves Roman Jakobson's preface to M. Yaguello's French translation of Marxism and the Philosophy of Language. In it, Jakobson makes it quite clear that he considers the Marxist elements to be an obvious expediency, a necessary evil and not a part of the exposition as such, while she in turn must delicately assert exactly the opposite in her introduction which immediately follows, and in which she wants to claim the work as a Marxist work. Titunik uses a comparative analysis of the role of Marxism in three works published and, he would contend, written by Voloshinov, to produce a very efficient argument (and here the word 'argument' is truly applicable) for the evolution of Voloshinov's views towards a clearly and consistently Marxist orientation which at the same time is at odds with Bakhtin's own works. Because his argument involves detailed textological maneouvres it is difficult to reproduce in an abbreviated form. He does not claim to have solved the puzzle, indeed, he suggests that there are perhaps now more puzzles, but he has cast the kind of doubt on the issue--actually more than I have related--which cannot be ignored or treated lightly.

In the last paragraph of his article, Titunik displays in a somewhat impassioned manner his genuine frustration with this problem, especially with those who refuse to admit there are serious questions to be resolved or, on the other hand, imply they have information which, for whatever reasons, they are not prepared to divulge.

> In sum, how is it conceivable that anybody could possibly accept the attribution of these and other works to Bakhtin without first learning the solution to the puzzles that the attribution generates? Good heavens, these puzzles of the Bakhtin legacy adhere in blatant, egregious, clamorous matters and issues. Why does nobody--particularly those "in the know"--seem able and willing to confront them squarely? [. . .] The story still waits to be told. [. . .] Isn't it time to let it all out? Won't we, all of us, be so much better off for the telling of it?[92]

I have presented this question at some length, because it is obviously very important. There is compelling, though perhaps not incontrovertible evidence in favor of leaving the attribution of the texts as they were published. The Soviet Copyright Agency VAAP does not see it this way, but I do. Until proof is forthcoming, which is clearly unlikely, or someone evinces some more compelling arguments based on extensive textual analysis, which is also unlikely, I suggest it is most prudent to assume that Medvedev and Voloshinov did write the books published under their names, which they were clearly capable of doing and likely did. It is also likely that they had some input from Bakhtin, the kind of input from which I suppose we all could benefit, namely the inspiration and guidance to exceed our limitations and see things in a way we probably could not achieve on our own. Accordingly, I will not take the disputed texts into account in my discussion of Bakhtin's works.

After the above discussion had been written, two new studies of immediate relevance by prominent Bakhtinian scholars came to my attention. One of these, (actually the second to appear), is a section of the introduction to Caryl Emerson and Gary Saul Morson's recent study dedicated to a critical re-appraisal of Bakhtin and his legacy.[93] They present a detailed analysis of the statements of some of the leading participants in the debate, especially Clark and Holquist, and Titunik. Their discussion is detailed, precise and well argued, and covers much of the same ground as my presentation above. In general, they reaffirm the majority of my arguments. Of course, they touch on a number of issues which I did not raise,[94] but overall, they arrive, by a similar route, at basically the same conclusions.

One work they refer to which I did not, is a recently published study by Perlina[95] which I had actually discovered just before the Emerson and Morson work. In this essay, Perlina adds three points of particular interest to this discussion.[96] The first concerns an article by I. Kanaev, "Contemporary Vitalism," written in 1926. Clark and Holquist had claimed Bakhtin was its author and they claimed Kanaev as their source. Perlina demonstrates very convincingly that whether or not Bakhtin had published the article under Kanaev's name, he had not written it, or at least not much of it. It was in fact culled and copied from a work by N.O. Losskii, an emigré philosopher, and in 1926, a *persona non grata* in the Soviet Union.

Her second contribution is rather light-hearted but at the same time has very serious implications. She proposes a model for attributing texts to Bakhtin, and in so doing she points up the folly of such an exercise in the absence of good reasons, and demonstrates just how facile the arguments of the attributors are.

Her third contribution concerns the question of how it came to be that so many scholars both in the Soviet Union and outside became involved in what now seems to be a serious misrepresentation of fact. (Although her tone is not that accusatory.)[97] She believes there was a conscious effort to create a "legend." The reasons for this *mifotvorchestvo*, as I would call it, she gives as the need to use Bakhtin's name in order to publish as much material as possible by other members of the Bakhtin school, to use his name to add validity to current (and competing) trends in literary and cultural studies in the Soviet Union, and so on. What neither she nor Emerson and Morson seem to consider is that such a full blown conspiracy--for this is precisely what it would be-- implies the tacit co-operation of several Soviet scholars who were--and this is not hyperbole--bitter professional and, to some extent, personal enemies.[98]

Unlikely as this hypothesis may seem, it nevertheless remains the only one which has been offered, and I can think of no other. It is complicated further by the passive acceptance and/or creative embellishment of the myth by so many western scholars with, up until just recently, very, very few exceptions. Hard as it may be to accept or countenance, this seems to be the only available explanation. Given Ivanov's nearly obsessive adherence to his claim, and no indication that anyone is prepared to divulge any secrets, it may be some time until we have a better, more precise explanation--if ever we do have one.

NOTES

1. This remark will be qualified below.
2. For historiographical and pragmatic reasons, I will remain, as far as possible, within the scope of Russian/Soviet literary theory. While it is necessary to contain the study within reasonable parameters, it should also be noted that this decision is not altogether arbitrary. Such western figures as e.g. R. Barthes and J. Kristeva can be excluded by premise, i.e. as being simply beyond the scope of the inquiry, but also by virtue of their not being at all central to the question at hand. Kristeva, in particular, has commented on Bakhtin, but the theories of both Barthes and Kristeva do not really touch or shed light on anything like a Bakhtin-Lotman connection. See e.g. Barthes, The Semiotic Challenge, tr. Richard Howard, (New York: Hill and Wang, 1988). Cf. also Viach. Vs. Ivanov's comments on Kristeva's reading of Bakhtin in Vyach. Vs. Ivanov, "The Significance of Mikhail Mikhailovich Bakhtin's Ideas on Sign, Utterance, and Dialogue for Modern Semiotics," in Semiotics and Structuralism: Readings From the Soviet Union, ed. and with an Introduction by Henryk Baran, (White Plains, N.Y.: International Arts and Sciences Press, 1976), 326-27, 354n. Cf. also e.g. Ann Shukman, Literature and Semiotics: A Study of the Writings of Yu.M. Lotman, Meaning and Art, vol. I (Amsterdam, New York, Oxford: North-Holland Publishing Company, 1977), 4-5, where she says "French Structuralism . . . has developed along lines rather different from those of the Soviet Semiotic movement"; and Tomas Venclova, Неустойчивое равновесие: Восемь русских поэтических текстов, (New Haven: Yale Center for International and Area Studies, 1986), 18.
3. On this point, see e.g. Clive Thompson, "The Semiotics of M.M. Bakhtin," University of Ottawa Quarterly 53, 1 (January-March, 1983), 11-12. Cf. Tzvetan Todorov, Mikhail Bakhtin: The Dialogical Principle, tr. Wlad Godzich, Theory and History of Literature, vol 13, Minneapolis: University of Minnesota Press, 1984), 3-13.
4. For specific details refer to the appropriate sections of the Bibliography.

5. Katerina Clark and Michal Holquist, Mikhail Bakhtin, (Cambridge, Mass. and London, England: Harvard University Press, 1984).
6. V. Kozhinov and Sergei Konkin, "Михаил Михайлович Бахтин: Краткий очерк жизни и деятельности," in Проблемы поэтики и истории литературы. (Сборник статей): К 75-летию со дня рождения и 50-летию научно-педагогической деятельности Михаила Михайловича Бахтина, Ed. Sergei S. Konkin, (Saransk: Kafedra russkoi i zarubezhnoi literatury, Mordovskii gosudarstvennyi universitet im. N. P. Ogareva, 1973), 5-19.
7. Tsvetan Todorov, The Dialogical Principle, ch. 1, "Biography," 3-13. Todorov's main contribution seems to be the questionable division of Bakhtin's life into a number of periods.
8. See also the much briefer bio-article by Holquist in Handbook of Russian Literature, ed. Victor Terras, (New Haven and London: Yale University Press, 1985), s.v. "Bakhtin, Mikhail Mikhailovich."
9. B.F. Egorov, "К 60-летию Юрия Михайловича Лотмана," in Finitis Duodecim Lustris: Сборник статей к 60-летию профессора Ю.М. Лотмана, comp. S. Isakov, (Tallin: Eesti Raamat, 1982), 3-20.
10. This is not a criticism of the article, simply a statement of fact.
11. Shukman, Literature and Semiotics, passim.
12. Handbook of Russian Literature, s.v. "Lotman, Yury Mikhailovich," by Victor Terras.
13. E.g., Ученые записки тартуского государственного университета, 139, Труды по русской и славянской филологии, VI, 1963, ed. B.F. Egorov, V.F. Adams, A.B. Pravdin, Iu.M. Lotman.
14. Of course, it also raises questions about Terras' editorship of the Handbook.

15. I have no doubt that someone is busy compiling materials for a biography, authorized or otherwise, but until such time as one is written, Lotman remains largely unknown as a man. "Уникальные человеческие качества Юрия Михайловича видны только лично его знающим, но его научный облик известен весьма широко: основатель и глава тартуской научной школы литературоведческого структурализма, один из пионеров семиотического изучения искусства, крупнейший теоретик-культуролог, автор фундаментальных исследований по русской культуре и литературе ХУИИИ−ХИХ вв." Ibid., 19-20.

16. A.A. Leont'ev, <u>Психолингвистика</u>, (Leningrad: n.p., 1967), 86-88. For the history and other details of the circle(s), including information on the members/participants, see Clark and Holquist, <u>Mikhail Bakhtin</u>, passim, Ann Shukman, "Introduction," in <u>Bakhtin School Papers</u>, <u>Russian Poetics in Translation</u>, 10 (1983), 1-4, Todorov, <u>The Dialogical Principle</u>, 3ff., and "М.М. Бахтин и М.И. Каган: (По материалам семейного архива). Публикация К. Невельской," <u>Память</u> 4, (Moscow, 1979, Paris, 1981), 249-52.

17. It should be noted that in so doing he set something of a trend. I refer to the fact that most of the concern with the Bakhtin circle and the disputed texts centres around this work which is, I would contend, although without the support of a real statistical analysis, the most quoted and referred to of all of "Bakhtin's" works.

18. Vyach. Vs. Ivanov, "On the Significance," 366-67, n. 1. Note that this article was based on an essay, apparently unpublished, read in 1970 on the occasion of a scholarly meeting celebrating Bakhtin's 75th birthday. Ibid., 343. See also O.G. Revzina's untitled report of the meeting in <u>Вопросы языкознания</u>, 2, 1971 (March-April), 160-162.

19. I am surprised no one has undertaken to do a computer based statistical-stylistic analysis of these texts. While I doubt it could produce definite results, still that would seem to be one

of the procedures which need to be pursued if the question is to be resolved, assuming it is resolvable. For a discussion of the current state of computer analyses of style in authorially disputed texts, see A.Q. Morton, "Authorship: The Nature of the Habit," The Times Literary Supplement, No. 4, 481, (February 17-23, 1989), 164, 174.

20. Irwin Titunik, "Bachtin &/or Voloshinov &/or Medvedev: Dialogue &/or Doubletalk?" in Language and Literary Theory: In Honor of Ladislav Matejka, ed. Benjamin A. Stolz, I.R. Titunik, Lubomir Dolezel, Papers in Slavic Philology, 5, (Ann Arbor: Department of Slavic Languages and Literatures, University of Michigan, 1984), 535. See also idem, "M.M. Baxtin (the Baxtin School) and Soviet Semiotics," Dispositio I, 3 (1976), 327-338. At least as late as 1986 his opinion remained unchanged, even, or especially, after reading Clark and Holquist's biography. " . . . Nothing I have read in that book has persuaded me to alter the attitude of skepticism expressed there [*i.e. in "Dialogue &/or Doubletalk"*]." Idem, "The Baxtin Problem: Concerning Katerina Clark and Michael Holquist's Mikhail Bakhtin," "Forum," Slavic and East European Journal XXX, 1 (Spring 1986), 94.

21. Clark and Holquist, Mihhail Bakhtin, give their list on pp. 356-57, Ivanov, "The Significance of Bakhtin's Ideas," gives his on pp. 342-3, while Titunik, "Dialogue &/or Doubletalk," gives a summary of lists on pp. 536-37. It should be emphasised that everyone seems to have his/her own list, but these are representative.

22. Pavel Nikolaevich Medvedev, Формальный метод в литературоведении: Критическое введение в социологическую поэтику, (Leningrad: Priboi, 1928, reprint, Hildesheim, New York: Georg Olms Verlag, 1974); V.N. Voloshinov, Марксизм и философия языка: Основные проблемы социологического метода в науке о языке, 2nd ed., Leningrad: n.p., 1930, reprint, The Hague, Paris: Mouton, 1972); idem, Freudism: A Marxist Critique, tr. I.R. Titunik, ed. I.R. Titunik and Neal H. Bruss, (New York: Academic Press, 1976).

23. Clark and Holquist, Mikhail Bakhtin, 147. Though this is not their first, nor necessarily their favorite argument, it is

24. See note 18 above.
25. E.g. Viach. Vs. Ivanov, "О Бахтине и о семиотике," Rossija/Russia, 2 (Torino, 1976), 284; and idem, Очерки по истории семиотики в СССР, (Moscow: Nauka, 1976), 215.
26. Cf. Titunik, "Dialogue &/or Doubletalk," 560-61.
27. Cf. Todorov, Mikhail Bakhtin, 7. "As far as the 'witnesses' whom Ivanov never identifies are concerned, one may well doubt their existence."
28. Unless, of course, they do not exist.
29. Ivanov, "О Бахтине," 284.
30. See Walter Lowrie, A Short Life of Kierkegaard, (Princeton, New Jersey: Princeton University Press, 1942).
31. Albert J. Wehrle, "Introduction: M.M. Bakhtin/P.N. Medvedev," in P.N. Medvedev/M.M. Bakhtin, The Formal Method in Literary Scholarship: A Critical Introduction to Sociological Poetics, tr. Albert J. Wehrle, (Baltimore and London: The Johns Hopkins University Press, 1978), ix-xxiii.
32. Ibid., x. This is the only reference in the literature to anyone considering the question prior not only to Ivanov's article but even prior to Leont'ev's mentioning of the Bakhtin circle in 1967. It should be noted that the reference is not supported in any way.
33. Ibid.
34. Ibid., ix.
35. Ibid., x.
36. As he puts it, "the speculations that follow are based on the premise that it is less likely that one of these accounts is erroneous than that both are somehow accurate within the situation as a whole." Ibid., x. He does not really confront the question of how that could be possible.
37. Ibid., xii.
38. Ibid., xii-xiv.
39. Ibid., xiv. Why not tell the story?
40. Ibid., xiv. Again, this is pure speculation. Indeed, Medvedev had some 35 published works by 1928! See the discussion of Perlina's analysis of Medvedev's authorship below.

[Note: entries above begin with item showing continuation; item 23 ends:] indicative of the sterility of their desire to prove or uphold their point. What is more, they repeat it in idem, "A Continuing Dialogue," "Forum," Slavic and East European Journal, XXX, 1 (Spring, 1986), 96-102.

41. Ibid., xxiii. This is, of course, conceivable, if just barely, but it is far from being *dialogical*.
42. B. Schnaiderman, "Semiotics in the USSR: (A Search for Missing Links)," Dispositio VI, 17-18 (Summer-Fall 1981), 103.
43. Thompson, "The Semiotics of M.M. Bakhtin," 12. "But Ivanov produced evidence to support his belief that three works published in the 1920's under the names of V.N. Voloshinov and P.N. Medvedev were in fact largely the work of Bakhtin. Ivanov's startling contention has been corroborated by both M. Holquist and T. Todorov, even though there is still considerable mystery . . ." This short passage contains at least three large errors: first, concerning Ivanov's evidence, of which there was and is none, at least in this context; second concerning the number three, which should be six; third, concerning Todorov's corroboration, for which see below. Accordingly, the word "corroborated" should be replaced by "repeated" or "echoed."
44. Thomas Winner, "Russian Theories of the Twenties and Thirties," Les littératures de langues européennes au tournant du siècle: Lectures d'aujourd'hui. Série D: La perspective critique soviétique. Cahier I, 1984, (Travaux du groupe de recherches international "1900"), Carleton University, 86 n. 1, and idem, "Jan Mukarovsky: The Beginnings of Structural and Semiotic Aesthetics," in Sound, Sign and Meaning: Quinquagenery of the Prague Linguistic Circle, ed. Ladislas Matejka, Michigan Slavic Contributions, No. 6, (Ann Arbor: University of Michigan, 1976), 451n.
45. Todorov, The Dialogical Principle, xi, and ch. I, "Biography," 3-13 passim.
46. Ibid., 8.
47. Ibid., 10-11.
48. Ibid., 12.
49. Ibid., 4.
50. Ibid., 12.
51. Shukman, "Introduction," 2. Cf. Titunik, "Dialogue &/or Doubletalk," 535, where he refers to the "unanswered--and even unasked--questions" involved in this issue.
52. Ibid., 2-4.
53. Note that Titunik also points to this in "The Baxtin Problem," 91-93.
54. Clark and Holquist, Mikhail Bakhtin, ch. 5, 120-145.

55. Ibid., 121.
56. Ibid., 370 n. 1. Elsewhere (376 n. 9) they also question Shklovskii's reliability as a witness, although they are far from consistent in this since they cite him as a firm authority in a closely related matter placed between these two notes, 375 n. 3.
57. Ibid., 370 n. 1.
58. Ibid., 120.
59. Молот, December 3, 1918, No. 47, quoted in "М.М. Бахтин и К.И. Каган," 273-274 n. 6.
60. Clark and Holquist, Mikhail Bakhtin, 43, 362n15.
61. Michael Holquist, Introduction to Mikhail Mikhailovich Bakhtin, Speech Genres and Other Late Essays, tr. Vern W. McGee, ed. Caryl Emerson and Michael Holquist, (University of Texas Press Slavic Series, No. 8, (Austin: University of Texas Press, 1986), xviii, (my emphasis, A.R.)
62. Michael James Holquist, "Bad Faith Squared: The Case of Mikhail Mikhailovich Bakhtin," in Russian Literature and Criticism: Selected Papers from the Second World Congress for Soviet and East European Studies, Garmisch-Parterkirchen, September 30-October 4, 1980, ed. Evelyn Bristol, (Berkely, Calif.: Berkely Slavic Specialities, 1982), 223.
63. Ibid., 151.
64. See note 56 above.
65. Which, incidentally, Titunik takes up at some length in "The Baxtin Problem," 93-94.
66. Clark and Holquist, Mikhail Bakhtin, 147.
67. Ibid., 147-48.
68. Ibid., 148-50.
69. Ibid., 150.
70. E.g. Ibid., 157, the paragraph beginning "Vladimir Propp . . ."
71. For an important examination of questions of style, in particular, see the discussion below of Nina Perlina's article "Bakhtin-Medvedev-Voloshinov: An Apple of Discourse," University of Ottawa Quarterly 53, 1 (January-March, 1983), 35-47. I will also note some of Titunik's arguments concerning ideology and Marxism.
72. Clark and Holquist, Mikhail Bakhtin, 158.
73. Bakhtin's discussion of *synchrisis* in Проблемы поэтики Достоевского, fourth edition, (Moscow: "Sovetskaia Rossiia," 1979), 127, merits comparison here.

74. Perlina, "B-M-V," 36.
75. Ibid., 38.
76. Ibid., 37.
77. Clark and Holquist, Mikhail Bakhtin, e.g. 151.
78. Perlina, "B-M-V," 39.
79. Mikhail Mikhailovich Bakhtin, "Проблема содержания, материала и формы," in Вопросы литературы и эстетики: Исследования разных лет, (Moscow: "Khudozhestvennaia literatura," 1975), (hereinafter ВЛЭ), 6-71.
80. Perlina, "B-M-V," 40-42.
81. Bakhtin, "Проблема содержания," quoted in Perlina, "B-M-V," 40.
82. Ibid., 40-42.
83. Ibid., 42-44. Clark and Holquist indicate that "Voloshinov graduated from the Philological Faculty of Leningrad University in 1927 and went on to graduate work under V.A. Desnitsky and N.A. Yakovlev in a group working on literary methodology at the Institute for the Comparative History of Literatures and Languages of the West and East. This institute represented a 'new Marxist approach' to linguistic study which challenged such undesirable approaches as the formalist. The topic of Voloshinov's dissertation was probably 'the problem of how to present reported speech' (*problema peredachi chuzhoi rechi*), which was cited as the topic of his research in an article on the institute published in 1928 in Literature and Marxism (*Literatura i marksizm*)." 110. It should not be too surprising to anyone that Voloshinov should be capable of writing a book on almost exactly the same topic as he was treating in his dissertation!
84. Perlina, "B-M-V," 44-47.
85. Titunik, "Dialogue &/or Doubletalk."
86. Ibid., 537-42 passim.
87. Ibid., 540.
88. Ibid., 542.
89. Ibid., 543-44.
90. Ibid., 544-46.
91. Ibid., 546-61.
92. Ibid., 560-61.

93. Rethinking Bakhtin: Extension and Challenge, ed. Gary Saul Morson and Caryl Emerson, (Evanston, Illinois: Northwestern University Press, 1989), 31-49.
94. E.g. the question of Bakhtin's possible motivations for publishing under others' names, and esp. some aspects of "what is at stake" in the whole problem.
95. Nina Perlina, "Funny Things are Happening on the Way to the Bakhtin Forum," Kennan Institute for Advanced Russian Studies, Occasional Paper #231, (March 1989).
96. Actually her paper makes several new points, but these three are of particular interest here.
97. Emerson and Morson also consider the question in somewhat similar terms. "Rethinking," 31-32.
98. Although it must be mentioned that they (the Moscow-Tartu scholars and the scholars grouped around the journal Контекст) did manage to co-operate on at least one project connected with Bakhtin, namely the publication of a *Festschrift* on the occasion of his 75th birthday, Проблемы поэтики и истории литературы.

II. THE STATE OF THE QUESTION

II.1 The Moscow-Tartu School on Bakhtin

There is a significant number of references to Bakhtin in the writings of the Moscow-Tartu school including some attesting to, though not elucidating, his influence on them. This is not unexpected, given that Bakhtin reappeared in print and in person around the same time as the Moscow-Tartu school was forming and emerging into prominence. Indeed, some members of the Soviet semiotics movement[1] figured prominently in the initiatives to see Bakhtin's works published and republished and to otherwise gain professional and official recognition and respect for him. Nevertheless, almost none of their references are of the kind which would help us understand how Bakhtin's thought changed or influenced the direction of their thinking either on specific questions or in general. One possible exception here is Boris Uspenskii's work on point of view.[2]

Still, by virtue of the large number of references to Bakhtin and to various related events, some of which will be referred to below, we can establish that Bakhtin was frequently "on their minds." He figured in major respects as a component of their analyses and evaluations of past developments and the tradition of literary scholarship in the Soviet Union (and Russia)--what they generally call the "pre-history" of structuralism. These discussions or analyses, for the most part, formed part of and took place within the context of the debates and polemics of the 1960s and 1970s on the question of precision and scientific methods in the study of literature, the state of literary scholarship in the Soviet Union, and the changing assessment of the contributions of Russian formalism to the theory and study of literature.[3]

In most respects, what the members of the Moscow-Tartu school have written about Bakhtin tells us more about them than about Bakhtin and his influence on them. As shall become evident, the majority of statements, some of which are quite extensive, are quite paradoxical insofar as, while they are generally full of praise for Bakhtin, they still do not say anything concrete or specific about his influence or role in the development of structuralism in the Soviet Union.[4]

One more problem further blurs this already largely indeterminate situation: I am aware of no evidence attesting to any but the most limited knowledge of Bakhtin's works prior to the republication of the Dostoevsky book in 1963.[5] This is peculiar if one recalls that its original publication in 1929 was debated in print, and it is unlikely that it was totally forgotten.[6] The same can be said of the Rabelais work which, though not actually published before 1965, did create quite a stir when Bakhtin defended it as his dissertation in 1946.[7] This must be seen to include a certain political dimension as well, since Bakhtin's name appears to have been proscribed until the early 1960s. Not to lose sight of what is known with certainty, however, it must be stressed that not only was Bakhtin not mentioned earlier, but there is also no evident trace of his influence.

The following discussion represents an analysis based on a review of certain core works of the Moscow-Tartu school[8] and a number of historical surveys from within the school which highlight its members assessment of and attitude towards Bakhtin.

The question of assessing historical developments in Soviet literary theory is one which has frequently attracted the attention of the members of the Moscow-Tartu School. It was, and presumably is, felt by Lotman and others that it is desirable and even necessary to study the trends and achievements of the past in order to better understand the *status quo*, and indeed, to be able to move forward.

> The history of literary studies as a discipline is basically undeveloped and undocumented (with the result that the level of *contemporary* scholarship, which sometimes commits carelessly to oblivion achievements of the past and disregards the level previously attained, has been lowered).[9]

Clearly, Lotman feels that an understanding and appreciation of past achievements is not only interesting but a necessary precondition for the development of the discipline.

In a series of papers, one from 1961,[10] and two from 1967,[11] Alexander Zholkovskii and Iurii Shcheglov discuss what they call the *prehistory* of Soviet structuralist poetics. In their works these two members of the Moscow-Tartu School tried to rehabilitate certain core concepts of Russian formalism which define the literary work of art immanently and synchronically in terms of its devices and mechanical organization.[12] Such notions are very nearly anathema to some other members of the movement including Ivanov, D. Segal, B.A. Uspenskii, Lotman, etc., and were also vehemently and vigorously opposed by Bakhtin.[13] These 1967 articles provoked cautionary rejoinders and rebuttals by Lotman and Ivanov.[14] While the Moscow-Tartu school was obviously never meant to be under the hegemony of any particular individual or ideology,[15] it was generally felt that it had, in broad terms, overcome the type of notions deriving from Russian formalism as were being enumerated and praised by Zholkovskii and Shcheglov.[16]

In his editorial comments preceding "Из предыстории"[17] Lotman cautions against accepting that version of the history in question as complete, but we have to look to his 1967 article in Вопросы литературы, to learn more precisely what he feels is missing.[18] Ivanov ranges widely in his article which takes up a number of dimensions of the question it addresses without exhausting it. He polemicizes in each case with varous opponents who are occasionally named (Palievskii, Zholkovskii, Shcheglov) but for the most part remain anonymous, though not likely unknown to the informed reader.

Confining the focus of attention to points relevant to the present discussion, it can be said that Ivanov has both restrained praise for the formalists[19] and their heritage and harsh, almost unrestrained criticism for Zholkovskii and Shcheglov. He calls their essay and the methodology it embodies unscientific, outdated, semiparodic, and sterile.[20] He decries their misrepresentation of Eisenshtein by foregrounding the "наименее оригинальное и содержательное" of all his ideas to which, moreover, they themselves subscribe.[21] Most importantly for the matter at hand, he presents Bakhtin as the model and inspiration for more adequate and fruitful studies of literature.

In particular, he refers to Bakhtin's trans-(meta-) linguistics and to his inter-relating of various cultural phenomena--history, social context, popular or folk consciousness, etc,--with literary phenomena.

Typically, however, he does not speak of Bakhtin's influence, only his achievements, which, it is implied, anticipated current studies in semiotics.[22] The case of Zholkovskii and Shcheglov demonstrates clearly that significant differences of opinion did (and do) exist inside the Moscow-Tartu School, and suggest that the appraisal and appreciation of Bakhtin is an important part thereof.

In view of this, Dmitri Segal's bold statement that "no author can be compared with Mikhail Mikhailovich Bakhtin as far as influence on modern Soviet Semiotics is concerned"[23] has a problematic ring to it. Segal, now in Israel, was a key figure in the rise of Soviet Semiotics and thus was in a privileged position to make such an assessment. However, he makes no attempt to substantiate the exact nature and modalities of this putatively incomparable influence, indeed, he does not even suggest what it may have involved. He does stress, without going into detail, the importance of the rediscovery of the works of the 1920s and 1930s. In reference to Bakhtin he simply defers to the above mentioned article by Ivanov from 1973 on Bakhtin's significance.[24] He makes no real contribution of his own to the discussion beyond the unsupported statement just quoted.[25]

Ivanov, in his article, attempts to establish Bakhtin as a precursor or, more precisely, anticipator of Soviet semiotics who made major discoveries in the field of semiotics which parallel the discoveries of other more recent scholars and anticipate the work being done by Soviet semioticians and especially by western scholars. He uses expressions such as *anticipates, is analogous with, parallels, precursor, had in common with*, etc., or occasionally such exceptional formulations as "virtually word-for-word correspondence with."[26] He seems to characterize his method in his paraphrase of G. Dumezil, who noted in 1969 that "the return to what had been discovered fully thirty years ago and then remained unnoticed has become normal in the humanities."[27] The re-discovery of a community of semiotic precursors from the 1920s and 1930s, including Eisenshtein, Vygotskii, and Florenskii, is seen as a positive factor in the current direction of investigations being undertaken within the Moscow-Tartu school.

Ivanov's aim, therefore, is to demonstrate the existence of a body of organic scholarly study in the 1920's and 1930's which both *anticipates* current work and which can make a contribution to it. However, on one level he makes little effort to demonstrate how the theories of Bakhtin, Eisenshtein, Florenskii and others arose and therefore he fails to contribute to our understanding of the historical process[28] which could have led in turn to a fuller understanding of the real relationship between Bakhtin and Soviet semiotics, whether in terms of legacy, anticipation, parallels or influence. On another level, practically all the parallels pointed to refer more to semiotics as it is practiced outside of the Soviet Union, or by other so-called precursors, especially Eisenshtein. While Ivanov has a very sympathetic attitude towards Bakhtin, it is clear from this essay and from his large work of 1976 entitled Очерки по истории семиотики в СССР,[29] that he is, at least as a scholar, more interested in Eisenshtein than in Bakhtin.[30] Of course, he is fully entitled to such a position. The only sense in which this is problematic is the manner in which Ivanov almost seems to use Bakhtin's name to make his points about Eisenshtein. This same deference to the classic film-maker is even more evident in at least two other essays, one "dedicated to the eternal memory of Mikhail Mikhailovich Bakhtin,"[31] and the other being Ivanov's contribution to the 1973 Saransk *Festschrift* dedicated to Bakhtin.[32]

While both Segal and Ivanov obviously have a clear sense of Bakhtin's genius and importance, their reader gets very little sense of how they view his relationship to Soviet Semiotics *in specific terms*, and, in general, gets confusing signals from both of them in this regard. There is, for example, reference to his acknowledged influence on Boris Uspenskii,[33] but there is little if anything to show how their discovery (or re-discovery) of Bakhtin changed, complemented, or reinforced particular areas of research or theory. Again, we look in vain for indications of how or if his published writings of the 1920's and 1930's were absorbed and handed down, whether via Soviet channels or via roundabout routes through Czech structuralism or French literary and anthropological studies, or combinations thereof. For example, are the similarities between Bakhtin's study of binary oppositions in carnival and Levi-Strauss' study of them in myth a result of the mediating influence of Roman Jakobson or simply coincidence?[34]

Ivanov's presentation leaves the reader wondering if, by virtue of anticipating--as he calls it--the work of an enormous number of outstanding scholars in a wide range of fields,[35] Bakhtin is just a curiosity or is there something more important to be discovered? Given their privileged position and their implicit and explicit acknowledgement of the importance of the question, it is unfortunate that Segal and Ivanov fail to take up the challenge of providing a more penetrating and meaningful analysis of the relationship between Soviet Semiotics and Bakhtin.

Boris Uspenskii, in his key work Поэтика композиции,[36] published in 1970, pays his respects to Bakhtin's role in opening up the area of point of view or perspective in relation to literature.[37] Although he extends it to painting as well, Uspenskii develops his project both on a more limited scale and on a more technical level than Bakhtin. He outlines four planes of point of view in literature: the ideological, phraseological, spatio-temporal, and the psychological. The one which is most directly related to Bakhtin's contribution, the ideological plane, is the one which he deals with the least. This is arguably because Bakhtin has already covered the ground, although more likely Uspenskii's interests are simply not in that sphere. Uspenskii clearly sees his work as dependent on contributions by Bakhtin, whose work receives a positive appraisal within a limited context.

While there appears to be no hard evidence of Lotman having direct knowledge of Bakhtin prior to the republication of the latter's study on Dostoevsky in 1963,[38] two points in particular made the establishment of contact around this time significant and fruitful. First of all, Lotman's training as a literary and cultural historian--as opposed to a stylistician or a prosodist, for example--made him highly receptive to Bakhtin's broad historical and cultural perspective.[39] Lotman had recently--beginning in the late 1950's--made the move towards a structural-semiotic approach to the study of literature (including close textual analysis), by concentrating on the recognition of various levels within the text, their functional dependence on mutual inter-relationships, including the consciousness of the author and reader, and the broad cultural system to which they relate referentially or "contextually." Like Bakhtin, Lotman, in appropriating aspects of the scholarly tradition of the 1920s and 1930s, had rejected the hegemony of the dualistic form-content distinction, the absoluteness of the synchronic-diachronic distinction, and perhaps most importantly in our context, he rejected the notion of literature as being, strictly speaking, a phenomenon of natural language use.[40] Bakhtin had proceeded similarly, and his focus on dialogue and communication, the cognitive and referential relations of literature to reality, and the overall semanticity of literature also echoed Lotman's own position.

One key factor in Lotman's appraisal of Bakhtin has been the latter's analysis of literature and culture in terms of various levels and oppositions, the tension between them, and the process of their neutralization in ambiguous texts.[41] Lotman stresses this very often in his references to Bakhtin and the importance of this concept in the work of both scholars is not to be underestimated.[42] Although there are as yet too many missing pieces to assert anything categorically, it would appear that one of the key factors in the development of Lotman's thought during the five or so years between the publication of his first and second major monographs[43] may well have been his discovery of and familiarization with Bakhtin.[44] This period also marks a movement away from Lotman's expressed desire for finding new applications for the use of statistical and mathematical methods in literary research,[45] which was, of course, anathema to Bakhtin.

Lotman has not made specific references to Bakhtin as anything like a formative influence. However, he has made many comments in which he clearly attempts to define his position relative to Bakhtin's, thereby establishing the nature of his great respect for the latter's ideas and acknowledging the need to define his own position in relation to them.[46] Clearly, he considers him to be an important part of the heritage of Soviet semiotics and of his own position. He has also made explicit the need to be cautious and to avoid exploiting Bakhtin's name and ideas in an imprudent and unscholarly manner.[47]

This demonstrates above all his sense of closeness to Bakhtin, and his sense of having come to terms with the latter's ideas in a dialogical sense. Frequently, he tries to develop Bakhtin's position, or to go beyond it.[48] In this context we might be able to speak of influence, which is surely an element here and elsewhere with Lotman and Bakhtin, but not the dominating factor of the relationship. It is probably best to view the relationship as a case of shared concerns, attitudes, values and methods. I would prefer to say that Bakhtin and Lotman have theoretical orientations which are compatible and mutually supportive or reinforcing on many levels: how and why remains to be shown.

II.2 Bakhtin on Soviet Semiotics

Clearly, analyzing the manner in which Bakhtin has been appraised by the Moscow-Tartu School reveals more about the appraiser than about the appraised. It is significant that certain divisions, trends, and perhaps shortcomings within the Moscow-Tartu School emerge from the analysis, and it is precisely the attitude of the Moscow-Tartu scholars to their own past which renders divisions among them concrete.

Despite his contacts with members of the Moscow-Tartu School,[49] and their fondness as a group (with notable exceptions) for him, Bakhtin, in his typically unpredictable fashion, had almost nothing to say, at least in print, about Soviet semioticians. In fact, I have located only three definite references to Lotman and his school.[50] All three should be considered within the context of the debates which were taking place in the Soviet Union between the structuralists and their various opponents during the 1960s and 1970s.[51]

The debates concerned, as mentioned above, questions of the applicability of precise methodologies in the study of literature, the evaluation of past contributions to the theory and study of literature in the Soviet Union, and other related questions. It should be remembered that the debate and polemic had dimensions which were not only theoretical, but political and economic as well. Like structuralism, the debate actually began in the mid-fifties during the post-Stalin thaw, and questions of the control of institutions, access to print media, and contact with western scholars and institutions were at stake. Bakhtin was not actively involved in these debates, although his Новый мир essay did bring him into the arena somewhat. He was, however, implicitly involved in two respects. First, his name occasionally appeared in articles written by other scholars, not just in the articles by Lotman and Ivanov mentioned above, but in others as well. Secondly, he published several essays[52] in the annual journal Контекст, which was in most respects an anti-structuralist publication. However, the debate and polemics of the period interest us here only as background, so I will not go into detail about any particular events or processes which formed and characterized it.[53]

The question which had been put to Bakhtin by the editors of Новый мир was "как я оцениваю состояние литературоведения в наши дни."[54] While recognizing a significant tradition--he mentions Veselovskii, Potebnia, Tynianov, Tomashevskii, Eikhenbaum, and Gukovskii--and an existing infrastructure, his overall evaluation is that literary studies in the Soviet Union are not in a good state, and are not taking advantage of their potential. He decries the lack of risk taking, bold hypotheses, and solid established methodologies. He does acknowledge that there is no shortage of truisms and clichés. He adds that one can find good work being done, occasional profound articles, and so on, but there are three large and relatively isolated positive phenomena to which he wishes to direct special attention: N. Konrad's book Запад и восток, D.S. Likhachev's book Поэтика древнерусской литературы, and Труды по знаковым системам, четыре выпуска (направление молодых исследователей, возглавляемых Ю. М. Лотманом)."[55] Bakhtin then indicates he will look at only two aspects of the study of the history of literature, ignoring other questions for the moment, and especially questions related to the study of contemporary literature and its history.

> Прежде всего литературоведение должно установить более тесную связь с историей культуры. Литература--неотрывная часть культуры, ее нельзя понять вне целостного контекста всей культуры данной эпохи. Ее недопустимо отрывать от остальной культуры и, как это часто делается, непосредственно, так сказать, через голову культуры соотносить с социально-экономичискими факторами. Эти факторы воздействуют на культуру в ее целом и только через нее а вместе с нею на литературу.[56]

He goes on to stress that it is insufficient both to study the specificity of literature--a remark directed at formalism and certain aspects of its heritage--and to study the history of literary movements in isolation. Here again, he would appear to be referring in the first place to the formal school and similar tendencies, but his criticisms also direct themselves to official notions of literature and culture. He goes on to expand and qualify his remarks and then confirms that Konrad, Likhachev, as well as Lotman and his school

> при всем различии их методологии одинаково не отрывают литературы от культуры, стремятся понять литературные явления в дифференцированном единстве всей культуры эпохи.[57]

This point, which could fairly be said to refer to the synchronic dimension of the question, i.e the view from an intersystemic perspective, is essential to Bakhtin's understanding of literature, and cannot be ignored. However, "еще более пагубно замыкать литературное явление в одной эпохе его создания, в его, так сказать, современности."[58] This, then, is the diachronic perspective. Bakhtin says that great literary works are prepared by centuries, that it is necessary to see their past, and how they grew into the future, enriched by new meanings.

> Автор——пленник своей эпохи, своей
> современности. Последующие времена
> освобождают его из этого плена, и
> литературоведение призвано помочь этому
> освобождению.[59]

Further, he speaks of each individual culture being not closed but open, and part of human culture.[60] While I could go on to present more individual statements he makes in this essay, this is its major point and thrust. It is important to see that it could almost be a manifesto of much of Lotman's writing from the periods both before and after its appearance. Much of the following chapters will be devoted to juxtaposing Lotman's and Bakhtin's ideas with regard to their compatibility, so I will not endeavor at present to provide quotes from Lotman to show precise details of how Bakhtin's program aligns with his. For now, it is important to stress that at this point Bakhtin feels that Lotman is carrying out a program which satisfies the criteria he is putting forward. I would add that of the three literary studies he mentions, Lotman's comes the closest to realizing Bakhtin's methodology and proposals.[61]

At approximately the same time as Bakhtin's essay was being published, he recorded in his notebook remarks referring to Lotman which are sharply and peculiarly at odds with what he stated in the essay. These notes were not published until 1979,[62] but that part which concerns us here, or a variation thereof, was repeated in print much earlier in the essay which will be taken up next. It should be remembered that the notebook records are just that: they are jottings, ideas recorded by Bakhtin without great regard for thematic unity, argument, cohesion, or flow. Some of them are reflections, others are critical observations of various phenomena, still others are ideas stored for further development. They must not be uncritically accepted as well-defined or definitive.

The reference to Lotman which interests us here occurs in the following fragment.

> Изучение культуры (и той или иной ее
> области) на уровне системы и на более
> высоком уровне органического единства:
> открытого, способного на гибель и обновление,
> трансцендирующего себя (то есть выходящего
> за свои пределы.) Понимание многостильности
> Евгения Онегина (см. у Лотмана) как

Literature as Communication and Cognition in Bakhtin and Lotman 41

> перекодирования (романтизма на реализм и
> др.) приводит к выпадению самого важного
> диалогического момента и к превращению
> диалога стилей в простое сосуществование
> разных версий одного и того же. За стилем
> цельная точка зрения цельной личности. Код
> предполагает какую-то готовность содержания
> и осуществленность выбора между данными
> кодами.[63]

Obviously, the passage is somewhat less than clear, or, to put it more directly, it is, at least in places, opaque and disjointed. We are not dealing with prepared lecture notes or a diary intended for other readers.

The reference to Lotman is to an article from 1965 published in Труды по знаковым системам II, i.e. to a part of the phenomena which Bakhtin so eagerly and openly praised in his Новый мир essay.[64] Why Bakhtin singled out this and only this particular article for criticism in his private notes is unclear, especially since by the end of 1970 Lotman had over 200 publications.[65] In this article Lotman wants to demonstrate how meaning is produced in different kinds of semiotic systems. He refers to what he calls internal (simple and multiple) transcoding and external (binary and multiple) transcoding. I will not go into detail on all of these variations, especially as Lotman does not sufficiently elaborate all aspects of the distinctions he makes between these processes. This is typical of Lotman: frequently he will raise a question, analyze it in terms of certain distinctions, and then take up only those aspects which concern him at the moment, leaving the reader to either take his word for the viability of the distinctions, or put his imagination and/or his own analytical skills to work. If the reader is unaware of this tactic, it can be quite confusing, but otherwise it is simply a means of getting to the heart of a problem as quickly as possible.[66]

As an example of multiple internal transcoding Lotman turns to romanticism, which he calls a closed semiotic system. By "closed," Lotman means it is inward-looking while claiming for itself universality, a monopoly on world views, and that it has a distinctively non-pluralistic perspective. He takes the example of the opposition

| genius--crowd |

and shows how its meaning is received from its relationship to certain other concepts in the system of romanticism, which are all variants of an invariant archeseme or archemeaning. These variants can be arranged as follows:

greatness--lowliness
uniqueness, exceptionalness--banality,mediocrity
spirituality--materiality
creativity--baseness
rebellion--submission[67]

To get a more **precise sense** of the meaning of these concepts within the romantic **conciousness** we can contrast them with yet further series of similar **antithetical pairs** which go into making up the semiotic system of romanticism. **What** results is several intersecting series of oppositions, all of **which generate** and elucidate the meaning of each of the variants and **ultimately** their invariant archeseme without there being any need to actually **step** outside the system.[68] Lest there be any doubt that Lotman holds **that these** concepts are the same for any and all romantics, he **had already** addressed the problem of the need to determine the distinct meaning of such concepts for individual thinkers or writers within a semiotic system as early as 1963.[69]

Lotman next turns to external transcoding. He takes an example from Евгений Онегин in which he says Pushkin is looking on romanticism as a realist, i.e. located outside of it, and tries to reveal the meaning of the former by transcoding it into the contrasting style of realism.[70]

> Показательно, что романтическая фразеология Ленского выступает как выражение, а авторская речь--как ее объективное содержание. Структура *не* романтического повествования воспринимается здесь не как один из многих возможных способов выражения, а как *содержание*, структура самой действительности.[71]

What was Bakhtin thinking about when he made his notes about Lotman? He is clearly mistaken about Lotman's undertaking in the article on meaning.[72] Consider some of the dimensions of his error. 1. Lotman is not talking about Евгений Онегин as a whole, he is simply using one stanza--actually only part of it--to illustrate a point. I would say he is quite successful in doing so, but he would not extend his limited analysis to the whole of the work without major amplification, and even then it is quite unthinkable. 2. He has not even tried to deal with the meaning of the entire stanza. He always stresses the need to base a reading on as complete an analysis as possible of all levels, internal and external. He has simply shown one way in which meaning is produced on the level of style. 3. In principle, Pushkin is being quite monologic here, yet there is still much dialogue, none of which Lotman denies. In fact, and it is this that is most incomprehensibly lacking in Bakhtin's reading of Lotman's essay, a good deal of the remainder of Lotman's article looks at much more complex forms of external transcoding in Lermontov, especially in his Герой нашего времени.[73] 4. Finally, Bakhtin's last sentence in the quoted fragment implies somehow that code, for Lotman, equals *langue*, which it most certainly does not.

Between 1970 and 1973, Lotman and various members of the Moscow-Tartu school were involved in a number of high-profile activities, including public relations, publishing, and other scholarly endeavors, to honor Bakhtin as a significant scholar, to disseminate his ideas and theories, and to further and deepen the study and understanding of his ideas and contributions.[74] It would seem that this period actually represents the peak of such activity, which neither started nor stopped there. This background makes something of a puzzle of Bakhtin's rather uncharitable assessment of Lotman and company in the publication entitled "К методологии гуманитарных наук," which was published posthumously.[75] According to the editors, it was based on a sketch Bakhtin had put together in the 1930s or early 1940s. What was published had been compiled by Bakhtin in 1974, and called "заметки" by the editors.[76] V.V. Kozhinov had prepared a special edition for publication in Контекст 1974,[77] which Bakhtin purportedly approved but which appeared after his death.[78] It differs in many respects from the original, a situation which adds one more chapter to the puzzles associated with the Bakhtin legacy, one which could possibly illuminate the role of some of Bakhtin's editors in shaping that legacy.[79]

There are two passages in the notes which mention structuralism and Lotman is mentioned in one of them. In the first,[80] Bakhtin says that contemporary literary scholars, especially structuralists, posit an ideal listener and an ideal author thereby losing all dialogue, *personification*, interaction, etc. He does not say that this refers to Lotman, and, of course, it can not. Later on, I will take up Lotman's model of communication and other aspects of his theory which demonstrate that interaction is the key to understanding his notion of the relationship between author, text and reader. Indeed, it is this concern that informs his refinement and substantial modification of Jakobson's well-established and broadly accepted model of communication.[81]

In the second passage,[82] Bakhtin makes a number of remarks which appear to be under the heading "Мое отношение к структурализму." He declares himself first of all "против замыкания в текст," which is also programmatic for Lotman. He then refers negatively to "opposition" as a mechanical category, which it is not for Lotman, and which Bakhtin himself has used very successfully and non-mechanically, especially in his study of Rabelais (верх и низ, etc.). Similarly, he refers to "смена кодов," which I have never seen anywhere in Lotman or anyone else, but which is likely meant to be equated with "перекодирование," since he refers again to Lotman's work on Евгений Онегин in "О проблеме значении." The shortcomings of his reading of this article have already been discussed above. He then turns once more to the problem of "деперсонализация," this time associated with formalization and logic, but again opposed to dialogicity, which has also been referred to above.[83] Before he reformulates that opposition in terms of precision and depth, there is a sentence which reads "Высокие оценки структурализма," and which makes no sense in or out of context. Finally, there is a paragraph which, to some extent, expands his comments on inter-subjectivity and personalism, concepts which are idiosyncratic in relation to Bakhtin's own theories, and properly so, but which are also present in Lotman's theories, and so insofar as they are intended as criticism of the latter, do not land solidly on him. More could be said about Bakhtin's comments in these notes. However, just as the notes themselves seem to have a somewhat *ad hoc* character, most comments are also of that nature. There is also Bakhtin's unfortunate lack of differentiation between structuralism and its practitioners, which is, after all, no less important than distinguishing between *langue* and *parole*, code and text, monologue and dialogue.

While I will not try to reduce Lotman to Bakhtin or Bakhtin to Lotman, I will, I believe, be able to demonstrate that Bakhtin's original assessment of Lotman in the 1970 article is the most valid, and I will also demonstrate that while Lotman does not practice Bakhtinian dialogism as such--in reality, only Bakhtin does--and despite a marked difference in use of terminology, Lotman is actually very close to Bakhtin. Indeed, I will show that he shares not only Bakhtin's central concern for "depth of penetration" as opposed to "precision"[84] but also a number of other very profound concerns touching on literature as cognition and communication.

Influence is an informative concept where it can be shown to be operative. In the case of Bakhtin and Lotman, its operativeness cannot be established, at least not yet. Nevertheless, there is a deeper dimension of interrelationship, one I have called compatibility, and it is this I will endeavor to demonstrate as forging a bond between the two theorists and at the same time setting them apart from a majority of others.

II.3 The Bakhtin-Lotman Connection in Western Scholarship

Non-Soviet works have not devoted a great deal of attention to analysis of the relationship between Bakhtin and the Moscow-Tartu School, and even less to the more specific question of the so-called Bakhtin-Lotman connection. When the question is raised it is usually deferred to the works by Ivanov and Segal cited above.[85] In 1976, Irwin Titunik could write:

> ... the relationship between Soviet semiotics and the Baxtin legacy is something of a problem, and a problem, what is more, the airing of which remains peculiarly untried.[86]

Little has changed up to the present in this respect. The main thrust of Titunik's very interesting and well-argued article is to show the inconsistencies and *non-sequiturs* which abound in the two articles by Ivanov and Segal.[87] Of course, he does add a number of constructive comments which indicate some possible directions for investigating the question of the relationship between Bakhtin and Soviet Semiotics, but for the most part, these do not come very close to the present problem. One exception is a reference to the notion of primary and secondary modelling systems as proposed and employed by Lotman. Here, Titunik feels Bakhtin's position is diametrically opposed to the position of the Soviet semioticians and especially of Lotman.[88] I will take up this question below in a manner which is at odds with Titunik's interpretation. It should be noted that besides the fact that Lotman's primary and secondary modelling systems are not incompatible with Bakhtin's notions of language and artistic activity, which I will try to demonstrate below, Titunik is relying for his assessment on texts which he himself does not believe Bakhtin wrote.[89] This is acceptable insofar as he is referring to the Bakhtin school, but he speaks of the "Bakhtin theory" and "the Bakhtin point of view"[90] and cites textual support from Voloshinov's works, although he himself has shown they are not equivalent.

As mentioned, the overriding tendency seems to be to defer to Ivanov's article (and less so to Segal's) on the question of Bakhtin's influence or connection with Soviet semiotics and Lotman. Stephen Rudy's detailed (if not exhaustive[91]) survey of Soviet semiotics is an example of this tendency.[92] Boris Schnaiderman, a Brazilian semiotician, similarly defers to Ivanov in his search for the antecedents of Soviet semiotics.[93] Schnaiderman's line of thought is often hard to follow when he sets out on his own. For example, he considers Bakhtin's criticisms of the formalists to be "rude" since

> these theorists of 'material aesthetics' were the ones who took up his theses again and perceived that they contained valuable and innovating material for literary and semiotic studies.[94]

It would appear he has in mind--despite the use of the plural--Jakobson, who, he says, "stands out as the one who contributed most to a revival of Bakhtin's ideas."[95] Naturally, he gives no references to illustrate this questionable claim, but one suspects the influence of Ivanov here, with whom Schnaiderman has had "talks."[96]

Boris Oguibenine, in his retrospective essay,[97] seems so dependent on Ivanov (and less so on Segal), as to give the impression that he has not read Bakhtin.[98] Still, he does offer something of an original proposition according to which at the source of Lotman's notion of two models of communication[99] lie Bakhtin's notions of dialogue and polyphony.[100] The chain of reasoning by means of which he arrives at this point is simply unclear. There is, however, good reason to sympathize with his conclusion, and I will be following a similar line of thought below. Moreover, he also seems to intuit Lotman's push to transform Jakobson's model of communication to allow for something like dialogue (he says polyphony here).[101] While I would change influence to something like reinforcement, it certainly seems he has opened the discussion of an important aspect of the Bakhtin-Lotman connection, although regrettably, he subsequently reformulates it somewhat in terms of a consumption/reception position.[102]

Henryk Baran notes that through writings but even more so through personal contact, the Moscow-Tartu school has had the unusual experience of having had contact and influence with such scholars and progenitors as Bakhtin, V.Ia. Propp, P. Bogatyrev, and "most important" Roman Jakobson.[103] He might have added that, although some of the Soviet semioticians did know Bakhtin, they never worked with him or even participated in conferences and seminars with him. They did work very closely with the other three scholars he mentions.

Ann Shukman, although she has written a great deal on both Lotman and Bakhtin, not to mention many aspects of Soviet literary theory and semiotics,[104] has been surprisingly silent on the question of the Bakhtin-Lotman connection. One indication--negative--she gives of her position is in her discussion of the origin of Lotman's concept and use of the notion of opposition. She claims he arrived at it through the works of Trubetskoy and Jakobson on structuralist phonology which Lotman discovered in the 1960s[105] and in another place she says that a second source was the notion of binary opposition in computer language.[106] There is nothing objectionable in what she says; it is what she does not say that is problematic: namely, her omission of the contribution of Bakhtin's notion of opposition, especially as he employs it in the Rabelais book.

Gitta Hammerberg's article on Tynianov and Jakobson seems to hold promise of revealing important findings relevant to this question insofar as its subtitle reads "(With Some Thoughts on the Baxtin and Lotman Connection)."[107] It is disappointing, within the present context, of course, to learn she has in mind connections between Roman Jakobson and each of Bakhtin and Lotman, and not between the latter two themselves.

Also promising in its title is D.W. Fokkema's article.[108] However, he sticks right to his title, and offers no indication of the role of Bakhtin in the picture he portrays--with one exception, that is. Here he falls under the influence of Ivanov, or at least cites him as authority in claiming that Lotman's notion of the impossibility of making a sharp distinction between expression and meaning is drawn from Bakhtin.[109] Since this notion is already present in Лекции,[110] we can almost certainly rule out any possibility of influence from Bakhtin.[111] Finally, Krystyna Pomorska identifies Bakhtin and L. Vygotskii as two outstanding adversaries and critics of the theories of OPOIAZ,[112] but, she says there is also a third.

> Jakobson was not merely a member and cofounder but the group's critic and "corrector" as well: it is thus natural that Jakobson's theories, rather than those of Baxtin and Vygotskij,

underlie the system of the Tartu-Moscow school, which is the continuation and corrective of the OPOJAZ today.[113]

Apparently feeling it to be self-evident, she simply leaves it at that.[114]

Another scholar who has taken up the question of the connection between Bakhtin and Lotman or, more specifically, Soviet Semiotics, is Thomas Winner. Winner clearly senses a significant connection between Bakhtin and his school and the Moscow-Tartu School. However, he is unable to establish unambiguously what the nature of that connection is. In 1977, in a paragraph which refers to three works by Bakhtin (including one of the disputed texts), Winner refers to at least eight important aspects of Bakhtin's theories, lumps them all together, and concludes that "Baxtin's ambitious approach underlies the later Tartu-Moscow scholars' complex analyses of culture texts of all types."[115] Not only is this not particularly clear, but it lacks any sequence of ideas which would enable the reader to make the causal links between Bakhtin and the later Soviet Scholars. In the subsequent discussion he does not in any way illuminate the matter. There are other problems with Winner's article, but for the present discussion it is not necessary to take them up.

In a later article, also a general overview, Winner makes statements which are not only somewhat unclear but unambiguously wrong:

> While Formalism focussed attention on the text and lies at the base of the early logocentrism of Soviet Semiotics, it is M.M. Bakhtin who, as early as the 1920s, laid the foundations for the broad intersystemic approach of contemporary Soviet semiotics.[116]

The statement about formalism and logocentrism is questionable on the grounds that it seriously equivocates the significance of logocentrism as applied to Russian formalism and Soviet semiotics respectively, and ignores other factors, most notably the influence of Prague structuralist theories, about which Winner, as a specialist in the field, is well aware.[117] The notion that Bakhtin could have "laid the foundations" for a major movement which emerged and established itself at a time when he was practically unknown, is both untenable, and carelessly made.[118] The whole notion of *foundations* is highly problematic. Taking Ivanov as an example, we see his unquestionable if unclear admission of Bakhtin's influence, but in his idiosyncratic manner he also includes others, especially Eisenshtein, and I would speculate that his answer to the question who actually laid the foundations for Soviet semiotics would put Roman Jakobson ahead of Bakhtin, as long as it is understood that the question refers to foundations. But Winner himself is unsure of what actually composes those foundations. In 1977, he had already made the claim that

> the fertile ideas which originated in Prague in the thirties laid the foundation for modern semiotics, shaping the Tartu-Moscow school of semiotics, the Polish and Czech schools, and much of the semiotics of Western Europe, the Western Hemisphere and Israel.[119]

There is a great need to distinguish between foundations and influence, and of the two, only the latter can possibly be applied to Bakhtin, and even then only in a proper chronological and conceptual perspective.

The same kind of problems inhere in Winner's assertion that Lotman's concept of primary and secondary modelling systems "evolved" from Bakhtin's views.[120] This is a no less blatant and careless anachronism than the previous assertion. Clearly, Winner fails to make the effort to distinguish between what may be commonly held by the two groups or their representatives, and what may be considered genuine influence.[121] To an important extent this is precisely what this dissertation will seek to establish.

Caryl Emerson has also posited an influence of Bakhtin on Lotman. "It is likely that Lotman's move from Structuralism to cultural semiotics was inspired in part by the powerful ideological field generated by Bakhtin's work."[122] Unfortunately, she does not elaborate. Again, the fact of Bakhtin's influence at this particular moment is almost unquestionable, but what is more important is how Bakhtin's ideas fused with Lotman's given the latter's deep roots in broad intersystemic thinking.

The most precise statements I know of concerning a connection between Bakhtin and Soviet Semiotics, with particular emphasis on Lotman, have been made by Simonetta Salvestroni.[123] Her point of departure concerning this connection, in particular, is formulated as follows. "The work of Michail Bachtin, ... is undoubtedly a fundamental reference point for research carried out in recent years in the Soviet Union."[124] Note the crucial difference in her statement as compared with Winner's where Bakhtin is said to have laid the foundations for Soviet theories. She further points out that while there is a convergence of ideas between Bakhtin and various trends in western scholarship, they likely developed independently, due above all to common concerns and interests.[125] The major focus of her wide-ranging and perhaps overly eclectic discussion is on epistemology, questions of the growth of knowledge, and the philosophy of science. While her presentation of these questions is not flawless--in particular, I would mention her failure to separate Einstein and Einsteinian relativity from quantum theory,[126] she makes a number of very interesting and perceptive points. I will not be concentrating on technical aspects of epistemology any more than Bakhtin or Lotman do, and certainly not on Salvestroni's level of abstraction and generalization. However, these questions are highly pertinent to the broader question of a Bakhtin-Lotman connection and must be raised if not resolved.[127]

    I know of no other studies which take up the question of a connection between Lotman and Bakhtin although passing reference to it is made occasionally, usually, as mentioned, in the context of Ivanov's and Segal's articles. I would like to avoid the type of error committed by Winner, as well as that made by Titunik--a normally cautious scholar--so I would repeat that I do not intend to try to prove Bakhtin was a *formative* influence on Soviet Semiotics or on Lotman. It is a more prudent and probabilistic strategy to argue for the existence of a common outlook and approach based on fundamental principles and methodological orientation, and manifesting itself in a profound and somewhat unique body of theoretical and applied studies on literature and culture. Much of what I have to say may not be altogether new or revolutionary as bits of information, but I see my task as putting these things together in a manner which will bring new light and new understanding to the work of these two scholars and by extension to the object of their studies, in particular, literature as communication and cognition.

NOTES

1. Especially, but not only, Ivanov. See Winner, "Russian Theories," 86; Todorov, <u>The Dialogical Principle</u>, 7; Shukman, <u>Literature and Semiotics</u>, 29.
2. See below.
3. For the details of these polemics and debates see Peter Seyffert, <u>Soviet Literary Structuralism: Background - Debate - Issues</u>, (Columbus, Ohio: Slavica Publishers, Inc., 1983); and Shukman, <u>Literature and Semiotics</u>, Appendix I.
4. See especially the discussion of Segal's article below.
5. In an article from 1962, V.V. Kozhinov suggests Bakhtin's work on Dostoevsky was known to many. However, I think it fair to say he does not sound very convincing. At the time, Kozhinov was working to get Bakhtin's book on Dostoevsky republished and to get his study of Rabelais published for the first time. V.V. Kozhinov, "Научность--это связь с жизнью," <u>Вопросы литературы</u>, year 6, no. 3 (March 1962), 86-87.
6. E.g. A.V. Lunacharskii, "О многоголосности Достоевского," <u>Новый мир</u>, 10, 1929. For details of its reception, see Clark and Holquist, <u>Mikhail Bakhtin</u>,
7. For a discussion of Bakhtin's submission and defense of his dissertation, and the attendant controversy see Ibid.
8. An exhaustive review would be nearly impossible. Karl Eimermacher and Serge Shishkoff, <u>Subject Bibliography of Soviet Semiotics: The Moscow-Tartu School</u>, (Ann Arbor: Michigan Slavic Pubications, 1977), lists over 2,000 entries as of 1977. The 1982 bibliography of Lotman's works includes over 500 entries. "Список печатных трудов Ю.М. Лотмана: (Материалы к библиографии)," comp. L.N. Kiseleva, *et al*, in <u>Finitis Duodecim Lustris</u>, 20-53. Both lists would be much longer if brought up to date as of 1989.
9. Iurii M. Lotman, "O. M. Friedenberg as a Student of Culture," in Henryk Baran, <u>Semiotics and Structuralism</u>, 257. A short space later he goes on to state: "We would consider it useful to direct attention to the way structural-semiotic methods formed

10. A.K. Zholkovskii and Iu.K. Shcheglov, "О возможностях построения структурной поэтики," in <u>Структурно-типологические исследования: Сборник статей</u>, ed.T. N. Moloshnaia, (Moscow: Izdatel'stvo AN SSSR, 1962) 138-141.

11. Idem, "Из предыстории советских работ по структурной поэтики," <u>Труды по знаковым системам</u> (hereinafter <u>TZS</u>) III, (1967), 367-72, and idem, "Структурная поэтика——порождающая поэтика," <u>Вопросы Литературы</u>, 11, no. 1 (1967), 74-89.

12. "Заслуга рационального в принципе подхода к литературе принадлежит 'формальной щколе' в русском литературоведении. . . . В центр внимания ставилось выявление отличии 'поэтического ряда' от 'практического'. Литература рассматривалась как особый объект, автономный по отношению к быту, религии, мифологии, биографии автора и пр." Idem, "О возможностях,"139. Cf. idem, "Структурная поэтика——порождающая поэтика," 74-75, for an equally bold statement of the same point with even greater polemical ramifications.

13. The first article predates Lotman's involvement in the semiotics movement, and while Ivanov did respond to it, it is not necessary for present purposes to outline the complex development of his position on these matters. Note that "Структурная поэтика——порождающая поэтика," is an expanded version of their 1961 article.

14. Most notably in Bakhtin, "Проблема содержания." Compare also Medvedev, <u>Формальный метод</u>; and Voloshinov, <u>Марксизм и философия языка</u>.

15. Viach. Vs. Ivanov, "О применении точных методов в литероведении," Вопросы литературы 11, no. 10 (1967), 115-26; Iu. M. Lotman, "О задачах раздела обзоров и публикаций," TZS III, (1967), 363-66; Lotman's article published in the same number of Вопросы литературы as Zholkovskii and Shcheglov's "Структурная поэтика--порождающая поэтика," should also undoubtably be seen as part of this exchange. Idem, "Литероведение должно быть наукой," Вопросы литературы 11, no. 1, (1967), 90-100. While his ostensible intent is to polemicize with articles by L. Timofeev, P. Palievskii, and especially V. Kozhinov ("Возможна ли структурная поэтика," Вопросы литературы 9, No. 6 (1965), 88-107, and see also Seyffert, Soviet Literary Structuralism, 204-208) the fact that his article follows Zholkovskii and Shcheglov's both in position in the journal and in content is significant. Notably, when referring to predecessors of structuralism, he mentions in the first place its deep traditions in relation to V. Propp, P. Bogatyrev, M. Bakhtin and A. Skaftymov. He goes on to mention Iu. Tynyanov, B. Tomashevskii, B. Eikenbaym, G. Gukovskii, V. Grib, L. Pumpianskii, G. Vinokur, S. Balukhatov, and A. Kukulevich, 92. The absence of Shklovskii and Eisenshtein from his list is striking in the context of comparison with the other article.
16. See e.g., "От редакции," TZS II, 1965, 5.
17. Iurii Lotman, "О разграничении лингвистического и литературоведческого понятия структуры," Вопросы языкознания 3, (1963), 44-52, and idem, Лекции по структуральной поэтике: Введение, теория стиха, Brown University Slavic Reprint V, (Providence, Rhode Island: Brown University Press, 1968), 3-12.
18. I.e. in Lotman, "О задачах рахдела обзоров и публикации."
19. Note also his prefatory remark to a statement quoted above, in n. 106: "Adopting a view of the prehistory of structural

poetics somewhat different from that sketched by A. K. Zholkovskii and Iu. K. Shcheglov, ... " Idem, "O. M. Friedenberg," 259.

20. Ivanov, "О применении," 124-25.
21. Ibid., especially p. 126.
22. Ibid., n. 1.
23. E.g., he suggests Bakhtin's studies of polyphony and internal dialogue preceded the appearance of these phenomena in modern literature (p. 126), but does not say that or how his ideas on these questions influenced contemporary literary scholarship or how contemporary scholars may have found confirmation or amplification of their ideas in Bakhtin.
24. Dmitri Segal, Aspects of Structuralism in Soviet Philology, Papers on Poetics and Semiotics, 2, (Tel-Aviv: Tel-Aviv University, 1974), 120. See also E.M. Meletinskij and Dmitri Segal, "Structuralism and Semiotics in the USSR," Diogenes 73 (1971), 88-125.
25. Ivanov, "On the Significance."
26. For an analysis of the two articles and their interrelationship, see Irwin Titunik, "M.M. Baxtin (the Baxtin School) and Soviet Semiotics," Dispositio I, 3 (1976), 327-338.
27. Ivanov, "On the Significance," 316.
28. Ibid., 316.
29. Examples of studies which do open up in this direction include Michael Holquist, "Bakhtin the Scientist: The Role of Physiology in His Thought," (abstract of an unpublished paper), in Mikhail Mikhailovich Bakhtin, His Circle, His Influence: Papers Presented at the International Coloquium, Queen's University, October 7-9, 1983, 72; Sagayesi Igeta, "Ivanov - Pumpianskii - Bakhtin," in Comparative and Contrastive Studies in Slavic Languages and Literatures: Japanese Contributions to the Tenth International Congess of Slavists, Sofia, September 14-21, 1988, ed. Japanese Asociation of Slavists, (Tokyo: College of Arts and Sciences, University of Tokyo, 1988), 81-91; Perlina, "Funny Things are Happening"; and Simonetta Salvestroni, "Bachtin in Soviet and West European Semiotic Research," in Mikhail Mikhailovich Bakhtin, His Circle, His Influence, 197-221.
30. Viach. Vs. Ivanov, Очерки по истории семиотики в СССР, (Moscow: Nauka, 1976).

31.	Cf. "One should avoid giving the impression, however, that such well-known antecedents of Soviet semiotics as Baxtin, Bogatyrev, Vygotskij, and Veselovskij, or less prominent figures like Florenskij and Spet, occupy the central stage in Ivanov's work. In fact their several entrances and exits in the first chapter and a few lines in the closing scenes constitute their entire role. The true hero in Ivanov's *Essays* is Sergei Eisenstein. He is, in effect, the *raison d'etre* of the work." R. and G. Vroon, "Ivanov's Essays on the History of Semiotics in the USSR," (Moscow: Nauka, 1976), in Dispositio I, 3 (October 1976), 356-360. See also Grete Neumann, "Signs on Signs on Signs on Signs." Review of Viach. Vs. Ivanov, Ocherki po istorii semiotiki v SSSR, in Semiotica 21, 3/4 (1977), 339-56.
32.	Idem, "The Semiotic Theory of Carnival as the Inversion of Bipolar Opposites," in Carnival, ed. Thomas E. Sebeok, Aproaches to Semiotics, 64, (Berlin, New York, Amsterdam: Mouton, 1984), 11.
33.	Idem, "Из заметок о строении и функциях карнавального образа," in Проблемы поэтики и истории литературы, 37-53.
34.	Ivanov, "On the Significance," esp. 322, 331, 350n. On Uspenskii's work, see below.
35.	Ibid., esp. 336-7. Any accounts of the meeting of Jakobson and Levi-Strauss which I have seen fail to mention the name of Bakhtin. Cf. Howard Gardner, The Mind's New Science: A History of the Cognitive Revolution, (New York: Basic Books, Inc., Publishers, 1985), 235-236; and Thomas E. Sebeok, "Vital Signs," American Journal of Semiotics, III, 3 (1985), esp. 11-15. Note that in another essay, Ivanov claims that Jakobson spoke often in America about Bakhtin and L.S. Vygotskii in the 1940s and 1950s but no one paid attention. Perhaps he did,--Ivanov typically gives no references--but there is no evidence for this, no historical trace: it reads more like wishful thinking or invention than anything else. A survey of the respective indices of the seven very hefty tomes of Jakobson's Selected Works produces no references to Medvedev, four passing references of no substance to Voloshinov, one paragraph in which he simply notes that "Voloshinov raised a certain question," and four passing references to Bakhtin. The results of such a cursory survey

clearly do not support Ivanov's claims, and again raise questions about their veracity. The point is that one really does not know what to make of all the claims he makes in the 1973 essay. See Ivanov, "Roman Jakobson: The Future," in <u>A Tribute to Roman Jakobson, 1896-1982</u>, (Berlin, New York, Amsterdam: Mouton, 1983), 47-57.

36. I will forego providing a list of these, but it is important to note he does cover a lot of ground.

37. Boris Uspenskii, <u>Поэтика композиции: Структура художественного текста и типология композиционной формы</u>, (Moscow: Izdatel'stvo 'Iskusstvo', 1970).

38. Ibid., 11. He also mentions Voloshinov, V.V. Vinogradov, and G.K. Gukovskii, but Bakhtin appears to be the major figure, and is given credit for influencing Voloshinov in this field, as well.

39. I am assuming that he did read the Dostoevsky book about this time insofar as its publication was something of an event. The earliest reference to Bakhtin by Lotman is in "Художественная структура *Евгения Онегина*," <u>Ученые записки Тартуского государственного университета</u>, 184, <u>Труды по русской и славянской филологии</u>, IX (1966), 6 n. 2.

40. Cf. Shukman, <u>Literature and Semiotics</u>, 2, and Appendix I which lists his "pre-structuralist works."

41. See e.g. Lotman, "О разграничении." See also the discussion of this question and its importance below.

42. "Несмотря на известную упрощенность предлагаемой Тыняновым схемы, ему принадлежит бесспорная честь первой попытки описания *механизма* диахронного движения литературы. Вершиной рассмотрения динамики литературы как борьбы, напряжения между культурным 'верхом' и 'низом,' нейтрализации этого напряжения в амбивалентных текстах и соотношения этого процесса с общей

эволюцией культуры, бесспорно, до сих пор остается книга М.М. Бахтина <u>Творчество Франсуа Рабле и народная культура средневековья и Ренессанса</u>." Lotman, "О содержании и структуре понятия 'художественная литература,'" in <u>Проблемы поэтики и истории литературы</u>, 30.

43. E.g. Lotman, "Gogol and the Correlation of 'The Culture of Humor' with the Comic and Serious in the Rusian National Tradition," in <u>Semiotics and Structuralism</u>, 297-300; idem, "Несколько замечании по поводу статьи проф. Марии Р. Майеновой, 'Поэтика в работах тартусского университета'," <u>Russian Literature</u>, 6 (1974), 82-89; idem, "Художественная природа русских народных картинок," in <u>Народная гравюра и фольклор в России ХУИИ–ХИХ вв. (К 150–летию со дня рождения Д.А. Ровинского.) (Материалы научной конференции)</u>, (Moscow: Sovetskii Khudozhnik, 1976), 247-67; idem, <u>Структура художественного текста</u>, Brown University Slavic Reprint IX, (Providence, Rhode Island: Brown University Press, 1971), esp. 300-301; etc.

44. Lotman, <u>Лекции</u>, 1964, and <u>Структура</u>, originally published in 1970.

45. Here I remind the reader of the assumption implicit in this analysis that Lotman probably read Bakhtin for the first time around 1964-1965. I should also repeat the fact mentioned above that although <u>Лекции</u> was published in 1964, it was composed between 1958 and 1962.

46. E.g. Ibid., 6, 9-10.

47. See the references above and the discussion in the following sections/chapters.

48. "This last point is especially vital, since we find more and more often that there is a tendency not to develop or interpret Bachtin's ideas, but mechanically to extend them into areas where their very application should be a subject of special

investigation. [. . .] Bachtin's complex and controversial ideas have been oversimplified and made into a handy decoration of scholarship." Iurii M. Lotman and Boris A. Uspenskii, "New Aspects in the Study of Early Russian Culture," a review of D.S. Likhachev and A.M. Panchenko, "Smekhovoi mir" drevnei Rusi, in The Semiotics of Russian Culture, 51 n. 5. Cf. also p. 37.

49. E.g. Iurii M. Lotman, "Текст в тексте," TZS XIV (1981), 3-18; idem, "Динамеческая модель семиотической системы," TZS X (1978), 18-33; idem, "От редакции: К проблеме пространственной семиотики," TZS XIX Пространство, 3-6; and idem, "Gogol and the Correlation."

50. See above.

51. Mikhail M. Bakhtin, "Ответ на вопрос редакции Нового мира," 328-35, (originally published in the journal Новый мир under the title "Смелее пользоваться возможностями."); idem, "Из записей 1970−1971 годов," 339; idem, "К методологии гуманитарных наук," 372. All three selections have been published in idem, Эстетика словесного творчества, (Moscow: Iskusstvo, 1979), hereinafter referred to as ЭСТ.

52. See Seyffert, Soviet Literary Structuralism.

53. Or allowed them to be published. See the discussion on this question below.

54. Again, Seyffert has gone into considerable detail in presenting many of the concerns and essays that conditioned and comprised the debate. Cf. also Shukman, Literature and Semiotics, appendix III.

55. ЭСТ, 328. The question was put to ten scholars between November 1970 and June 1971. Seyffert, Soviet Literary Structuralism, 295. Judging by Seyffert's work and other indicators, only Bakhtin's reply has retained any lasting interest.

56. ЭСТ, 329. Konrad's book does not appear to be particularly well known, at least outside its rather specific field, Likhachev's book has become a classic text in the study of old

Russian literature and culture, and, of course, Труды по знаковым системам continues as a vital part of the publishing activity of the Moscow-Tartu school.

57. ЭСТ, 329.
58. Ibid., 330.
59. Ibid., 331.
60. Ibid., 332.
61. Ibid., 333.
62. Lotman even found it appropriate to quote from this essay for help in explicating certain aspects of his theory which had come under attack. Lotman, "Несколько замечании по поводу статьи Проф. Марии. Р. Майеновой," 87.
63. ЭСТ, 336-360.
64. ЭСТ, 339.
65. Lotman, "О проблеме значении во вторичных моделирующих системах," TZS II, (1965), 22-37. The article was incorporated into Структура, 44-64.
66. "Список печатных трудов Ю.М. Лотмана."
67. Cf. Alexander D. Nakhimovsky and Alice Stone Nakhimovsky, preface to The Semiotics of Russian Cultural History: Essays by Iurii M. Lotman, Lidiia Ia. Ginsburg, Boris A. Uspenskii, ed. Alexander D. Nakhimovsky and Alice Stone Nakhimovsky with an Introduction by Boris Gasparov, (Ithaca and London: Cornell University Press, 1985), 8: "The rules of academic discourse in the Soviet Union are different from those of the West. In the Soviet Union, the primary mode for communication is oral: conversations, seminars, talks. A published article is a record of thoughts that have been put forward elsewhere. It is accepted as a kind of shorthand for work in progress, and the way it is written--as opposed to what it says--is not subject to particular scrutiny. Lidiia Ginsburg is a writer of great elegance, but Lotman and Uspenskii do not try in their writings for a particular precision of expression, nor do they see it as their task to do so."
68. Lotman, "О проблеме значении," 25-26. (Величие---ничтожество\необычность, исключительность--пошлость, заурядность\духовность---материальность\

творчество--животность\
мятеж--покорность).
69. Ibid.
70. Lotman, "О разграничении." There he looks at the different content of the concept "natural state" for various 18th-century thinkers.
71. Lenskii's romantic text runs: "Он мыслит: Буду ей спаситель. /Не потерплю, чтоб развратитель /Огнем и вздохов и похвал /Младое сердце искушал; /Чтоб червь презренный, ядовитый /Точил лилей стебелек; /Чтоб двухутренний цветок /Увял еще полураскрытый'. /Все это значило, друзья: /'С приятелем стреляюсь я.'" A.S. Pushkin, Евгений Онегин, VI, 17, quoted in Lotman, "О проблеме значении," 26.
72. Ibid., 27.
73. If it is too much to say he is mistaken, then he is at least being unfair, although I would hold to the former.
74. Esp. Ibid., 31-33.
75. I have in mind e.g. the special session at the university of Moscow in 1970 to celebrate Bakhtin's 75th birthday, Ivanov's article "On the Significance," and the special *Festschrift* dedicated to Bakhtin in 1973 to which Lotman, Ivanov, and Toporov were significant contributors (Проблемы поэтики и истории литературы).
76. ЭСТ, 361-373.
77. ЭСТ, 409.
78. (Moscow: 1975), 203-212. It appeared under the title "К методологии литературоведения."
79. ЭСТ, 409.
80. There are three or, actually, four texts: The ЭСТ version, the Kontekst version, the original authorial text from the 1930s or 1940s, presumably held in Bakhtin's archives, and the text given in the notes to ЭСТ (409-411) which is said to be the original, and is entitled "К философским основам гуманитарных наук" and which the editors reprint "с

некоторыми сокращениями." Ibid., 409. Cf. also Ladislav Matejka, "The Roots of Russian Semiotics of Art," in <u>The Sign: Semiotics Around the World</u>, ed. R.W. Bailey *et al*, Michigan Slavic Contributions No. 9, (Ann Arbor: Michigan Slavic Publications, 1978), 168-169, where he relates a similar publishing history concerning versions of "Проблема содержания."

81. Ibid., 367-68.
82. This will be discussed in detail below.
83. <u>ЭСТ</u>, 372-73. All references in the following section are to this passage.
84. And see the discussion below of personality in Lotman's theory.
85. <u>ЭСТ</u>, 372. In "К методологии гуманитарных наук," this opposition does not play anywhere near the role ascribed to it by Kozhinov in the <u>Контекст</u> version.
86. See below.
87. Titunik, "M.M. Baxtin (The Baxtin School)," 329.
88. "Owing to the unavailability of numerous key facts and the everpresent peril of sticking one's finger into God knows what, no attempt will be made here to come to grips with the problem on such a scale. Instead, attention will be directed only to a few points of a conceptual nature, having to do with the approach to and appreciation of M.M. Baxtin by V.V. Ivanov and D. Segal, in the hope that thereby the discussion might be at least opened." Ibid.
89. Ibid., 333-34.
90. See the references to Titunik in the discussion on the disputed texts above.
91. Titunik, "M.M. Baxtin (The Baxtin School)," e.g. 332.
92. He concentrates primarily on the Moscow branch of the "school."
93. Stephen Rudy, "Semiotics in the USSR," in <u>The Semiotic Sphere</u>, ed. T.A. Sebeok and J. Umiker-Sebeok, (New York and London: Plenum Press, 1986), 555-582. On Bakhtin see esp. 561-62, 564, 565.
94. Boris Schnaiderman, "Semiotics in the USSR." The discussion of Bakhtin is on pp. 102-106.
95. Ibid., 105.
96. Ibid.

97. Ibid., 104. See above for Ivanov's speculations about Jakobson and Bakhtin
98. Boris Oguibenine, "Linguistic Models of Culture in Russian Semiotics: A Retrospective View," PTL 4 (1979), 91-118.
99. Ibid., esp. 111.
100. Iurii. M. Lotman, "О двух моделях коммуникации в системе культуры," TZS VI (1973), 227-243, and see below.
101. Oguibenine, "Linguistic Models," 114-115.
102. Ibid., 115.
103. Ibid., 116. It should also be added that his overall position in this article (in terms of influence or predecessors) is to show not only the role of Bakhtin, but also of Jakobson, setting them off as the metalinguistic and linguistic backgrounds respectively. While I do not feel he is totally successful, it is an interesting and necessary balance that he seeks to find.
104. Henryk Baran, Introduction to Semiotics and Structuralism, ix-x.
105. See titles listed under her name in the bibliography, which is neither exhaustive, nor does it include all of her extensive translating and editorial contributions.
106. Ann Shukman, "Soviet Semiotics and Literary Criticism," New Literary History IX, 2 (1978), 193.
107. Ibid., 196.
108. Gitta Hammarberg, "A Reinterpretation of Tynianov and Jakobson on Prose (With Some Thoughts on the Baxtin and Lotman Connection)," in Language and Literary Theory, 379-401.
109. D.W. Fokkema, "Continuity and Change in Russian Formalism, Czech Structuralism, and Soviet Semiotics," PTL I (1976), 153-196.
110. Ibid., 182-183.
111. Lotman, Лекции, e.g. 41-43.
112. Since Fokkema gives no page reference to Ivanov ("On the Significance") and his page references to Lotman are to the German translation of Структура, it is not a simple matter to follow through and check up on what he feels he has inferred.
113. Krystyna Pomorska, "Poetics of Prose," in Verbal Art, Verbal Sign, Verbal Time, by Roman Jakobson, ed. Krystyna

114. Pomorska, Stephen Rudy, (Minneapolis: University of Minnesota Press, 1985), 169.
115. Ibid. I think it is very likely she is polemicizing with someone, but she gives no indication who that may be.
116. Tomas Venclova also mentions Bakhtin as an important influence but does not develop his observations. Неустойчивое равновесие, e.g. 15, 17, 18.
117. Thomas G. Winner, "The Semiotics of Texts and its Application to Contemporary Poetics," in Papers in Slavic Philology, I: In Honor of James Ferrell, ed. Benjamin A. Stolz, (Ann Arbor: Michigan Slavic Publications, 1977) 309.
118. Idem, "Russian Theories of the Twenties and Thirties," 86.
119. Cf. Idem, "Jan Mukarovsky: The Beginnings of Structural and Semiotic Aesthetics," in Sound, Sign and Meaning: Quinquagenary of the Prague Linguistic Circle, ed. Ladislas Matejka, Michigan Slavic Publications, No. 6, (Ann Arbor: University of Michigan, 1976), 433-435.
120. Cf., e.g. Rudy, "Semiotics in the USSR," 556, where he makes the comment that Toporov and Ivanov "laid the foundations for the development of semiotics in the USSR." Though not indisputable, it surely is a much more reasonable position.
121. Winner, "Jan Mukarovsky," 443. Incidentally, this statement is probably much more defensible than the one concerning Bakhtin.
122. Winner, "Russian Theories," 87. Compare this with Titunik's statement above concerning the essential incompatibility of the notions of primary and secondary modelling systems with Bakhtin's views.
123. There is also the fact that something like a notion of secondary modelling system exists prior to Lotman's association with the Soviet semiotic movement, and prior to any discernible influence of Bakhtin. See Dmitri Segal's article from 1961 quoted below.
124. Caryl Emerson, Foreword to Russian Views of Pushkin's "Eugene Onegin," tr. with an introduction and notes by Sona Stephan Hoisington, (Bloomington and Indianapolis: Indiana University Press, 1988), xi.
125. Simmonetta Salvestroni, "Bachtin in Soviet and West European Semiotic Research," in Mikhail Mikhailovich Bakhtin, His Circle, His Influence, 197-221.

125. Ibid., 197-8. And she makes a special reference to Lotman.
126. Ibid., 198
127. Ibid., 207, 211.
128. Compare Shukman's treatment of the question of epistemology in Lotman, which is for the most part at odds with Salvestroni's, in "The Canonization of the Real: Jurij Lotman's Theory of Literature and Analysis of Poetry," PTL, I (1976), 317-338.

III LITERATURE, LANGUAGE, AND LINGUISTICS

In this chapter I will examine relationships among the key notions of literature, language and linguistics in the theories of Russian formalism, Prague school structuralism, Roman Jakobson, Bakhtin, and Lotman. I will attempt to demonstrate that these are the notions which more than any others separate the theories of Bakhtin and Lotman from those of their immediate predecessors. Insofar as "logocentrism" has been characteristic of so much of twentieth-century criticism and literary theory--formalism, structuralism, post-structuralism, deconstructivism, etc.--this must be seen as a crucial area for detecting and understanding differences and similarities. The decision concerning which theoretical positions were to be examined was motivated by two primary considerations. First, both Lotman and Bakhtin made serious and significant efforts to clarify their positions and define a stance relative to Russian formalism, while the Prague school is obviously closely related to the latter. The historical-genetic and geographical link is therefore manifest. Secondly, other major traditions such as the French schools of Kristeva, Barthes, Todorov, and the deconstructivists, for example, as mentioned above, simply do not have a great deal in common with the theories of Lotman and Bakhtin. Thus a principle of exclusion applies here.

The characterization of each school or position will necessarily be somewhat general, however, it is hoped that the points of primary significance will emerge with sufficient clarity so as to illuminate the crucial differences upon which my argument rests.

III.1 Russian Formalism and the Question of Literariness (*Литературность*)

Russian formalism arose as a movement or school in the middle of the second decade of the twentieth century.[1] It was in effect a hybrid of two separate groups of young scholars, the Moscow LInguistic Society, founded in 1915, and the Общество изучения поэтического языка (OPOIAZ), founded in St. Petersburg (Petrograd) in 1916. They considered the current state of literary studies to be, in general, unsatisfactory, especially insofar as it did not seem to be an independent field of inquiry and study.[2] They perceived a need to establish a branch of learning with its own principles, methods and object of study. With this end in mind they set out to discover and establish the *specificity* of literature and literary studies, i.e. what they called literariness or *литературность*.

Current theories of literature were found seriously wanting. In particular, the young formalists rejected the popular theories of Aleksander Potebnia (1835-1891), especially his insistence on the notion of poetry as thinking in images,[3] while, as Erlich points out, they owe a large and largely unacknowledged debt to his--Potebnia's--affirmation of the need to align poetry with linguistics and see it as a special form of verbal behaviour;[4] they also took issue with the position of Aleksander Veselovskii (1838-1906), especially his genetic approach, although his recognition of the need to define a science of literature and his interest in identifying constant motifs and 'formulae' in literature were very important stimuli for the formalists;[5] and they rejected sociological, utilitarian, and ideologically oriented theories of all varieties. At the same time it should be noted that they found the theoretical studies of Russian symbolists--which were strongly influenced by the theories of Potebnia--almost totally unacceptable, objecting in particular to the emphasis of the symbolists on inspiration, transcendentalism, the image, 'impressionism,' and so on.[6]

Under the influence of the linguistic theories of Bauduoin de Courtenay[7] and Ferdinand de Saussure,[8] the philosophical impetus of Husserlian phenomenology as presented especially by Gustav Spet,[9] and to a great extent the poetic practice of Russian futurism, especially of Velimir Khlebnikov and Vladimir Maiakovskii, with whom some of the formalists had close personal contacts,[10] they identified literature as a linguistic activity with a specifically aesthetic function.[11] In this way, they sought to rid literature of the burdens of religious, philosophical and other ideological trappings,[12] as well as relieving its study of the need to pursue causal or genetically oriented studies. Literature was seen as a specially organized linguistic activity,[13] which was to be distinguished by its formal,[14] and not its ideational or cognitive aspects. It was deemed important in this respect to study literature not in relation to other systems of ideas or other social and historical processes or series, but immanently, in terms of its own particular formal organization and linguistic functioning,[15] i.e. in terms of its devices.[16] It needed to be freed from its subjugation to other disciplines and interests. A colorful analogy put forward by Roman Jakobson in 1921 illustrates the formalists' view of the prevailing situation and why it was in need of being overcome.

> Таким образом, предметом науки о литературе является не литература, а литературность, т.е. то, что делает данное произведение литературным произведением. Между тем, до сих пор историки литературы преимущественно уподоблялись полиции, которая, имея целью арестовать определенное лицо, захватила бы на всякий случай всех и все, что находилось в квартире, а также случайно проходивших по улице мимо. Так и историкам литературы все шло на потребу--быт, психология, политика, философия. Вместо науки о литературе создавался конгломерат доморощенных дисциплин. Как бы забывалось, что эти статьи отходят к соответсвующим наукам--истории философии, истории

культуры, психологии и т. д., и что последние могут естественно использовать и литературные памятники, как дефектные, второсортные документы. Если наука о литературе хочет стать наукой, она принуждается признать 'прием' своим единственным 'героем.'[17]

While the so-called Formal school evolved significantly from its maximalist position as declared in the first five years or so of its existence, and not all its members shared that position equally,[18] no attempt will be made here to outline the full development of the school or all its achievements and contributions. The major contribution of the school was surely in its re-orientation of literary studies by attempting to determine the specificity of literature and study it within the context of human linguistic activity. The political situation in the Soviet Union did not permit formalism to evolve and develop its enormous potential. Instead, as a movement, it was definitively halted by about 1928, but in many respects even earlier. At any rate, the present focus of attention is on the innovations and insights brought forward by the formalists precisely in relation to the matrix of literature, language and linguistics.

Having established to their own satisfaction the basic linguistic nature of literature, the formalists held that, within the field of linguistic phenomena, the further necessary distinction of literature from non-literature[19] was made largely through the teleological notion of function (цель): literature had a different function than other linguistic phenomena.[20] Within a given work it was necessary to recognize that there might be other functions as well, but the aesthetic or poetic function was the 'dominant' one.[21] Thus poetry or literature is not equal to its poetic function, but is *dominated*, or determined by it.

Having identified the notion of aesthetic function[22] and of the dominant it was possible to recognize a hierarchy of functions within the poetic work[23] and the specific characteristics of the aesthetic function.[24] Thus the aesthetic function is what makes the work literary (artistic) and the aesthetic function is manifested within the work in or through various formal artistic devices. These devices are used "чтобы эти вещи (i.e. poetic works, A.R.) по возможности наверняка воспринимались, как художественные."[25] This can best be understood in the context of a general definition of art:

> Целью искусства является дать ощущение вещи, как видение, а не как узнавание: приемом искусства является прием 'остранения' вещей и прием затрудненной формы, увеличивающий трудность и долготу восприятия, так как воспринимательный процесс в искусстве сомоцелен и должен быть продлен: искусство есть способ пережить деланье вещи, а сделанное в искусстве не важно.[26]

Thus devices function to make the reader aware of them, of form, of language; they do not point to something else, but to themselves,[27] to the organization of the work. They are self-referential. Literature should be analyzed in terms of these devices.[28]

At a later period some of the formalists expanded their horizons somewhat and went beyond linguistic and formal analyses,[29] but this can, in a sense be considered a transition out of or beyond formalism strictly viewed. The important point of this cursory presentation of Russian formalism is that all significant concepts and conclusions revolve around language--around literature as a linguistic phenomenon with a dominant aesthetic function realized through creative manipulation of formal devices.

By 1928 formalism had become a well-entrenched term of vilification in the Soviet Union and, indeed, up until relatively recently, it has been used to cover a number of the gravest sins, often where nothing else seemed to be strong enough. Formalism as such ceased to exist, while the now ex-formalists either recanted--sincerely or otherwise--and/or turned to less conspicuous or less potentially dangerous occupations such as more general literary historical scholarship, biography, or literary prose. Some emigrated. In 1928 Roman Jakobson and Iurii Tynianov published a brief manifesto of sorts which it has become customary to refer to as the "1928 theses."[30] In this publication they broke officially with a number of problematic tenets associated with the formal method dating from its origins, most notably with the notion that literature evolves on its own and can be studied synchronically and independently of other cultural phenomena. In other words they rejected both the purely synchronic and immanentist positions associated with formalism. They did not, however, which is obvious even from the title of their essay, reject the notion of literature as a fundamentally linguistic phenomenon whose specificity is in its self-referentiality (the aesthetic function). This avowed acceptance of literature's relationship to other cultural series was a major step in the direction of a fuller understanding of literature but literature and literary scholarship still remain dominated by considerations of technique (device) and self-referential language use.

III.2 Czech Structuralism and the Aesthetic Function

At about the same time as formalism was being wound down, the Prague linguistic circle was forming in Czechoslovakia.[31] It arose out of a felicitous collision of several factors not least of which were the personal contacts of the Czech scholars with some erstwhile members of the Russian formalist movement who had relocated temporarily or permanently during the twenties to Czechoslavakia, in particular, one can mention Roman Jakobson--who, at the age of thirty, was already active in founding his second school!, as well as Prince N. Trubetskoi and Petr Bogatyrev.[32] The Prague school made a number of highly significant contributions to linguistics and literary studies, not the least of which was to further the interrelationship between the two branches of study.

> One of the most characteristic features of the Prague school . . . is the close association between linguistics and literary studies. . . . it was based on a clear perception of the essential unity of goals and research methods in the two areas. [. . .] The essential unity of linguistic and literary studies is, in my opinion, the most precious heritage of the Prague school.[33]

Some even consider it to be a watershed in the intellectual development of the twentieth century,[34] which is probably not unreasonable given its enourmous influence not only on linguistics but also given the methodological example it provided for other disciplines.[35] Here we will not be interested in particular achievements of Prague school members in linguistics *per se*, but in their theory of and approach to literature. They saw literature as an integral part of linguistic research. They had a fundamental "conviction that language analysis without regard to poetry is as incomplete as an analysis of poetry without regard to words."[36]

To what part of language, then, does literature belong? "Functional linguistics views language as a sum of expedient means which are defined by various functions of the language"[37] or, in other words, "language is a totality only when viewed from the angle of purpose."[38] They distinguished between intellectual and emotional characteristics of utterances, with intellectual speech being addressed to someone (communication) and emotional speech being sometimes addressed and sometimes not (possible communication). Communication is necessarily social, but the social function of language distinguishes utterances by their "relationships to extralinguistic reality."[39] If the utterance is aimed at an object its function is communicative, if it is aimed at itself, it is poetic.[40]

"Each functional language utterance has its own system of conventions--its own language (*langue*)."[41] Therefore, the different functions are not related like *langue* and *parole*. Poetic language must be studied in such a way as not to confuse it with communicative language, but any poetic expression (*parole*) should be evaluated in relation to both poetic and communicative languages,[42] this being in accord with the standard structuralist strategy of defining features dynamically in terms of relationships.

The individual levels of poetic language, whether morphological, phonetic, grammatical, or whatever, are much more closely linked together than in communicative language. The levels are ascribed independent values:

> Poetic language aims at expression in and of itself and . . . all levels of a language system that have only an ancillary function in the communicative idiom acquire more or less independent values in the poetic language.[43]

Nevertheless, from the point of view of analysis, they cannot be considered in total isolation from one another. Art, here literary art, is characterized primarily by this concentration on verbal expression, on the sign itself.[44] Also, poetic language is to be understood and investigated not in reference to other phenomena, whether historical, sociological, psychological, etc. but "in and of itself, . . . [i.e. not in terms of] mysticism, of causal relationships between heterogeneous systems."[45] The means by which the poetic function is achieved is called 'foregrounding'[46] which is roughly, though not totally, equivalent to what the formalists called defamiliarization (остранение).

The progress achieved by the Prague school in comparison with the formalists, at least as far as the subject of this discussion is concerned, seems to be precisely in terms of the relation of literature to language in general. Their notion of the role of function in language makes it easier, from the formalist-structuralist point of view, to see where literature fits into the system of language. This is obtained by maintaining the notion of dominant function, particularly as it pertains to the communicative and aesthetic functions, and by the differentiation between poetic language and other types, especially the standard language (also called the standard literary langage). While the poetic and standard languages are defined in terms of each other, and they interact in manifold ways at various levels, they belong to different fields. The Prague scholars do not make their point unambiguously, but it is possible to distill a clear trend. Havranek's staement that "the regular foundation of *poetic language* is the standard,"[47] may have statistical validity, but it is in no way a valid definition with normative or prescriptive status. The standard is less extensive than the poetic, since the latter "has at its disposal . . . all the forms of the given language--often of different developmental phases thereof,"[48] and they both constitute different '*langues*'[49] bearing in mind the structural notion of separate but related.[50] While the definition of the standard language which the Prague school presents[51] is in some ways controversial, especially the presuppositions it maintains concerning culture, language and social class,[52] it contributes a great deal to establishing and clarifying the school's position.

Despite advances made on many fronts, in terms of a linguistic approach to literature and the notion of the dominant determining influence of the so-called aesthetic function, the Prague school added little to the position already taken up by Russian formalism.[53] Peter Steiner isolates five main contributions of Russian formalism to Czech structuralism, beginning with that which has already been mentioned: "The most important for poetics was the use of linguistics as a tool for the study of verbal art."[54] The second point of influence concerned the functional approach to language,[55] including the crucial notion of the aesthetic function, and something which was stressed by the Prague school, namely, multi-functionality, originating with Jakobson's notion of the dominant. The third point he mentions is the notion of остранение "as the principle of artistic form."[56] This, as we have seen, is closely bound up with the emphasis on the notion of art as device.57 What emerges from this, and it is confirmed in the writings of the school, is a view of art which maintains the notions of self-referentiality and aestheticism - albeit in a somewhat diminished form. This seriously impedes, and in the case of the Prague school, arguably prevented, a more satisfying approach to the fullness of verbal art, which will be seen to be located precisely in its communicative, referential and cognitive functions.

While I have not presented anything like a complete picture of the Prague school, especially having foregone a discussion of their interests in semiotics and later concerns with communication and dialogue, what I have presented remained central to their aesthetic and literary theory, and of their worldview, throughout. The Prague school ceased to exist officially by 1948 as a result of political changes in Eastern Europe, but its considerable legacy has not yet ceased to grow and is felt in many spheres of scholarly activity.58 An example, negative in my view, of what can happen when the notion of the self-referentiality of literature is taken one step farther is to be found in the work of Lubomir Dolezel, who emerged from the Prague school tradition. His work on narrative worlds takes the self-referentiality of literary texts to a very high level of abstraction in which all contact with the world of reality is fundamentally severed,59 certainly severed to an extent much greater than was attempted by the formalists or the Prague scholars.

III.3 Roman Jakobson--Poetry and Linguistics

The name which comes up most often in all these discussions is, of course, Roman Jakobson. He was a key figure in the rise of Russian formalism, and again in the Prague school, and from the 1940s has been a towering figure in linguistics as well as literary and folklore studies in the United States and, without exaggeration, throughout the world.60 Although he died in 1982, his influence continues to be felt to an enormous extent.61 From almost the very beginning up to the end of his career, Jakobson held that the study of literature was the purview of the science of linguistics.62 Moreover, he held that what made literature literature, i.e. *literariness* (литературность), was precisely its determination as verbal expression or language use with a dominant aesthetic, or self-referential, function. This is arguably *the* leitmotif which unites his early writings, ("Поэзия есть язык в его эстетической функции," 1921)[63] his contributions of the 30s and 40s

> (Only when a verbal work acquires poeticity, a poetic function of determinative significance, can we speak of poetry. But how does poeticity manifest itself? Poeticity is present when the word is felt as a word and not a mere representation of the object being named or an outburst of emotion, when words and their composition, their meaning, their external and internal form acquire a weight and value of their own instead of referring indifferently to reality. 1933-34)[64]

his model of communication[65] which he apparently developed in response to the inroads made by the new science of information theory,[66] and many of the other numerous contributions he made to the study of literature, linguistics, and related disciplines.[67]

Here I would simply like to refer to his model of communication and then briefly to his notion of the relationship between linguistics and poetry, i.e. literature. Jakobson's model of communication is essentially a schematic representation of the multi-functionalist theory of language held by members of the Prague linguistic circle and, to a certain extent, by the Russian formalists--with the addition of notions of how communication is organized which he appropriated from the then relatively new science of communication theory or information theory.[68] Within the context of the present discussion, it is not what is new in this model which stands out, but what is old.[69] Jakobson's theory of the dominant--which in some form or other seems to have come to be accepted and employed by a great variety of scholars involved in the study of literature--along with the notion of the aesthetic function, have been given a new graphic representation. For the purposes of identifying the specificity of literature, literary texts are still those which are self-referential, in other words, those in which the aesthetic function is dominant.

As concerns the relationship between linguistics and literature, Jakobson never appears to have substantially altered or modified his earliest position, i.e. that the study of literature is part of the study of language, or in other words, that poetics is part of linguistics. Certainly, at first look, this is hardly controversial or problematic. However, an anlysis of the positions of Bakhtin and Lotman on this question will reveal how very problematic it is. Essentially, it is bound up with a definition of literature which depends on the concept of the aesthetic function, that is to say, that literature is not *primarily* communicative or referential, i.e. that it is not primarily about something other than itself, which for Bakhtin and Lotman it most surely is.[70]

What I wish to demonstrate in what follows is that Bakhtin and Lotman in turn assumed positions which are fundamentally at odds with the notions of literature as self-referential verbal expression, and explicitly rejected not only the hegemony but also the primacy of linguistics in the study of literature. Furthermore, in so doing they define a ground and theoretical positions which are very close to each other and are highly compatible. The key factor in their strategies is their recognition of the dominant communicative and cognitive aspects of literature (and all of art) and the concommitant and concurrent rejection of the notion of self-referentiality. They stress the content, meaning and ideological levels of literature, the notions of world-view, and the inter-relationship of literature with other cultural series and with "life" or extra-textual reality. In order to arrive at such fundamentally different positions, they have to take as their ultimate starting point the rejection of literature as a functional component of natural language. At the risk of being repetitive, their starting point is the rejection of the starting point of the other schools and scholars discussed above, which for them had been critical in their development.

The notion of the importance of a starting point is often underestimated, but even small differences at the origin can eventually lead to enormous divergences. Some recent discussions in mathematics and related sciences have termed this factor the "butterfly effect," basing it on the realization or discovery that:

> tiny differences in input could quickly become overwhelming differences in output--a phenomenon given the name "sensitive dependence on initial conditions." In weather, for example, this translates into what is only half-jokingly known as the Butterfly Effect--the notion that a butterfly stirring the air today in Peking can transform storm systems next month in New York.[71]

In a strange twist, as Gleick indicates for the emerging science of chaotics or chaology,[72] the butterfly effect was the starting point, i.e. the recognition of the importance of the starting point was the starting point.[73] Bakhtin and Lotman also demonstrate an awareness of the importance of the starting point and, I would contend, this is a major consideration in establishing what sets their theoretical positions apart from those referred to above and others like them. Formalism and Prague school structuralism began from the notion that the specificity of literature is in the fact that it is a special form of language use.

Bakhtin and Lotman begin not only by rejecting formalism and its narrow understanding of the aesthetic function, but by affirming the need to study and understand literature in a broadly based context.[74] So, while the term butterfly effect is used in the context of the study of chaos to highlight the crucial importance of even the smallest initial differences, it still can be used to refer to the larger scale differences we are dealing with here.

III.4 Bakhtin--Content, Material and Form

While the formalists and Czech structuralists made it their clearly defined objective to determine what the specificity of literature was, Bakhtin set out to do almost the exact opposite. Poetics, or literary theory, according to Bakhtin, must be founded on a general systematic aesthetics, and only then can one look at the specific nature of literary art.[75] Although it seems reasonable to expect to find a discussion of the relationship of literature to language and linguistics in some of his later essays which bear titles ostensibly alluding to such topics, for example "Слово в романе"[76] or "Проблема речевых жанров,"[77] this is not, in fact, the case. In these later essays he is primarily concerned with questions of discourse and dialogue in general, the novel as genre, and related questions, but he does not specifically take up the question of how literature differs from other verbal events or texts. To a great extent, the later works assume the principles and framework he establishes in the early works. What he has to say in these essays does bear on the present question but it is first necessary to turn to one of his earliest works to find his only systematic attempt to present his views on the question of what literature as a whole actually is.[78]

In many of his subsequent writings he discusses the question of *the novel* as differentiated from other speech genres, but, even though Bakhtin may occasionally give the impression of believing it, the novel is not coterminous with literature. I will return to the question of Bakhtin's theory of the novel below, but it will not be at the centre of the present inquiry. As Caryl Emerson has pointed out in her most recent

Literature as Communication and Cognition in Bakhtin and Lotman 77

work,[79] Bakhtin actually does take up the question in another place, i.e. in the essay "Автор и герой в эстетической деятельности,"[80] however, it is not developed at length, and is largely formulated on the basis of the ideas set out in the essay "Проблема содержания." The archivists/editors are not sure when "Автор и герой" was written,[81] but it dates from the same period as the finished work "Проблема содержания."

This raises the question of why "Проблема содержания" has been almost totally ignored, and certainly never discussed at any length. It was omitted from the English translation of the volume in which it was published[82] because it did not relate to the question of novelistic discourse,[83] and it has never recovered the status it surely should have had, and perhaps otherwise would have. On the other hand, it was translated into French,[84] but has not fared better in French language discussions than it has in English. Caryl Emerson and Gary Saul Morson, in their re-evaluation of Bakhtin,[85] write as if the work did not exist, directing all their considerable skills and efforts to unfinished fragments containing, alongside more powerful ones, "hazy and inadequate" formulations which Bakhtin subsequently "abandoned."[86]

Finally, it should be pointed out that Bakhtin did complete "Проблема содержания" by 1924, and that it did not appear in print only because the Journal in which it was to appear "прекратил свое существование" as the editors of ВЛЭ, so euphemistically put it.[87] It was one of the first works which Bakhtin worked on and authorized for publication during the 1970s, appearing in abridged form in the journal Контекст[88] under the title "К эстетике слова." However, Bakhtin's anti-formalist and anti-structuralist editors may have been or indeed likely were pushing him to get this work out in a hurry.[89]

In a certain sense, i.e. insofar as it contains at least one of the central roots of his later thinking, we can turn to his first and briefest published work, "Искусство и ответственность" (1919)[90] to find a concise, if almost aphoristic statement of what art and--by implication--literature, are for Bakhtin. Here he formulates his notion of the three axiological domains of culture, i.e., science or cognition, art or the aesthetic, and the practical or ethical, which together "обретают единство только в личности, которая приобщает их к своему единству."[91] His search for integration and unity within human subjectivity or personhood, which will occupy an enormous portion of his energies for the rest of his life, here receives a very terse, yet, in context, very forceful formulation: "Искусство и жизнь не одно, но должны стать во мне единым, в единстве моей ответственности."[92]

The significance of this essay only really becomes clear in the light of his later writings, but it is important to note how early he had arrived at some of his most fundamental ideas. In his early essay on the problem of content, material, and form, he formulates his fundamental theoretical position concerning the nature of art, its relation to the other fields of human culture, the specific nature of literature, and its relation to language and linguistics.[93] It is extremely important to note that his point of departure is a criticism of Russian formalism, which was at the height of its development, and of the formalists' notion of the linguistic specificity of literature.[94] As mentioned, Bakhtin locates aesthetic activity within the unity of human culture, the three domains of which must be understood in relation to one another. They are not to be understood as three separate fields, but as boundaries, or limits, where cultural activities meet or come together. Given the notions of culture and aesthetic activity, poetics should be considered within this unity, and therefore should be seen as an aesthetics of verbal artistic creation.[95] As such it must be dependent on a general systematic aesthetics. Approaching literature from the point of view of linguistics as the formalists and their fellow travellers do leads to a narrow and unsatisfactory materialist aesthetic. This is similar to trying to found a theory of music on accoustics, of architecture on geometry and dynamics, of painting on optics, and so on. Such an aesthetics sees man's aesthetic activity directed only at the material of art, in this case language, and excludes all other possibilities, including the notion that artistic and creative activity is axiological and is intentionally directed at the world, at reality, at man, at his social and other ethical relations.[96] Bakhtin readily grants that materialist aesthetics, such as that practiced by the formalists is very productive and has yielded important results in technical studies on such questions as rhythm and metrics. However, in this positive light it must be viewed only as a "working hypothesis."[97]

Perhaps it is necessary to point out that Bakhtin is upholding a key distinction in the context of the philosophy of science or methodology. What he has in mind by the notion of a working hypothesis is a concept or proposition which makes no claim to veracity. It is capable of producing results within a narrowly defined sphere, but if its proponents attempt to apply it in any general sense, it cannot be

maintained. Bakhtin opposes this notion to a general theory which
purports to be capable of explaining all of the phenomena within its
purview. In other words, while the so-called working hypothesis may be
capable of producing significant results, it can be shown to be
demonstrably false by the general theory. The argument has had numerous
manifestations throughout the history of philosophy and science, but
ultimately it can be reduced to the question of whether the theoretician is
primarily concerned with results or with truth. Bakhtin, like Galileo and
Copernicus, believes his theory is a true description of the phenomena it
would describe, while he implies that formalism is simply a convenient
hypothesis for resolving certain limited problems, but is ultimately false,
or at least can make no ultimate claims to truthfulness.[98] In this regard,
Boris `Eikhenbaum's statement that "в своей научной работе
мы ценим теорию только как рабочую гипотезу,"[99]
is both a confirmation of the basis of Bakhtin's criticism, if not a
justification for it, as well as a fairly adequate restatement of the medieval
notion of *apparentes salvare*, as held by such figures as Ossiander and
Galileo's antogonist, Cardinal Bellarmino, and which Karl Popper has
redubbed *instrumentalism*.[100]

    Bakhtin gives a number of reasons why a materialist aesthetics is
deficient as a genuine theory of aesthetics. 1) It cannot ground or provide
a basis for artistic form. Form here can only be a relationship to material,
while for Bakhtin it defines an attitude which includes higher valorising
emotional-volitional activities of the artist or perceiver. Ultimately, for
materialist aesthetics, aesthetic experience is simply one of pleasure, i.e.
as organized material a work of art can only be understood as having a
practical, utilitarian determination, as a stimulus to a psycho-physical
condition, and he notes the tendency of the formalists to use expressions
such as "ощущать форму," "сделать художественное
произведение," and so on.[101] As a counter-example Bakhtin notes
that in the case of sculpture, artist and perceiver direct their aesthetic
activity not to the marble but to the valorised human form. The marble,
like the sculptor's chisel, is meaningful, but secondary. The same can be
said of other arts: while in the case of such arts as music or literature the
situation may be more complicated, it is, nevertheless, essentially the
same.[102]

    2) Material aesthetics cannot differentiate between the tangible
external work and its larger manifestation which Bakhtin calls the
aesthetic object. This is what the object of aesthetic analysis is and he
defines it broadly as "содержание эстетической

деятельности (созерцания), направленное на произведение."[103] He identifies three moments or tasks of aesthetic analysis: a) to understand the artistic uniqueness and structure of the aesthetic object, i.e. its architectonics, that is to say, its organization independent of its material;[104] b) to refer to the work in terms of its physical, material properties, i.e its strictly cognitive dimension, independent of the aesthetic object;[105] c) and finally, to understand the external, material work as realizing the aesthetic object, as a technical apparatus for aesthetic completion. This involves a teleological method of analysis, and the object of this part of the analysis Bakhtin calls the composition of the work. He describes it as an accumulation of the factors of artistic impression, the external relations of the intentional whole. Materialist aesthetics can only deal with the second of these three tasks.[106]

3) Materialist aesthetics cannot differentiate between architectonic and compositional form.

> Архитектонические формы суть формы душевной и телесной ценности эстетического человека, формы природы--как его окружения, формы события в его лично-жизненном, социальном и историческом аспекте и проч.: все они суть достижения, осуществленности, они ничему не служат, а успокоенно довлеют себе,--это формы эстетического бытия в его своеобразии.
>
> Композиционные формы, организующие материал, носят телеологический, служебный, как бы беспокойный характер и подлежат чисто технической оценке: насколько адекватно они осуществляют архитектоническое задание. Архитектоническая форма определяет выбор композиционной: так, форма трагедии (форма события, отчасти личности--трагеческий характер) избирает адекватную композиционную форму--драматическую. Отсюда, конечно, не следует, что архитектоническая форма существует где-то в

готовом виде и может быть осуществлена помимо композиционной.[107]

Bakhtin holds that all arts, given the similarity of their architectonic aims, share analogous compositional forms, although their different materials differentiate them.[108]

4) Materialist aesthetics cannot account for artistic or aesthetic vision outside of art. These are hybrid or impure areas of aesthetic activity, but materialist aesthetics cannot even approach them since there is a total absence of *material* or *technique*.[109]

5) Materialist aesthetics cannot ground a history of art. Since history cannot admit of an isolated series, and materialist aesthetics sees its object in isolation, separated by virtue of its material determination, and lacks a general systematic aesthetic, it can at best produce a pattern of exchange of various technical devices within a given art over time, but it cannot enter the complexity of history.[110]

Having thus cast doubt on the ability of materialist (formalist) aesthetics to provide a basis for an adequate view of art in general or for any specific art, Bakhtin then proceeds to examine the three basic phases or aspects of aesthetic activity: content, material and form. He begins with a discussion of content, central to which is a restatement of his notion of the three fields of human culture--the cognitive, the ethical, and the aesthetic--which are not to be understood territorially, but in contiguity. They have what he calls attached autonomy or autonomous attachment.[111] Only thus understood within the unity of culture can any cultural act cease to be a bare fact and acquire significance and meaning, becoming like a sort of monad, reflecting everything and reflected in everything.[112] An activity of any member of the cultural triad encounters not a neutral reality, but a reality already valorised by the other two, in an atmosphere of responsive mutual determination, therefore life or reality "opposed" to art is always reality already cognitively and ethically valorised.[113] There is no neutral reality which can be opposed to art or aesthetic reality.[114]

Bakhtin discusses briefly the differences between the cognitive, ethical and aesthetic approaches to reality, but does not go into great detail concerning the former two.[115] At present I feel uncertain about entering into the discussion of the texts where he does apparently expand on the ethical.[116] The matter of these new texts has all the makings of a new controversy in the fashion of the disputed texts. Certainly, Bakhtin's editors, Bocharov and Kozhinov *et al.*, have a bad track record and are simply not to be trusted. Nina Perlina notes that "when placed next to one another, Bocharov's highly selective publications impede proper textual attribution and textological analysis of the whole."[117] Further on she notes, for example, that "in many instances, the epistemological, thematic, and compositional connection of "K filosofii postupka" to "Author and Hero" has to be simply divined."[118] Given the doubts that Emerson and Morson themselves express concerning the textology here,[119] it would seem prudent to await a thorough textological study such as Perlina has promised,[120] before extensively incorporating these studies into the picture.

One further note, which throws one more wrench into the works, concerns the question of Kantianism, or anti-Kantianism. While Bakhtin may have singled out Kant[121] as a particular object of criticism, his framework still owes a considerable debt to Kant and the neo-Kantian tradition, especially as concerns the division of human cultural activity into the three fields of cognition, act, and the aesthetic, and this would need to be analyzed and elaborated. Certainly, the first and clearly necessary step is to begin the process of analyzing the only complete essay from this early period so that the ideas it expresses can be brought to bear on any further discussion.[122]

Returning to the differences between the cognitive, ethical, and aesthetic approaches to reality, essentially, he stresses the negative character of the cognitive and ethical, the fact that they, each in their own way, operate, at least analytically viewed, independently of the other two.[123] The aesthetic, on the other hand, is all-embracing in its receptivity.

> Преднаходимая эстетическим актом, опознанная и оцененная поступком действительность входит в произведение (точнее в эстетический объект) и становится здесь необходимым конститутивным моментом. В этом смысле мы можем сказать: действительно, жизнь находится не только вне искусства, но и в нем, внутри его, во всей полноте своей ценностной весомости: социальной, политической, познавательной и иной. Искусство богато, оно не сухо, не специально: художник специалист только как

мастер, то есть только по отношению к
материалу.*124*

Everything enters into art, it rejects nothing. Art transforms reality without changing its cognised and ethically valorised nature. While cognition and act create a new reality, art enriches, embellishes, and fulfills reality. It unifies the worlds of cognition and act, it humanizes nature and naturalizes man.[125]

Art creates new form as a new valorising attitude towards that which has already become reality for act and cognition. This is the basis for novelty and originality in art: what was previously valorised cognitively or ethically is now, by virtue of the free creative activity of the artist and the perceiver seen and experienced in a new way.[126] These and several other observations especially on the relationship between the three areas of cultural activity, allow Bakhtin to propose the following definition of content in art:

Действительность познания и этического поступка, входящую в своей опознанности и оцененности в эстетический объект и подвергающуюся здесь конкретному, интуитивному объединению, индивидуации, конкретизации, изоляции и завершению, то есть всестороннему художественному оформлению с помощью определенного материала, мы ––в полном согласии с традиционным словоупотреблением ––называем содержанием художественного произведения (точнее, эстетического объекта).

Содержание есть необходимый конститутивный момент эстетического объекта, ему коррелятивна художественная форма, вне этой корреляции не имеющая вообще никакого смысла.*127*

The artist, in principle, is detached from, does not participate in, or directly experience this valorised reality. He experiences it in a correlative way (сопереживает).[128] From an external position, the aesthetic activity of the artist imposes an artistic form on the content, according to which the traditional formulation of form and content is acceptable.[129] Thus content in art is neither form nor material. Content is always *informed*; the notions of form and content are separable only for purposes of analysis.[130]

Bakhtin next sets out three aspects of how content is realized in artistic creation and perception, and what the tasks and methods of analyzing it are. 1) It is necessary, he says, to distinguish between cognitive and ethical moments which are part of content and those which are directed at or involve the content but do not enter into it. 2) Content cannot be purely cognitive, ideed, the ethical is primary in content.[131] Content is not an idea, it must be related to the world of human action.[132] 3) The ethical moment of artistic creation and perception must be experienced immediately, not through theoretical analysis. It is a *direct* experience between two consciousnesses: "путем сопереживания или вчувствования и сооценки."[133] It is the relation of the ethical to the cognitive that makes a judgement or statement within a work of art artistic and not simply theoretical.

Turning to the problem of material, Bakhtin first notes that material is to be understood in its strict scientific determination, i.e. without any embellishments or additions. Leading from this he strictures against those who would treat language as some sort of metaphysical, mythical, religious, or otherwise enriched substance. He would include here those who refer to anything as remote as the biblical *logos*. He also strictures against those who misrepresent culture as being totally co-terminous with language; both notions, he says, are greatly deformed in the process.[134] Language as the material of poetry must be understood linguistically.[135] While on the one hand, there is no such thing as a neutral statement, on the other hand, linguistics *qua* linguistics finds itself forced to ignore the political, social, ethical, artistic or other values of a statement; it is indifferent to these values. Any statement is equal for linguistics, whether it be by Newton, Dostoevsky, or John Doe. Accordingly, without the aid of aesthetics, linguistics cannot deal with poetry.[136]

Unlike any other area of culture, literature uses *all* of language. It leaves no aspect of language outside of its purview, including not only all lexical and dialectical aspects, but also sound, intonation, syntax, grammar, etc. It uses these to the fullest extent, but in doing so, literature overcomes language, this being the fundamental characteristic of their relationship. The artist uses the material, but at the moment of artistic perception it remains outside, excluded. "Язык в своей *лингвистической определенности в эстетический объект словесного искусства не входит.*[137] Bakhtin gives examples from other arts illustrating how their materials do not enter into the aesthetic object as independent, self-sufficient signifiers, and by extension, he also excludes technique from the aesthetic object, since it most properly relates to the material.[138]

The artist does not deal with objects, but with their values as represented by language. It is not the language (material) which enters the aesthetic object, but the values and meanings it conveys. An aesthetic object contains ethico-aesthetical moments (события) which have been completely determined and artistically completed, and these are made of what he calls images. These "informed moments of content" must be sharply excluded from any visual association.[139]

> *Итак, эстетический компонент――назовем его пока образом――не ест ни понятие, ни слово, ни зрительное представление, а своеобразное эстетическое образование, осуществляемое в поэзии с помощью слова, в изобразительных искусствах――с помощью зрительно воспринимаемого материала, но нигде не совпадающее ни с материалом, ни с какой-либо материальной комбинацией.*[140]

Material is important insofar as the aesthetic object is realized only through material. In this respect, "техника в искусстве все."[141] Therefore technique is not a word with immediately pejorative connotations, and it is not mechanical except in bad works or in bad investigations. Still, one must bear in mind what the limitations of technical and material analyses are: by definition they cannot enter into the aesthetic object itself, only into the material object through which it is realized.[142] Such analysis cannot, as the formalists claimed, "exhaust" the aesthetic object.

The final problem to be discussed is that of artistic form:

> *Художественная форма есть форма содержания, но сплошь осуществленная на материале, как бы прикрепленная к нему. Поэтому форма должна быть понята и изучена в двух направлениях: 1) изнутри чистого*

> эстетического объекта, как архитектоническая форма, ценностно направленная на содержание (возможное событие), отнесенная к нему и 2) изнутри композиционного материального целого произведения: это изучение техники формы.[143]

Needless to say, this division involves some very fine and abstract distinctions. Bakhtin seems most concerned to point out, first of all, that form in the second orientation must not be understood as the form of material, but as form realized "on" and through the material.[144] In his discussion, Bakhtin's intent is to examine form on a non-technical, strictly aesthetic plane. As such his question is: How can form, being realized entirely on material, become the form of content, axiologically related to it, or how can form as the organization of material unite and organize cognitive and ethical values of the aesthetically active subject in a work of art?[145] The resolution lies in the notion of authoring or creating. Cognitive or practical acts do not have an aesthetically active author/creator, while aesthetic activity does have one as a basic constitutive element.[146] Cognitive form is found or discovered, while aesthetic form is created.[147] And the author/perceiver is a constitutive moment of that form, this being probably the crucial point in the whole discussion, that which provides the impetus and unity to Bakhtin's whole theory.

> В форме *я нахожу себя*, свою продуктивную ценностно оформляющую активность, я живо чуствую свое созидающее предмет движение, притом не только в первичном творчестве, не только при собственном исполнении, но и при созерцании художественного произведения: *я должен пережить себя в известной степени творцом формы, чтобы вообще осуществить художественно-значимую форму как таковую.*[148]

The artist/perceiver not only expresses but experiences aesthetic form. It is his/her active valorising relationship to content. It is necessary to internalize, to appropriate a work of art, to make it one's own, in order for it to be experienced aesthetically.[149] Form is the expression of the

Literature as Communication and Cognition in Bakhtin and Lotman 87

active valorising relationship of the artist/perceiver to content; characteristically in this relationship, in the experiencing of form, we not only overcome the limitations of the material, but we sense both ourselves and this active valorising activity.[150] Cognitive activity is not individualized, not directed at the personality. Content is inherently passive in relation to form, and only becomes aesthetically realized via the agency of creative artistic activity in and through form.[151]

The primary function of form in relation to content is that of isolation or separation.[152] This relates to the work not as material, but to its meaning or content. It is a question of severing the ties of the cognitive and ethical moments of the work with cognitive and ethical reality--without destroying them--allowing for individuation of that which would otherwise by its very nature be a non-isolable and non-completable moment of existence (событие бытия).[153] Content is then a moment of existence freed by form from responsivity (ответсвенность) towards the future, completed and separate. This isolation removes all aspects of thingness from content. Once isolated it cannot be a thing.[154] The formalist notion of "остранение" is related to this notion of isolation, but Bakhtin holds that they simply dealt with it primitively, on a material and sometimes psychological level.[155] Isolation is the first component of form, being a negative condition ("отрицательное условие") for the personal subjective character of form; "она позволяет автору-творцу стать конститутивным моментом формы."[156] In form the author/creator experiences his aesthetic activity, feels his freedom in creation.[157] At the same time, isolation renders the material conditional, making it that in which the artist works with values of isolated reality, transcending the material itself without going outside of it. An utterance in literature ceases to require a response from reality, a request in a lyric does not expect a reply from its addressee, nor does a prayer in literature require God. "Форма, пользуясь одним материалом, восполняет всякое событие и этическое напряжение до полноты свершения."[158] The creator enters this isolated moment as creator without becoming a direct participant. This isolation makes the material, here the word or utterance, formally creative.[159]

Bakhtin identifies five hierarchically organized[160] levels of language-material which enter a work of verbal art, and which he lists in reverse hierarchical order: **1.** the accoustical, **2.** lexical, **3.** syntactic, **4.** intonational, and **5.** what he calls a sense or feeling of verbal activeness, or a sense of active production of verbal meaning, which includes internal and external non-verbal components of a given utterance such as gesture and movement and still others such as the personal origin of the meaning or value or intent of the utterance. This fifth is the highest level and reflects the other four, being that side of the utterance which is oriented to the personality of the speaker.[161] The artist and perceiver employ all levels of language both to express content and to realize form. By contrast, in a cognitive utterance the second, lexical level is the most important. It is the importance of the fifth level in poetry which characterizes its uniqueness, since only this level returns the creative personality back upon itself, upon its active, creative unity, returns it back to the source of the meaningful moment, of the created meaning of the work of art.[162]

Form and the formal moments of a work of art do not depend on what they are about, but on how they create the unity of moment and object in the artistic and aesthetic activity. It is the activity of experiencing this specially isolated moment in which, by returning to myself as origin and end of this aesthetic activity, and in which I discover myself in this activity that characterizes aesthetic form.

> Единство эстетической формы есть, таким образом, единство позиции действующей души и тела, действующего цельного человека, опирающегося на себя самого.[163]

Bakhtin looks at how the five levels of language are involved in the creative activity of artistic form,[164] and, while they will not be examined here, how they aid in determining the manner in which artistic form is realized through language by the artist/perceiver in defining his relationship to content.

> Творцом переживает себя единичный человек—субъект только в искусстве. Положительно—субъективная творческая личность есть конститутивный момент художественной формы, здесь субъективность ее находит своеобразную объективацию, становится культурно—значимой творческой субъективностью: здесь же осуществляется своебразное единство органического—— телесного и внутреннего——душевного и

> духовного — — человека, но единство — — изнутри переживаемое. Автор, как конститутивный момент формы, есть организованная, изнутри исходящая активность цельного человека, сплошь осуществляющего свое задание, ничего не предполагающего вне себя для завершения, притом — — всего человека, с ног до головы: он нужен весь — — дышащий (ритм), движущийся, видящий, слышащий, помнящий, любящий и понимающий.[165]

In his conclusion, Bakhtin stresses the centrality to aesthetic analysis of the aesthetic object, its organic quality or non-thingness, the presence of the artist/perceiver as active subject in the artistic form of the content, and the special position of verbal art among the other arts due to its material--language--which grants its creator/s a non-mediated position, and, perhaps most importantly, he stresses the all inclusive and *personal* nature of art:

> Художественно-творящая форма оформляет прежде всего человека, а мир — — лишь как мир человека, или непосредственно его очеловечивая, оживляя, или приводя в столь непосредственную ценностную связь с человеком, что он теряет рядом с ним свою ценностную самостоятельность, становится только моментом ценности человеческой жизни. Вследствие этого отношение формы к содержанию в единстве эстетического объекта носит своеобразный персональный характер, а эстетический объект является некоторым своеобразным осуществленным событием действия и взаимодействия творца и содержания.[166]

As stated above, this essay has been largely overlooked by scholars in their studies of Bakhtin. When it has been briefly referred to, it is largely in the context of it being a criticism of formalism. That it most certainly is, but it is much more. It should be remembered that Bakhtin set out not only to criticise the formal school and what he calls materialist aesthetics, but to sketch out a general, systematic, and philosophical aesthetics. Nowhere does he return in any detail to the concerns he expresses here, but it seems safe to assume that by virtue of his return to this text in the 1970s with apparently only minor revisions that he still held to the ideas set forth in it some 40 years after it was written. Moreover, practically all subsequent works contain unelaborated references to the three areas of human culture and to the notions of content, material and form as presented in this essay.

A curious and problematic dialectic is created when "Проблема содержания" is confronted with his later works. First of all, this essay does not deal with his notion of dialogue or even the communicative nature of literature together with other speech genres. Nevertheless, the subjective, in the sense of personal, nature of aesthetic activity is certainly brought out, and it will be a key factor in his later essays. He does not mention here the possibility or need for a science of meta-linguistics, although the basis for this claim is certainly present in his criticism of poetics based on linguistics. In subsequent works, the nature of the utterance in literature and non-literature will differ only as ends of a continuum;[167] he will be more interested in the difference between the novel and non-novelistic genres, than between literature and non-literature.

Some of his studies look at the problem more immanently, examining such questions as the relationship between author and hero, the specific nature of discourse in the novel, the image of the author (образ автора), polyphony as the hallmark of Dostoevsky's poetics, and so on. Scholarship has fixated on Bakhtin's theory of discourse and speech genres, while regrettably ignoring what was obviously important for him, i.e the general aesthetic and philosophical basis for discussing any form of art or aesthetic activity.

While his essay on the problem of methodology in the humanities and science returns to and reaffirms some notions of the essay discussed above, his focus is both different and more limited. Insofar as the focus of the discussion in this chapter is the relationship between literature, language, and linguistics I do not need to go much further than the essay on content, material and form. In it Bakhtin has already set out his central notions, i.e. that language is neither content nor form in literature, but material, and literature in employing it transforms and overcomes it. Linguistics is not capable of studying or investigating literature except in relation to material. A different approach, a different branch of learning is necessary to study verbal art, what Bakhtin will later call meta-linguistics.[168] Art is concerned not with grammar, syntax, images (traditionally understood), devices, or technique, but with values, with the valorising activity of man. Literature is clearly not primarily about language somehow reflecting itself.

Subsequently Bakhtin will set out how languages represent value systems, points of view, worldviews,[169] and how these are presented in literature, especially in novelistic literature. Literature (primarily novelistic literature) is an artistic representation of worldviews through language. Bakhtin's position will emerge as basically, though not necessarily traditionally or naively, representational. The basis for this is to be found in the essay on material, content and form, where he most clearly affirms the presence of cognitively and aesthetically valued yet artistically transformed reality in works of art or aesthetic objects.

III.5 Lotman's Definitions of Literature

In discussing Lotman's position relative to the question of literature, language and linguistics, I will employ a significantly different methodology than that employed in preceding sections. This arises from the nature of his writings on the subject and the manner in which he has arrived at and formulated his position. With regards to the matter of ascertaining his stance on the formalist/Prague school notion that literature is natural language in its aesthetic function, that in literature we are dealing with self-referential language use, there is no problem: Lotman programmatically and philosophically dissociated himself from any such conceptions at the very outset.[170] Literature is a communication[171] system organized in the same way as natural language (по тыпу языка) but is not a part of the system of natural language functions.[172] Moreover, it cannot be studied by linguistics *qua* linguistics, although linguistics has a contribution to make, both methodologically, and to the extent to which language is the material of verbal art.[173] Language enters the work of art and is then transformed.[174] Right from the moment Lotman joined the semiotic-structural movement in the Soviet Union he has distanced himself, and to a lesser extent the movement, from the study of linguistically oriented semiotic systems, i.e. natural language, and any other primary modelling systems, and from the strict application of linguistics.[175]

Given the rather unambiguous nature of Lotman's position on this question, I will present several aspects of what Lotman says literature is, and how it relates to several notions fundamental to Lotman's general theoretical position. What emerges should allow me to formulate some significant points of comparison and compatibility between the theoretical positions of Lotman and Bakhtin, which will already have been seen to be seriously at odds with fundamental notions in the theoretical positions of the other major schools and scholars discussed above. Throughout the following discussion it should be remembered that in place of the aesthetic function, i.e. self-referentiality, Lotman takes literature to be, first of all, a form of cognition, operating by means of a reflection (отображение) of reality (life), including the structure of the artist's consciousness or his worldview[176] and, secondly, a form of communication, i.e. transmission of information.

> 1) Искусство познает жизнь, пользуясь средствами ее отображения.
>
> 2) Познание в искусстве всегда связано с коммуникацией, передачей сведений.[177]

In the case of Lotman, it seems most appropriate to examine some of the definitions he has offered concerning the nature of literature. While the formalists and the members of the Prague school preferred to specify what literature is in terms of a functional determination, Lotman, while he has not totally eschewed this strategy,[178] has frequently made statements of a typically definitional type, and would seem to have a predilection for such statements. Still, it could, and no doubt will, be argued that a clear, categorical definition of what literature is does not emerge from these statements as a group or individually considered, but that is perhaps bound up with various problems associated with the generation of definitions. Lotman's definitions, as will be shown, do help to clarify at least what he considers literature to be, even if they do not provide an unassailably unified concept. It must be remembered that Lotman's position has not remained static, although I would caution against positing a marked evolution of his fundamental position. More apt, I would contend, is to say his position has been shifting, expanding and refining itself. These internal movements account for some of the variance in his definitional statements. Such shifts could reasonably be expected of any thinker in a project of such a scale and scope, i.e. the study of all of culture. But there are, as will be shown, other factors at work here as well.

It is important to know what we expect from definitional statements. As a minimal criterion I would suggest that definitions ought to be capable of assisting us in classification, identification, description and understanding of the thing being described. Aristotle, who, through his writings, is responsible for much of the history of definition in the western world, felt that we need not, or indeed ought not to expect the same degree of precision in all areas of knowledge. In particular, he was referring to his own endeavors in the field of ethics or moral science, which he saw as succumbing to less terminological precision than, say physics, metaphysics, or logic.[179] This is not to say that Aristotle is encouraging sloppiness or laxness, or that we should hide behind his allowance for greater or lesser precision but, and this is the thrust of Aristotle's remarks, it is necessary to bring to bear a certain amount of common sense on our expectations. I make no appeal to Aristotle's authority for shortcomings in my own use of terms or concepts, or in my re-creation of Lotman's use of them, but this notion of degree of precision is important.[180]

As an example of how difficult it can be to find correct and useful conceptualizations and to define them, I would relate a historical moment from the field of theoretical physics. This is a field of knowledge which operates with almost unbearable precision and omni-quantification. Yet, in 1984, when Nobel laureate physicist Sheldon Glashow, in his search for a *Grand Unified Theory* (GUT) of all the known forces at work in the universe, suspected he had discovered a new fifth force, he had difficulty in describing it in "English."[181] Here is how he paraphrased the published version of his suspected discovery:

> In it I claim that what we're seeing is the first manifestation of a fifth force of nature--the "smelly force." It has to do with a previously unknown property I call "odor." Odor goes along with color, right? I note that the O(18) group, which I'm pushing, predicts that there could be hundreds of odoriferous particles--or maybe I said "odorous." Anyway, I'm really talking *structure*.[182]

The published version is reportedly no less metaphorical, but how *does* one deal with "256-dimensional representation," when most of us have problems with two or three dimensions?

What I hope to arrive at, therefore, is mainly a better understanding of how Lotman views literature, how his theory of literature and culture is constructed, and to a certain extent, how he differs in his approach from the other positions discussed above with which he is often mistakenly and dangerously confused. Lotman is difficult and somewhat confusing when one attempts to arrange and systematize what has not been presented by him in a systematic fashion. I would refer to the words of a one-time collaborator of Lotman's to highlight how difficult it can be to unwind the sometimes labyrinthine twists of Lotman's thought. According to Boris Ogibenin, many of Lotman's writings,

> while proposing novel ideas concerning the two basic concepts, *contain many statements which need clarification. These latter are indeed sometimes so cryptic, so concisely formulated, and at times so utterly confusing, that one may easily be at a loss when trying to apprehend them systematically* with a view to using them as guidelines for practical purposes. Many of the notions are so intuitively formed that except for Lotman himself--who has done the major work on the semiotic approach to culture, along with Uspenskii--none of the most active semioticians has attempted consistently and systematically to apply the concept of culture as message or text . . . in concrete analysis.[183]

Definition #1: Literature is those texts which a given collective calls literary. One of the clearest statements by Lotman of what literature is, but in many ways one of the least helpful, comes from his 1973 article entitled "О содержании и структуре понятиия 'художественная литература.'"[184]

> Если рассматривать художественную литературу как определенную сумму текстов, то прежде всего, придется отметить, что в общей системе культуры эти тексты будут составлять часть. Существование художественных текстов подразумевает одновременное наличие нехудожественных и то, что коллектив, который ими пользуется, умеет проводить различие между ними. Неизбежные колебания в пограничных случаях только подкрепляют самый принцип: когда мы испытываем сомнения, следует ли отнести русалку к женщинам или к рыбам, или свободный стих к поэзии или прозе, мы

заранее исходим из этих классификационных делений как данных. В этом смысле представление о литературе (логически, а не исторически) предшествует литературе.[185]

According to the tenets of the functional approach, those texts will be considered literary which fulfill a poetic or aesthetic function, and this will be determined by its self-referentiality, or "установка на выражение."[186] According to Lotman, however,

Новейшие семиотические исследования подводят к прямо противоположным выводам. Эстетически функционирующий текст выступает как текст повышенной, а не пониженной, по отношению к нехудожественным текстам, семантической нагрузки.[187]

Lotman proposes a totally different aproach to determining which texts are, in fact, literary. It is based on the internal organization of the text; in other words, he is working towards an objective standard for determining what is and what is not literature. I will return below to the question of how literary texts are organized internally. If, in this definition, Lotman is saying that literature is whatever a given collective thinks it is, to paraphrase weakly, in subsequent definitions he will be seen to suggest more technically sophisticated and intentional formulations--indeed, in the remainder of the same article he elaborates considerably on the initial formulation as given above.[188]

An important aspect of Lotman's theory of literature and culture is his incorporation of principles and ideas from a number of disciplines and theoretical orientations into his program. The major elements obviously include structuralism and semiotics, but also cybernetics and information theory, as well as various elements of literary and cultural history, aspects of anthropology, philosophy, psychology, neurophysiology and, in special brackets, linguistics--bearing in mind that he rejects the above-mentioned distinction of poetic language as a functional variation of natural language. He does not study natural language as such, although he studies other communication systems as languages, and--a point which is crucial to understanding certain aspects of his methodology--the model of investigation employed by structural linguistics has been extensively appropriated by him.[189]

I propose, then, to discuss a number of definitional statements with at least one from each of the major confluent streams within Lotman's theory. The list is not meant to be exhaustive, but fairly representative. Such an overall perspective, i.e. a view of Lotman's theory considering all or at least most of these streams has, for the most part, been lacking, and remains a major desideratum in the study of Lotman.[190]

Definition #2: Let us turn, then, to the concept for which Lotman is perhaps best known. *Literature (art) is a secondary modelling system.*[191] According to Lotman,

> В науках семиотического цикла *язык* определяется как механизм знаковой коммуникации, служащий целям хранения и передачи информации.[192]

Languages can be divided into three basic groups: **1.** natural languages;[193] **2.** artificial languages;[194] **3.** secondary languages, i.e. secondary modelling systems.[195] These latter are

> коммуникационные структуры, надстраивающиеся над естественно-языковым уровнем (миф, религия). *Искусство-- вторичная моделирующая система.*"[196]

It is important to note that he refers to all secondary modelling systems in this way, not only to verbal art, because secondary in relation to language does not imply the use of language as material, but rather structured along the lines of language (*по типу языка*). Natural languages, or primary modelling systems, are one-to-one models of the world whose signs are conventional and which have easily distinguishable levels of expression and content. Secondary modelling systems are much more complex models of the world which seek to model the world in its general features from a certain perspective. They are superimposed on language and have unique and much more complex relations between content and expression, which in fact are, if not indistinguishable, inseparable. Their signs are representational and iconic (rather than conventional or indexical).[197]

Secondary modelling systems are used to express highly complex messages which cannot be transmitted by other means--including paraphrase or alteration--without significant loss of information.[198]

Literature as Communication and Cognition in Bakhtin and Lotman 97

This can be considered a test of whether something is literature or not, although we have no precise rules for carrying out such a test. Again it is also seen as evidence of the cultural need for literature, art and other secondary modelling systems, i.e. we do have such texts and such messages to send, they cannot be sent through the channels of primary modelling systems, and yet no known culture has existed without them in some form.[199]

Definition #2a: Here it must be observed that a sub-definition has been generated: *Literature is a representation of reality, of life.* This is unambiguously implied by the meaning of modelling,[200] but is also stated explicitly by Lotman.

> Художественное сообщение создает художественную модель какого-либо конкретного явления--художественный язык моделирует универсум в его наиболее общих категориях, которые, будучи наиболее общим содержанием мира, являются для конкретных вещей и явлений формой существования.[201]

Literature, in Lotman's view, does not create fictional worlds which are epistemologically and/or axiologically separate from reality, as some might have it.[202] This problem of representation is surely controversial, and in some places even tabu, but the notion of literature as cognition of reality (as Lotman states many times), and communication or one might say shared cognition, via secondary modelling systems, necessarily gives rise to the notion of representation,[203] or the less intentional but probably less appropriate notion of reflection. The Russian words Lotman uses most often are *отображать, воссоздавать,* and *воспроизводить,* each of which adds its own slight nuance of meaning. In his conclusion to the first, theoretical part of Анализ поэтического текста, he refers to the question this way:

> Одновременно поэтический мир-модель реального мира, но соотносится с ним чрезвычайно сложным образом. Поэтический текст мощный и глубоко диалектический механизм поиска истины, истолкования окружающего мира и ориентировки в нем.[204]

Definition #3: We can now shift from the perspective of semiotics to the perspective of structuralism. It must be remembered that such shifts are arbitrary and reflect not absolute distinctions but distinctions which can enable us to see how the whole operates. If literature is information or a message which is too complex to be transmitted by means of the semiotic system of natural language, then in terms of structuralist principles, Lotman holds that, *literature is a complicated structure, a set of complex and dynamic intersecting hierarchical but shifting relationships between its various levels and elements.*

> Реляционная структура--не сумма вещественных деталей, а набор отношений, который первичен в произведении искусства и составляет его основу, его реальность. Но набор этот строится не как многоэтажная иерархия без внутренних пересечений, а как сложная сруктура взаимопересекающихся подструктур со многократными вхождениями одного и того же элемента в различные конструктивные контексты.[205]

The nature of these intersecting relationships[206] is reducible to two basic patterns of relationships:

> со-противопоставления повторяющихся эквивалентных элементов и со-противопоставления соседствующих (не эквивалентных) элементов.
> Все разнообразие конструктивных построений текста можно свести к этим двум началам.[207]

In other words, the nature of the structural organization of literature involves a constantly shifting tension between sets of co-oppositional pairs in various combinations. Because the planes of expression and content are indistinguishable or inseparable in literature, all elements are meaningful or content-bearing, and can enter into structural relationships which would not be realized or realizable in a primary modelling system, such as natural language. It is this fusion of the levels of expression and content and the resultant dialectical relationships which produce the meanings, that semanticize all elements of the text.

> Итак, *стихотворение——сложно построенный смысл*. Это значит, что, входя в состав единой целостной структуры стихотворения, значащие элементы языка оказываются связанными сложной системой соотношений, со— и противопоставлений, невозможных в обычной языковой конструкции. Это придает и каждому элементу в отдельности, и всей конструкции в целом совершенно особую семантическую нагрузку. Слова, предложения и высказывания, которые в грамматической структуре находятся в разных, лишенных черт сходства и, следовательно, несопоставимых позициях, в художественной структуре оказываются сопоставимыми и противопоставимыми, в позициях тождества и антитезы, и это раскрывает в них неожиданной, вне стиха невозможное, новое семантическое содержание. Более того: . . . семантическую нагрузку получают элементы, не имеющие ее в обычной языковой структуре. . . .[208]

The notion of structure also includes the notions of text and system which are related--but in Lotman's usage not equivalent--to the notions of *langue* and *parole* as used by Ferdinand de Saussure.[209] Frequently, Lotman will use the terms code and language (язык) as rough equivalents of system. This creates considerable potential for confusion.[210] It must be pointed out in the first place that, for Lotman, system or code is not a fixed or a static entity. This has several ramifications. For Lotman, natural languages do exist, although he stresses that their mode of existence is not to be confused with the existence of individual utterances or "texts"; they exist just as algebra, planetary systems, or other abstractions do. Secondly, he does not categorically establish which is primary, text or system:

> Мы не беремся утверждать что́ чему предшествует: язык романтизма романтическим текстам или наоборот. Мы полагаем, что в таком виде сама постановка вопроса исключает удовлетворительное решение.[211]

Next, and what would seem to follow directly from the preceding point, there is a fluid relationship between text and system, i.e. what is text from one perspective can be system from another.[212] To understand this more clearly it is necessary to say what a text in literature is or more precisely what a cultural text is. A text is first of all an invariant structure which may be the basis of any number of variants. A given poem is an invariant text when considered as the product of a given author[213] and without reference to a particular instantiation. In other words, if I have three copies of the same edition of a poem in front of me which therefore do not differ in their appearance to any significant degree, they will be considered one text. However, if I have three recordings of readings of the poem by different readers, I will no doubt have three variants of the Text.[214] In that case, the text will stand as system in relation to the variant texts. Therefore "invariants" prove to be variable dependent on their contextual relationships.

The text is the conglomerate of the *internal* hierarchically organized structure of the work of art, i.e. that which is graphically or, to include oral texts, linguistically expressed.[215] This includes such levels of the work as the phonemic, metric, rhythmic, lexical, stanzaic, etc. In another sense, the text is that which interests textologists in their reconstructive efforts; in fact, Lotman considers the fact that scholars do work to reconstruct lost or unfinished or otherwise problematic texts a proof or at least a strong indication of the fact that there is a core or invariant Text.[216] Another important feature of texts, is that they must be seen to contain not only present elements and relationships, but also absent or what Lotman calls minus-devices (*минус—приемы*), or artistic silence.[217] To summarize somewhat, a text is characterized by the following three features: выраженность, отграниченность, структурность.[218]

Text is not, of course, a self-sufficient notion, any more than anything else is within a structural framework. Text must always be seen in its relationship with system. System is essentially the text seen in terms of its external or extra-textual relationships. System or code is that

Literature as Communication and Cognition in Bakhtin and Lotman 101

through which the text is organized and decoded or understood.[219] It is not the work of art any more than the text itself is. The relationship of text and system constitutes the work of art. System is always understood in relationship to non-system: the fact of non-inclusion of a certain element into the literary work or lack of relationship to a given code can be structurally meaningful. The minimum number of systems or languages needed to decipher a literary work is two,[220] otherwise the characteristic semantic tension which produces the wealth of meaning in a work is not possible, however, normally there will be many more:

> В отличие от нехудожественных текстов, произведение искусства соотносится не с одним, а с многими дешифрующими его кодами. Индивидуальное в художественном тексте--это не внесистемное, а многосистемное. Чем в большее количество дешифрующих структур входит тот или иной конструктивный узел текста одновременно, тем индивидуальнее его значение. Входя в различные ьязыкь культуры, текст раскрывается разными сторонами. Внесистемное становится системным и наоборот. Однако это не означает безграничного произвола, безбрежной субъективности, в которой порой видят специфику искусства. Набор возможных дешифрующих систем составляет некоторую свойственную данной эпохе или культуре величину, и он может и должен быть предметом изучения и описания.[221]

Thus, while in a scientific text, for example, ambiguity must be seen as a shortcoming, in a literary text, ambiguity or variant readings, not to be confused with gross or unlimited subjectivism, are a *sine qua non*. The existence of two interpretations of a scientific text implies either a mistake or a poorly written text. Ambiguity in daily conversation or in journalism is usually a defect and reduces the informativity of the text. In an artistic text (literary work of art) ambiguity is a function of the interaction of text and system/s to generate meaning, both at a given moment and over time.[222]

As an indication of the complex relationship between text and system, or between internal and extra-textual structures, I would quote from an article by Dmitrii Segal, which complements Lotman's position, and in which he is discussing the difference betwen a myth (also considered a secondary modelling system) which would be generated according to rules similar to those outlined by the quasi-formalist Vladimir Propp for fairy tales, and a real myth.

> Однако такой анализ недостаточен, если целью исследования является установление правил моделирования мира в умах членов группы. Если мы хотим искусственным образом (хотя бы с помощью электронных вычислительных машин) создать миф, который не только по своей структуре был бы мифом, но и мог быть принят как таковой членами некоторой группы, необходимо понять, с какими объектами вне мифа связываются его мотивы, герои,— —необходимо смоделировать не только структуру мифа, но и мир, им моделируемый.[223]

Definition #4: This high level of organization in literature, and the semanticization of all of its elements because of the fusion of the planes of expression and content permits Lotman to offer a definition of literature in terms of information theory. *Literature involves those texts in which redundancy or entropy approaches zero.*[224] Redundancy is the opposite of meaning or content or, in other words, of information.[225] If, in a literary text everything is semanticized, then there is no room for redundancy. Whereas in a normal language utterance or in other communication channels there is a relatively high level of redundancy,[226] in a poetic text, given its ability to interact with constantly changing cultural codes and therefore produce an almost infinite series of meanings, redundancy is close to zero. If the quantity of information is equal to the quantity of noise in a message, there is no message.[227] However, because literature is anti-entropic, i.e. because of its ability to transform non-systemic elements into systemic, in it entropy can be seen to actually lead to information.

Искусство——и в этом проявляется его структурное родство с жизнью в природе—— обладает способность преображать шум в информацию, усложняет свою структуру за счет корреляций с внешней средой (во всех других системах всякое столкновение с внешней средой может привести лишь к затуханию информации).[228]

According to the second law of thermodynamics, on which the notion of entropy is based, there is a constant irreversible process of decreasing order in the universe. For Lotman, and many others in the field of information theory, the law is not as universal as once thought.[229] Moreover, for Lotman, information is a precondition of both social and biological existence. Information theory is broader than semiotics[230] and provides the broad philosophical base for Lotman's theory needed to complement the methodological base provided by structuralism.

At one time Taylor defined culture as the aggregate of tools, technological equipment, social institutions, faiths, customs and language. Today one could give a more general definition: the aggregate of all non-inherited information and the means for organizing and preserving it. From this emerge very diverse conclusions. Above all it substantiates the concept of mankind's need for culture. Information is not an optional indication of, but one of the basic conditions for man's existence. The battle for survival--both the biological and the social one--is a struggle for information. An understanding of culture's essence as information explains the passionate involvement in this matter of both the bearers and the destroyers of culture whose conflicts with each other constitute the history of mankind.[231]

Culture, however, is not a storehouse of information. It is an extremely complex mechanism which preserves information while constantly working out the most efficient means to do this: it receives new information, encodes and decodes communications and translates them from one sign system into another. Culture is a versatile and highly organized mechanism of cognition. . . . [232]

Lotman is aware of the shortcomings of attempts to apply the statistical and stochastic methods of information theory to literature and culture,233 however he does hold out as a desideratum that such an eventuality would be beneficial. "Когда мы научимся точно измерять избыточность, мы получим объективный критерий художественного достоинства."234 Since information is a (negative) function of predictability--what is predictable is redundant in a message--but communication depends on a certain degree of commonality in the codes of receiver and sender, Lotman sees literature as a tension between fulfillment and violation of expectation.

> Из этого вывод: хорошие стихи, стихи, несущие поэтическую информацию,--это стихи в которых все элементы ожидаемы и неожиданны одновременно. Нарушение первого принципа сделает текст бессмысленным, второго—тривиальным.235

This step towards a more evaluative stance breaks another tabu, but there is no question that Lotman's theory has a considerable allotment of evaluation which frequently emerges in his applications and has been stated outright more than once.236 Following the same line, his views on information have led him to a proposal which is, although controversial, consistent with his overall position, namely that "красота есть информация."237 In other words, beauty, that which has traditionally been seen as the end of aesthetic practice, is located within the framework of information, i.e. a particular organization of texts and codes within a given culture,238 i.e. not all information is equal to beauty; the formulation refers to those kinds of structures--and structural violations of structures--characteristic of art.

Definition #4: Literature is those texts the communication of which involves the greatest number and degree of difficulties in understanding and a profound decrease in the possibility of unambiguous decoding.

One of the tangible results of Lotman's synthesis of semiotics, structuralism, and information theory is his model of communication. It has had several formulations, like most of Lotman's ideas, but the invariant structure, if I may borrow his terminology, seems to emerge in an article originally published in 1973.239 Lotman seeks to overcome the limitations of Jakobson's model, which he sees as idealizing communication by disregarding "lack of understanding, partial understanding, or varying perceptions of one and the same message," or at least seeing them as being located outside the phenomenon of communication.[240] Lotman substitutes for Jakobson's ideal addressee who shares a comon code with the addresser a "real" addressee who has a different code, one which only partially intersects with the code of the addresser. As a result, communication is not passive transmission of messages, but a difficult process of translation or transcoding.[241] "Непонимание, неполное понимание или переосмысление--не побочные продукты обмена информацией, а принадлежат самой ее сути."[242]

The more highly organized the text, as with literature, the greater the difficulties in understanding it, i.e. in giving it a single interpretation.[243] Various semiotic processes are at work in society tending both towards and against a creation of homogeneous codes. Both tendencies are necessary, but "окончательная победа любой одной из них сделает коммуникацию или ненужной, или невозможной."[244] For Lotman this process of transcoding has very serious ramifications for the ability of cultures to thrive and develop, to maintain stability and viability. It is bound up not only with the functioning of collectives, but also with the maintenance of individual personalities.

He describes the process whereby transcoding creates dialogues and polylogues on the one hand, and shared cultural codes on meta-levels on the other, and locates the individual as sender and receiver of messages within this complex system of shifting texts and codes. The central general thrust of his thought seems to inhere in the following polemical and somewhat programmatic statement:

> Кратко охарактеризованный выше принцип заставляет критически отнестись к установке структурного исследовательского анализа на доминирующее описание 'языка' систем. 'Случайные,' с точки зрения языка, явления не могут быть оставлены без внимания: они представляют собой работающие механизмы в семиотической структуре культуры, и следует искать пути к их описанию. В связи с этим актуальность приобретают исследования семиотической природы непереводимости и разного рода

создаваемых культурой шумов, а также
степени пересечения различных действующих
в единой системе культуры, кодов.[245]

     In regards to literature, Lotman's model of communication serves to reinforce the notions of its communicative function, its ability to generate meanings in proportion to its degree of structural organization, and its importance within the cultural system, insofar as the culture's viability depends on the individualizing tendency inherent in communication of this type at least as much as on levels involving less complex transcoding.[246]

     Specialization in the structure of individual codes--the possibility of a purely personal representation in texts of extralinguistic reality--meets deep needs of the collective as a whole, since a shortage of information typical of any human collective can most effectively be compensated for by the stereoscopic quality, polyglottism, and multi-level character of specialization. Under these circumstances, the difficulty of a synonymous interpretation of the text no longer seems to be a structural defect. It would be possible to show convincingly that certain cultural mechanisms work in the direction of making it difficult to decipher a text adequately; the more complex the structure of a message, the more individual is its interpretation by each recipient of the information.[247]

NOTES

1. For the history of the movement the standard work is Victor Erlich, <u>Russian Formalism: History - Doctrine</u>, Third Edition, Slavistic Printings and Reprintings, IV, (The Hague, Paris: Mouton, 1969). See also Medvedev, Формальный метод; Aage Hansen-Love, "Russian Formalism," tr. Alison Herford, <u>Essays in Poetics</u> VI, 2 (1981), 54-62; Krystyna Pomorska, <u>Russian Formalist Theory and Its Poetic Ambiance</u>, Slavistic Printings and Reprintings, 82, ed. C.H. van Schooneveld, (The Hague, Paris: Mouton, 1968); Tony Bennett, <u>Formalism and Marxism</u>, (London and New York: Methuen and Co. Ltd, 1979); and Introduction to <u>Russian Formalist Criticism: Four Essays</u>, tr. and with an Introduction by Lee T. Lemon and Marion J. Reis, (Lincoln and London: University of Nebraska Press, 1965), ix-xvii. For concise information concerning the biographies and bibliographies of leading members of the formalist school see Igor Chernov, "Brief Biographical and Bibliographical Notes on Leading Formalists," tr. Ann Shukman, <u>Formalist Theory</u>, <u>Russian Poetics in Translation</u>, 4, 1977, 1-12. See also, in the same volume, idem, "A Contextual Glossary of Formalist Terminology," tr. Ann Shukman and L.M. O'Toole, 13-48.

2. For many of the basic texts of Russian formalism, see Поэтика: Сборники по теории поэтического языка, St. Petersburg: np, 1919. Reprint, Bibliotheca Slavica, No. 1, Reprint Series, (Zug, Switzerland: Inter Documentation Company Ag., 1967), (hereinafter referred to as <u>Сборники</u>); <u>Texte der Russischen Formalisten</u>, Band I, <u>Texte zur Allgemeine Literaturtheorie und zur Theorie der Prosa</u>, mit einer einleitenden Abhandlung herausgegeben von Jurij Streidter, ed. Witold Kosny, (Munich: Wilhelm Fink Verlag, 1969); <u>Texte der Russischen Formalisten</u>, Band II, <u>Texte zur Theorie des Verses und der poetischer Sprache</u>, Eingeleitet und herausgegeben von Wolf-Dieter Stempel, ed. Inge Paulman, (Munich: Wilhelm Fink Verlag, 1972), (hereinafter referred to as <u>Texte</u> I and <u>Texte</u> II); and <u>Russian Poetics in Translation</u>, 4.

3. And lacked scientific reliability. See e.g. Iurii Tynianov, "О литературной эволюции," in <u>Readings in Russian Poetics: Russian Texts</u>, comp. Ladislav Matejka, second revised edition, Michigan Slavic Publications, No. 2, (Ann Arbor: University of Michigan, Department of Slavic Languages and Literatures, 1971), 100.
4. See Erlich, <u>Russian Formalism</u>, 23-26, and Viktor Shklovskii, "Искусство как прием," in <u>Сборники</u>, esp. 101-102, and idem, "Потебня," in <u>Сборники</u>, 3-6.
5. Cf. Erlich, <u>Russian Formalism</u>, 23-26, and for an example of how his influence was realized cf. Boris Tomashevskii, "Тематика," in <u>Теория литературы: Поэтика</u>, fourth edition, (Moscow and Leningrad: Gosudarstvennoe Izdatel'stvo, 1928, Reprint, The Slavic Series, 6, New York and London: Johnson Reprint Corporation, 1967), 131-204.
6. Erlich, <u>Russian Formalism</u>, 26-32.
7. See e.g. Shklovskii, "Искусство как прием," 102-103, and Boris `Eikhenbaum, "Теория 'формального метода,'" in <u>О литературе: Работы разных лет</u>, (Moscow: Sovetskii Pisatel', 1987), 105-106, 112-115. For a very brief description of symbolist poetics see Erlich, <u>Russian Formalism</u>, 33-41.
8. See Edward Stankiewicz, <u>Baudouin de Courtenay and the Foundations of Structural Linguistics</u>, PdR Press Publications in the History of Linguistics, 3, (Lisse: Peter de Ridder Press, 1976), and Erlich, <u>Russian Formalism</u>, esp. 60-62.
9. See Ferdinand de Saussure, <u>Course in General Linguistics</u>, ed. Charles Bally and Albert Sechehaye, with Albert Reidlinger, tr. Wade Baskins, (New York: Philosophical Library, 1959); Jonathon Culler, <u>Ferdinand de Saussure</u>, revised edition, (Ithaca, New York: Cornell University Press, 1986); and Erlich, <u>Russian Formalism</u>, 65.
10. Erlich, Ibid., esp. 61-63.
11. Cf. Erlich, Ibid,, 41-50, Pomorska, <u>Russian Formalist Theory</u>, esp. 77-92, and for an example of shared concerns of formalists and futurists, see Vladimir Maiakovskii, "Как делать стихи?" in <u>Собрание сочинений в</u>

	восьми томах, vol. 5, (Moscow: Biblioteka "Ogonek," Izdatel'stvo "Pravda," 1968), 466-500.
12.	"Литература . . . относится к *словесной деятельности человека*." Boris Tomashevskii, <u>Краткий курс поэтики</u>, (Moscow, Leningrad: Gosudarstvennoe izdatel'stvo, 1928; second edition, Russian Study Series, No. 70, Chicago: Russian Language Specialties, 1969), 18.
13.	E.g. Viktor Shklovskii, "Воскрешение слова," in <u>Texte</u>, II, 8-10.
14.	E.g. Lev Iakubinskii, "О поэтическом глоссемосочетании," in <u>Сборники</u>, 12, and idem, "О звуках стихотворного языка," in <u>Сборники</u>, 37, and compare Shklovskii, "Искусство как прием," 102-103.
15.	Idem, 113.
16.	Shklovskii, "Потебня," 6, Tomashevskii, <u>Краткий курс</u>, 18-19.
17.	Shklovskii, "Искусство как прием," and Tomashevskii, <u>Краткий курс</u>, 20
18.	Roman Jakobson, "Новейшая русская поэзия. Набросок первый: Велимир Хлебников," in <u>Texte</u>, II, 30-32.
19.	Cf. Erlich, <u>Russian Formalism</u>, 70ff.
20.	E.g.: "Создание научной поэтики должно быть начато с фактического, на массовых фактах построенного признания, что существуют 'прозаический' и 'поэтический' языки, законы которых различные, и с анализа этих различий." Shklovskii, "Потебня," 6. See also Tomashevskii, <u>Краткий курс</u>, 18-19.
21.	Cf. e.g. Iakubinskii, "О звуках стихотворного языка," in <u>Сборники</u>, 37, and Roman Jakobson, "What is Poetry," in <u>Semiotics of Art: Prague School Contributions</u>, ed. Ladislav Matejka, Irwin R. Titunik, (Cambridge, Mass., London, England: The MIT Press, 1976), esp. 174.

22. Cf. Roman Jakobson, "The Dominant," in <u>Readings in Russian Poetics</u>, 82-4.
23. The terms 'aesthetic function' and 'poetic function' are essentially interchangeable here, as are the terms 'poetic language' and 'literary language'. These pairings, especially the latter, reflect a peculiarity of Russian usage not nearly as strongly evidenced in English, in my experience. However, while the distinction poetic language--prose language generally refers to literature--non-literature, for the formalists and not only for them, there is a question of how literary prose relates to poetry on the one hand and non-literary prose on the other. The distinction varies among theoreticians, but I will somewhat arbitrarily--where it is not strongly counter-indicated by context--use literature for literary language and non-literature for non-literary language, thus hopefully avoiding any unnecessary misconceptions. The reader should have at least a preliminary awareness of these distinctions, although their full ramifications do not impact on the present discussion.
24. Jakobson, "The Dominant," 84.
25. Idem, 85.
26. Shklovskii, "Искусство как прием," 103.
27. Ibid., 105. The extent to which all members of the so-called formal school shared Shklovskii's "definition" is debatable. Nevertheless, it does point up a generally held emphasis on the aesthetic function as a part of a perceptual process and as a defining feature of poetry, and the overall aestheticism of the movement.
28. Cf. Iakubinskii, "О звуках," 37, and "О поэтическом глоссемосочетании," 12, and `Eikhenbaum, "Теория," 384-85.
29. See e.g. Shklovskii, "Искусство как прием," and Tomashevskii, "Тематика," for theoretical statements of this principle, and e.g. Shklovskii, "Пародийный роман. <u>Тристрам Шенди</u> Стерна," in <u>Texte</u>, I, 244-298, and `Eikhenbaum, "Как сделан 'Шинель' Гоголя," in <u>Texte</u>, I, 122-58 for applications to specific literary texts.
30. A good indication of this expansion of interests is given in `Eikhenbaum,"Теория," esp. 408.

31. Iurii Tynianov and Roman Jakobson, "Проблемы изучения литературы и языка," in Texte, II, 386-90. It would be interesting and probably enlightening to learn the circumstances and motivations for this publication. It has been customary to publish the theses without the ninth and last paragraph, which calls for the revival of OPOIAZ under the leadership of Viktor Shklovskii. This paragraph changes significantly the tonality of the entire text (while not changing its substance to a great degree) and suggests it was written at least as much for polemical and especially practical reasons as for the expression of theoretical considerations. Readings in Russian Poetics, Russian Texts, does not print paragraph 9, without explanation. In their introduction (no page number) to Russian Poetics in Translation, 4, where the theses can be found in English translation, 49-51, Shukman and O'Toole emphasize that theirs is the first *full* translation of this work, referring, of course, to paragraph 9. Perhaps these editorial peculiarities reflect a trend to amplify the relatively positive reputations of Jakobson and Tynianov as opposed to the somewhat ambiguous reputation of Shklovskii. At any rate, such editorial interference is not acceptable.

32. Peter Steiner gives the date as October 6, 1926. The Prague School: Selected Writings, 1929-1946, ed. Peter Steiner, tr. John Burbank, Olga Hasty, *et al*, University of Texas Press Slavic Series, No. 6, (Austin: University of Austin Press, 1982), 3. For a description and history of the Prague school, see e.g. Peter Steiner, "The Roots of Structuralist Esthetics," in idem, The Prague School, 174-219; René Wellek, The Literary Theory and Aesthetics of the Prague School, Michigan Slavic Contributions No. 2, (Ann Arbor: University of Michigan, Department of Slavic Languages and Literatures, 1969); Erlich, Russian Formalism, esp. 153-163; Sound, Sign and Meaning; Ladislav Matejka, "The Sociological Concerns of the Prague School," in The Prague School and Its Legacy in Linguistics, Literature, Semiotics, Folklore, and the Arts, ed. Yishai Tobin, (Amsterdam and Philadelphia: John Benjamins Publishing Company, 1988), 219-26; and Fokkema, "Continuity and Change." For collections of Prague Circle writings see e.g., Praguiana: Some Basic and Less Known Aspects of the Prague Linguistic School, ed. and tr. Josef Vachek and Libuse Dusková, with an introduction by Philip

A. Luelsdorff, (Amsterdam and Philadelphia: John Benjamins Publishing company, 1983); and <u>Semiotics of Art: Prague School Contributions</u>, ed. Ladislav Matejka and Irwin R. Titunik, (Cambridge, Mass. and London, England: The MIT Press, 1976); and <u>The Prague School</u>.

33. See e.g. Steiner, "Roots," esp. 174-75.
34. Lubomir Dolezel, "Narrative Worlds," in <u>Sound Sign and Meaning</u>, 542.
35. Cf. e.g. Peter Steiner, "To Enter the Circle: The Functionalist Structuralism of the Prague School," in <u>The Prague School</u>, ix.
36. E.g. Gardner, <u>The Cognitive Revolution</u>, 200-202.
37. Bohuslav Havranek et al, "By Way of Introduction," in <u>Recycling The Prague School</u>, ed. M.K. Johnston, (Ann Arbor: Karoma Publishers, 1978) 39.
38. "Manifesto Presented to the First Congress of Slavic Philologists in Prague," in <u>Recycling</u>, 26.
39. Havranek, "By way of Introduction," 33.
40. "Manifesto," 9.
41. Ibid.
42. Ibid.
43. Ibid., 13.
44. Ibid., and also Havranek, "By Way of Introduction," 34.
45. "Manifesto," 26, and Jan Mukarovsky, "Standard Language and Poetic Language," in <u>A Prague School Reader</u>, 22. Cf. Jan Mukarovsky, <u>On Poetic Language</u>, tr. and ed. John Burbank and Peter Steiner, PdR Press Publications in Poetic Language, 1, (Lisse: The Peter de Ridder Press, 1976): " . . . poetic discourse has expression itself as its aim," 11.
46. "Manifesto," 27, and Mukarovsky, "Standard Language and Poetic Language," 22.
47. Havranek, "The Functional Differentation of the Standard Language," in <u>A Prague School Reader</u>, 9ff, and Mukarovsky, ibid., 19ff.
48. Havranek, "Functional Differentiation," 3.
49. Mukarovsky, "Standard Language and Poetic Language," 17.
50. Cf. esp. "Manifesto," 9.
51. Cf. Mukarovsky, "Standard Language and Poetic Language," 28-30.
52. Havranek, "Functional Differentation," and "Manifesto," 10-12.

53. Ibid.
54. Compare Steiner "The Roots of Structuralist Esthetics: "The emphasis on the material of art, traditional in Czech esthetics, was a factor that spurred a spontaneous acceptance of the Russians' linguistic approach to the analysis of the material of verbal art." 181.
55. Ibid., 198.
56. Ibid., 198-99.
57. Ibid., 199.
58. Steiner's other points do not directly relate to the present topic as closely as the first three, and therefore I have chosen not to deal with them here.
59. There are many testimonials to the vitality and importance of the Prague school today, but for just one example, cf. The Prague School and its Legacy.
60. E.g. Dolezel, "Narrative Worlds"; idem, "Truth and Authenticity in Narrative," Poetics Today I, 3 (1980), 7-25.
61. As far as I know there is no definitive biography of Jakobson to date, although I have not tried overly hard to locate one, but there are many briefer references concerning his life and work. For a small sample of the esteem in which he was and is held by his peers see A Tribute to Roman Jakobson, 1896-1982, (Berlin, New York, Amsterdam: Mouton, 1983). There have also, of course, been numerous *Festschriften* and collections of articles including, e.g. Roman Jakobson: Echoes of His Scholarship, ed. Daniel Armstrong and C.H. van Schooneveld, (Lisse: The Peter de Ridder Press, 1977), and Roman Jakobson, Verbal Art, Verbal Sign, Verbal Time, ed. Krystyna Pomorska and Stephen Rudy, (Minneapolis: University of Minnesota Press, 1985).
62. Cf. Krystyna Pomorska and Stephen Rudy, Preface to Verbal Art, Verbal Sign, Verbal Time,: "Roman Jakobson . . . ranks among the seminal thinkers who shaped the 'human sciences' in the twentieth century." vii.
63. Cf. Ibid., viii, C.H. van Schooneveld, "By Way of Introduction: Roman Jakobson's Tenets and Their Potential," in Roman Jakobson, 1, and Roman Jakobson, "Поэзия грамматики и грамматика поэзии," in Poetics--poetyka--poètika, (Warsaw: Panstwowe Wydawnictwo Naukowe; Gravenhage: Mouton & Co.'S, 1961), 397-417.
64. Jakobson, Новейшая русская поэзия, 30.

65. Jakobson, "What is Poetry?" in Semiotics of Art, 174.
66. See especially Jakobson, "Linguistics and Poetics," in Style in Language, ed. Thomas Sebeok, (New York: John Wiley, 1960), 350-77.
67. Cf. "Linguistics and Communication Theory," in Selected Writings, II, (The Hague: Mouton, 1971), 570-571. I am speculating about the causal relationship, but it seems probable.
68. See also Jakobson, "The Dominant," and Linda R. Waugh, "The Poetic Function and the Nature of Language," in Verbal Art, Verbal Sign, Verbal Time, 143-168.
69. And cybernetics. I have in mind such fundamental notions and terms as sender, receiver, message, medium, code, channel, and so on. A comparison of Jakobson's model with Shannon and Weaver's is very suggestive, although I am not aware of any studies in which the two models are confronted. Cf. Warren Weaver, "Recent Contributions to the Mathematical Theory of Communication," in Claude E. Shannon and Warren Weaver, The Mathematical Theory of Communication, (Urbana: University of Illinois Press, 1949), esp. 98.
70. If one were trying to reconstruct the history of communication theory models as applied to fields outside of their traditional domain, it might be seen as a revolutionary achievement, (although Weaver had already anticipated the applicability of the theory to practically all sorts of communication, including, as he said music, photography, and moving pictures. Weaver, "Recent Contributions," 95.). However, from our perspective, it is simply a restatement of longstanding ideas, dating back to the Prague school era, if not earlier.
71. I have not raised the question of the inherent absurdity of any language being considered self-referential, but it would most certainly have to be raised sooner or later. Of course, this would involve an incursion into post-structuralism and deconstructivism, which would be a detour, since Lotman and Bakhtin find different means of dealing with the problem.
72. James Gleick, Chaos: Making a New Science, (New York: Viking Penguin Inc., 1987), 8. See also, ch. 3, "The Butterfly Effect" and passim. Gleick notes the traditional roots of this notion, locating it even in folklore: "For want of a nail, the shoe was lost;/For want of a shoe, the horse was lost;/ For want of a horse, the rider was lost;/For want of a rider, the

battle was lost;/ For want of a battle, the kingdom was lost!" 23. Indeed, it really is all-pervasive.
73. For unknown reasons, while he names the subject matter, i.e. chaos, he never names the discipline, but it has been called both chaotics and chaology.
74. Gleick, Chaos, e.g. 8, 20, 304.
75. Mikhail M. Bakhtin, "Проблема содержания," and Lotman, Лекции, esp. 3 and ff.
76. Bakhtin, ВЛЭ, 6.
77. Bakhtin, "Слово в романе," in ВЛЭ, 72-233.
78. Bakhtin, "Проблема речевых жанров," in ЭСТ, 237-280.
79. I.e. "Проблема содержания."
80. Caryl Emerson, "Problems With Bakhtin's Poetics," Slavic and East European Journal, XXXII, 4 (1988), 505.
81. М. М. Bakhtin, "Автор и герой в эстетической деятельности," in ЭСТ, esp. 170-175.
82. ЭСТ, 384.
83. M. M. Bakhtin, The Dialogic Imagination: Four Essays, ed. Michael Holquist, tr. Caryl Emerson and Michael Holquist, University of Texas Press Slavic Series, No. 1., (Austin: University of Texas Press, 1981).
84. Ibid., xiii.
85. Esthétique et théorie du roman, 21-82.
86. Emerson and Morson, "Introduction."
87. Ibid., 2.
88. "От издательства," ВЛЭ, 3.
89. Контекст. 1973: Литературно-теоретические исследования, (Moscow: Izdatel'stvo "nauka," 1974), 258-280.
90. See the discussion above.
91. Bakhtin, "Искусство и ответственность," in ЭСТ, 5-6. Cf. Caryl Emerson, "Problems with Baxtin's Poetics," 504, and Clark and Holquist, Mikhail Bakhtin, 55-57.
92. Bakhtin, "Искусство и ответственность," 5.
93. Ibid., 6
94. Because this essay is so little known and discussed. and because its argument is rather complex, or at least

complicated, I will present it here in some detail following the text for the most part.
95. Bakhtin, "Проблема содержания," 8.
96. Ibid, 10.
97. Ibid, 12.
98. Ibid, 13.
99. See "Foreword by Andreas Ossiander: 'To The Reader Concerning the Hypotheses of This Work,'" in Nicholas Copernicus, Complete Works, II, On The Revolutions, ed. Jerzy Dobrzycki, tr. and commentary by Edward Rosen, (Warsaw-Cracow: Polish Scientific Publishers, 1978), XVI.
100. `Eikhenbaum, "Теория 'формального метода'," 376.
101. Cf. Karl R. Popper, Conjectures and Refutations: The Growth of Scientific Knowledge, (New York, Hagerstown, San Francisco, London: Harper Torchbooks, 1963), esp. ch. 3, "Three Views Concerning Human Knowledge," 97-119.
102. Bakhtin, "Проблема содержаниа," 14.
103. Ibid., 15.
104. Ibid., 17.
105. Ibid., 17.
106. "В его первичной, чисто познавательной данности." Ibid., 17.
107. Ibid., 17-19.
108. Ibid., 20-21.
109. Ibid., 22.
110. Ibid. Bakhtin does not elaborate on how his theory deals with these areas, but I assume it would involve the directed valorising activities of the perceiver; still, that does not yet even approach a satisfactory explanation.
111. Ibid., 22-23. Again, he does not elaborate, but the lack of a diachronic perspective in the formalist movement is well known. Cf. Jakobson and Tynianov, "Proposals," for their attempt--only partially successful in my estimation--to overcome this, and Tynianov, "О литературной эволюции," in Readings in Russian Poetics, 99-113. True, it was at the same time as Bakhtin was writing this essay that the formalists were beginning to move towards a more diachronic and less "formalistic" position.

112. Bakhtin does elaborate his position on the question of literature and/in history in a much later essay, namely "Ответ на вопрос редакции Нового мира."
113. Bakhtin, "Проблема содержания," 25.
114. Ibid. This also has a notable parallel in Lotman's theory of secondary modelling systems as generalized or universal models of reality, e.g. Анализ, 42.
115. Bakhtin, "Проблема содержания," 26.
116. *"Никакой нейтральной действительности противопоставить искусству нельзя: тем самым, что мы о ней говорим и ее противопоставляем чему-то, мы ее как-то определяем и оцениваем: нужно только прийти в ясность с самим собою и понять действительное направление своей оценки.*
117. *Все это можно выразить коротко так: действительность можно противопоставить искусству только как нечто доброе или нечто истинное -- красоте."* Ibid., 27, (italics in original). It should be noted that the term 'beauty'--*красота*-- is intended as a general reference to the domain of aesthetic activity.
118. Ibid., 27-29.
119. I.e. M. M. Bakhtin "Архитектоника поступка," ed. S. G. Bocharov, Социологические исследования, 1986, 2 (April-June), 157-170; idem, "К философии поступка," ed. S. G. Bocharov, Философия и социология науки и техники, (Moscow: Nauka, 1986), 80-160; idem, "Автор и герой в эстетицческой деятельности (фрагмент первой главы)," ed. S. G. Bocharov and V. Kozhinov, in Литературно-критические статьи, (Moscow: Khudozhestvennaia literatura, 1986), 5-26; cf. Emerson "Problems" and Emerson and Morson, "Rethinking."
120. Perlina, "Funny Things are Happening," 7.
121. Ibid.
122. E.g. Emerson and Morson, "Rethinking," 2.

123. Perlina, "Funny Things," 7.
124. Emerson and Morson, "Rethinking," 6.
125. Bakhtin does follow up the distinction between the cognitive and the aesthetic somewhat in the later essay "К методологии гуманитарных наук," in ЭСТ, 361-73, however, the problem itself as well as his approach there are somewhat different.
126. Bakhtin, "Проблема содержания," 27-29.
127. Ibid., 29, (italics in original).
128. Ibid., 30.
129. Ibid., 30-32.
130. Ibid., 32, (italics in original). Note that the aesthetic activity is directed to pre-valorised reality in its fullness, and not to the material, which is in no need by itself of being unified, individualized, completed or otherwise altered. Ibid.
131. Ibid.
132. Ibid.
133. Ibid., 34.
134. Ibid., 37.
135. Ibid.
136. Ibid.
137. Ibid., 43. No doubt a great number of Bakhtin scholars would do well to reflect on this passage!
138. Ibid.
139. Ibid., 44.
140. Ibid., 46, (italics in original). See the extended illustration from a text by Pushkin on pp. 48-52, in which he clarifies how it is that the material (language) does not enter into the esthetic object, but serves to create what he calls images.
141. Ibid., 47.
142. Ibid., 52.
143. Ibid., 53.
144. Ibid., 55.
145. Ibid., 54-55.
146. Ibid., 56.
147. "На нем и с его помощью," ibid., 56. Bakhtin uses "на" here and not the standard "в" apparently to emphasize the auxilliary--if I can use that word--role of the material. To keep this emphasis foregrounded, I will follow his usage, even though it is more troublesome in English than in Russian.
148. Ibid., 57.

149. Ibid., 57-58.
150. Again, it may be appropriate to refer to the article "К методологии" to get a sense of some of the differences between what he here calls cognitive and aesthetic and in which the latter becomes humanistic thinking.
151. Ibid., 57.
152. "То есть я направлен при восприятии не на слова, не на фонемы, не на ритм, а со словами, с фонемою, с ритмом активно направлен на содержание, обымаю, формирую и завершаю его . . . Я становлюсь активным в форме и *формою занимаю ценностную позицию вне содержания — — как познавательно — — этической направленности,* — — и это впервые делает возможным завершение и вообще осуществление всех эстетических функций формы по отношению к содержанию." Ibid., 59, (italics in original).
153. Ibid., 59.
154. Ibid., 58.
155. Ibid., 59,
156. Ibid., 60.
157. "Изолированная вещь есть *contradictio in adjecto*." Ibid. On this distinction between things (objects) and subjects, see "К методологии." Bakhtin also associates the notion of invention (вымысел) *in art* with the notion of isolation from the cognitive and ethical aspects of reality and experience. What is invented is not a thing but something valorised, meaningful, personal and human.
158. Ibid., 60-61.
159. Ibid., 61.
160. Ibid., 60.
161. Ibid.
162. Ibid., 62.
163. See below, where Lotman will propose a similar, though not equivalent, hierarchy.
164. Bakhtin, "Проблема содержания," 62.
165. Ibid., 63.

166. Ibid., 64. This return to the origin of the aesthetic activity also distinguishes aesthetic activity from cognitive, since cognition does not have a beginning or end in the personal sense.
167. Ibid., 64-69.
168. Ibid., 69-70.
169. Ibid., 71, bearing in mind that when he says creator, he also means perceiver.
170. E.g. in "Проблема речевых жанров."
171. E.g., Bakhtin, Проблемы, 210, 211, and passim.
172. E.g. Ibid., 214.
173. See below, Chapter IV.
174. And/or semiotic.
175. E.g. Lotman, Структура, 13-17.
176. E.g. Lotman, Лекции, 24; idem, Структура, 210. Lotman's earliest statement on the non-identity of the lingustic and literary orders, and one which remains essentially operative within his theory, is "О разграничении лингвистического и литературоведческого понятия стуктуры." In this essay he demonstrates the fundamental difference between the approaches of linguistics and literary history to the question of lexical meaning. For the latter it is necessary to consider the relationship of the lexical unit to a much more complex system of relationships outside of its strictly linguistic usage, such as the individual's worldview, and its connnection to other intersecting series. The analysis sets up or anticipates the distinction between primary modelling systems and the much more complex secondary systems.
177. Cf. Lotman, "Несколько замечаний по поводу статьи проф. Марии Р. Майеновой, Поэтика в работах тартуского университета,'" Russian Literature, No. 2, 1977, 87-90.
178. Cf. Lotman, "От редакции," TZS II, 1965, 6; and Shukman, Literature and Semiotics, 22-23; and note the following editorial comment: "It is in the name of history, cultural relativism and Hegelian dialectics that Lotman challenges the concept of poetics as an integral part of linguistics, the very fundament of Jakobson's recent search for grammar of poetry and poetry of grammar. In sharp contradistinction to Jakobson, Lotman sees the language of

verbal art as a special secondary modelling system which is superimposed on the natural language and does not belong to the domain of linguistic studies. Lotman's paper ("Динамеческая модель семиотической системы," A.R.) is just one of an entire series of studies indicating that the development of Tartu semiotics of culture conceptually deviates from the development of Jakobson's poetics seen as an integral part of linguistics." <u>Readings in Soviet Semiotics</u>, 76.

179. E.g. "...ибо не моделировать образа автора, его мировоззрения искусство не может." Lotman, <u>Лекции</u>, 30.

180. Lotman, <u>Лекции</u>, 14. Cf. also ibid., e.g. 15, 29-32, 37: "Особая природа искусства как системы, служащей для познания и информации одновременно, определяет двойную сущность художественного произведения—— моделирующую и знаковую. . . . В аспекте: художественное произведение и действительность——мы рассматриваем искусство как средство познания жизни, в аспекте: художественное произведение и читатель——искусство как средство передачи информации." Cf. also idem, <u>Структура</u>, 9.

181. Although his notion of function is significantly different from theirs. Cf. Yu.M. Lotman and A.M. Piatigorsky, "Text and Function," tr. Ann Shukman, <u>New Literary History</u> IX, 2 (1978), 233-244.

182. "Our discussion will be adequate if it has as much clearness as the subject matter admits of, . . . We must be content, then, in speaking of such subjects and with such premisses to indicate the truth roughly and in outline and in speaking about things which are only for the most part true and with premisses of the same kind to reach conclusions that are no better. In the same spirit, therefore, should each type of statement be *received*; **for it is the mark of an educated man to look for precision in each class of things just so far as the nature of the subject**

admits;..." (My emphasis in bold, A. R.) Aristotle, <u>Nichomachean Ethics</u>, 1094b 12-26.

183. Note Bakhtin's remarks concerning the degree of precision which can be justifiably expected or desired in the humanities as opposed to the exact sciences ("К методологии гуманитарных наук"), yet he strove for some precision (or at least clarity) himself as exemplified especially in such works as <u>Поэтика творчества Достоевского</u>, and "Ответ на вопрос редакции." Those who would find something meritorious in a certain lack of precision in some of Bakhtin's work should remember that most of them are unfinished as we have them.

184. The other four forces are electro-magnetic, weak, strong and gravity.

185. Robert P. Crease and Charles C. Mann, "How the Universe Works," <u>The Atlantic</u>, August 1984, 93. The point made is not intended to be only anecdotally interesting; it underlines the profound difficulties in producing conceptually complete and consistent definitions which are also intuitively accessible.

186. Boris Oguibenine, "Linguistic Models of Culture," 99.

187. In <u>Проблемы поэтики и истории литературы</u>, 20-36.

188. Ibid., 20-21.

189. Ibid., 21. There are, of course, other considerations, but this is pivotal.

190. Ibid.

191. E.g.: "Мы стремились показать, что литература как динамическое целое не может быть описана в рамках какой-либо одной упорядоченности. Литература существует как определенная множественность упорядоченностей, из которых каждая организует лишь какую-то ее сферу, но стремится распространить область своего влияния как можно шире. При 'жизни' какого-либо исторического этапа литературы противоборство этих тенденций составляет интересы различных социальных сил, борьбу нравственных,

политических или философских концепции эпохи." Ibid., 35.
192. See e.g. "От редакции," TZS, II, 1965, 6. This notion of recognizing the various streams flowing into his theory is not as trivial as it might seem. For example, in one place Lotman chides a critic for not recognizing that he is using one word--language--in two senses, first in its linguistic sense, and secondly in its semiotic sense. "Несколько слов по поводу рецензии Я.М. Мейера 'Литература как информация,'" Russian Literature 9, (1975), 114.
193. The most obvious possible exception would be Walter Rewar, "Cybernetics and Poetics: The Semiotic Information of Poetry," review of Анализ поэтического текста, by Iu. M. Lotman, in Semiotica, 25 3/4. (1979), 273-305, and idem, "Tartu Semiotics," Bulletin of Literary Semiotics, 3, (1976), 1-16.
194. E.g. Lotman, Структура, 16.
195. Lotman, Анализ, 18. (My emphasis, A.R.)
196. E.g., Russian, English.
197. E.g., languages of the sciences, mathematics, traffic lights, etc.
198. Lotman, Структура, 16.
199. Ibid., emphasis in original.
200. Lotman, Лекции, esp. 29-43, Структура, esp. 29-34. Cf. also 72-74. Also on the difference between indexical and iconic signs see Lotman, "Несколько слов по поводу рецензии Я.М. Мейера," 116-117.
201. Ibid., 30-31, 78. For the question of information, see below.
202. See e.g. Lotman, "Primary and Secondary Communication-Modelling Systems," in Soviet Semiotics: An Anthology, ed., tr. and with an introduction by Daniel P. Lucid, (Baltimore and London: The Johns Hopkins Press, 1977), 95, and cf. "Давно уже было указано на то, что *необходимость искусства родственна необходимости знания, а само искусство-- одна из форм познания жизни, борьбы человечества за необходимую ему истину.*" (My emphasis, A.R.) Структура, 6-7. "Искусство

отличается от некоторых других видов познания тем, что пользуется не анализом и умозаключениями, а *воссоздает* окружающую человека действительность второй раз, доступными ему (искусству) средствами. То, что познание в искусстве достигается в процессе воссоздания действительности, — —чрезвычайно существенно." (Emphasis in original). Лекции, 15

203. E.g. Лекции, 27.
204. And he goes on: "Таким образом, изучение художественного языка произведений искусства не только дает нам некую индивидуальную норму эстетического общения, но и воспроизводит модель мира в ее самых общих очертаниях. Поэтому с определенных точек зрения информация, заключающаяся в выборе типа художественного языка, представляется наиболее существенной." Структура, 26.
205. E.g. L. Dolezel.
206. Lotman is not referring to some sort of naive one-to-one representation, or simple mirroring. Representation is mediated by the consciousness or worldview/s of the sender and receiver of the message, i.e. it models the content of their consciousness, including the model of reality presented by the natural language system. Compare Lotman, "О проблеме значений во вторичных моделирующих системах," TZS, II, "Вторичная моделирующая система художественного типа конструирует свою систему денотатов, которая является не копией, а моделью мира денотатов в общеязыковом значении." 35. Cf. also e.g. idem, "О статье проф. Марии Р. Майеновой," 83-87, where he very carefully expands on the question of modelling, and idem, "Primary and Secondary."
207. Lotman, Анализ, 131.

208. Lotman, Структура, 101, and he goes on, "Эти—то пересечения и составляют 'вещность' художественного текста, его материальное многообразие, отображающее причудливую бессистемность окружающего мира с таким правдоподобием, что у невнимательного зрителя возникает вера в идентичность этой случайности, неповторимой индивидуальности художественного текста и свойств отображаемой реальности." Cf. also ibid., e.g. 33, 70-71, 96, etc.

209. For a discussion of some aspects of the manner of these intersections in relation to the question of meaning in artistic texts see Lotman, "О проблеме значений."

210. Idem, Структура, 102-103. The discussion which follows the quoted passage refers to what is known in another terminology as the paradigmatic and syntagmatic axes.

211. Lotman, Анализ, 38, and cf. Структура, esp., 24-27.

212. E.g. Структура, 67.

213. Cf. Анализ, 123, where in one paragraph he uses all three; they are not, however, always co-terminous.

214. Lotman, "Несколько слов по поводу рецензии Я.М. Мейера," 113. But cf. idem, "Текст как динамическая система," in Структура текста: Тезисы симпозиума, ed. Viach. Vs. Ivanov, T.M. Sundik, T.V. Tsiv'ian. (Moscow: Institut slavianovedeniia i balkanistiki, AN SSSR, 1981), 104: "Однако, если говорить, по крайней мере, о таких понятиях, как 'текст искусства' (художественный текст) и 'текст культуры,' то все основания считать текст исходным, а язык производным от него явлением. . . . текст есть не реализация некоторого языка, а генератор языков."

215. Lotman, Структура, 70-71.

216. Ibid., and cf. also Анализ, 91-92. "Для того, чтобы стать 'текстом,' *графически закрепленный документ должен быть определен в его отношении к замыслу автора, эстетическим понятиям эпохи и другим, графически, в тексте не отраженным величинам.*" Лекции, 155 (emphasis in original).
217. E.g., Структура, 70.
218. E.g. Лекции, 57.
219. Ibid., 155ff, and Структура, 70-71, Анализ, 91-92.
220. Структура, 66-67.
221. Ibid., 67-69. It should be pointed out that Lotman recognizes that "text" can have different meanings for a general reader and for the literary scholar. This is particularly manifested in that the reader will read only a given text, an individual work of verbal art, while the literary scholar may study a given level of the text which then becomes the text and what was text becomes system, or on the other hand, he might study a genre, movement, or period, in which case the text will become either a variant or one level of the text. Cf. esp. Структура, 70-72.
222. Анализ, 119.
223. E.g. ibid., 123.
224. Ibid. Additionally, different portions of a text may be correlated with or constructed according to different artistic systems or codes. 124.
225. On this last point see e.g. Анализ, 90-92.
226. Dmitri M. Segal, "О некоторых проблемах семиотического изучения мифологии," in Симпозиум по структурному изучению знаковых систем, (Moscow: Izdatel'stvo AN SSSR, 1962), 94. Note that a myth is less complex than literature. Cf. Ju.M. Lotman and B.A. Uspenskij, "Myth--Name--Culture," in Soviet Semiotics, 233-52. Cf. also e.g. Анализ, 42.
227. E.g., Лекции. 187.
228. There are two senses of Information, one quantitive and technical, and one more theoretical and qualitative, being a

general notion of degree of organization. Lotman claims to be more interested in the latter. Cf. "Несколько слов по поводу рецензии Я.М. Мейера," 111-112,
229. E.g. Структура, 98-99.
230. Ibid., 99. Noise is an entropic force.
231. Ibid., 99. The association of art (literature) with life is not a capricious remark by Lotman or a flight of speculation; it is a view held by many or perhaps most information theorists. "Biologists as well as philosophers have suggested that the universe, and the living forms it contains, are based on chance, but not on accident. To put it another way, forces of chance and of antichance coexist in a complementary relationship. The random element is called entropy, the agent of chaos, which tends to mix up the unmixed, to destroy meaning. The nonrandom element is information, which exploits the uncertainty inherent in the entropy principle to generate new structures, to inform the world in novel ways." Jeremy Campbell, Grammatical Man: Information, Entropy, Language, and Life, (New York: Simon and Schuster,1982), 11. Compare Gleick, Chaos, writing in a section dealing with information theory, "Truly random data remains spread out in an undefined mess. But chaos (chaos here should be understood as a field of study, or certain natural occurrences, A.R.)--deterministic and patterned--pulls the data into visible shapes. Of all the possible pathways of disorder, nature favors just a few." 266-267. He also notes, quoting Erwin Schrodinger, the quantum physicist and occasional biologist, that "a living organism has the 'astonishing gift of concentrating a *stream of order* on itself and thus escaping the decay into atomic chaos.'" 299.
232. For a critical assessment of Lotman's view, see Richard W. Bailey "Maxwell's Demon and the Muse," Dispositio I, 3 (1976), 293-301.
233. Lotman, Структура, 77.
234. Incidentally, Lotman's writings contain numerous remarks of this sort which can be seen as attacks on the repressive Soviet controls on the production, storage and transmission of information.
235. Jurij Lotman, "Culture and Information," Dispositio, I, 3 (1976), 215. For the most part, where he says "culture" it is

236. E.g. <u>Лекции</u>, 186-187, <u>Структура</u>, 38ff., <u>Анализ</u>, 35.
237. <u>Лекции</u>, 187, and cf. <u>Анализ</u>, 34. His emphasis on the objectivity associated with his theory underlies somewhat my decision to present his position in the form of definitions.
238. <u>Анализ</u>, 128.
239. E.g. in a footnote in <u>Анализ</u>, 35, he equates readers' intuition of what good poetry is with results based on an empirical experiment to measure the redundancy of various texts. Given other remarks concerning the applicability of such tests to literary texts, one is led to suspect that he considers intuition to be even more reliable. "Проделанные нами эксперименты не только подтвердили данные венгерского ученого, но и показали, что стихи, интуитивно ощущаемые данным информантом как хорошие, угадываются с большим трудом, то есть имеют для него низкую избыточность. В плохих же стихах она резко растет. Это позволяет ввести объективные критерии в область, которая была наиболее трудной для анализа и традиционно покрывалась формулой: 'О вкусах не спорят.'"
240. <u>Лекции</u>, 98. He vigorously defends this formulation (as late as 1975) against a rather naive criticism in "Несколько слов по поводу рецензии Я.М. Мейера," 111-112.
241. "Красота есть некоторый особый вид организации," ibid, 112.
242. Lotman, "Знаковый механизм культуры," in <u>Сборник статей по вторичным моделирующим системам</u>, (Tartu: Tartuskii gosudarstvennyi universitet, 1973), 195-199.
243. Ibid., 196.
244. Ibid.

245. Ibid.
246. Ibid., 196-197.
247. Ibid., 197.
248. Ibid., 199. Bound up with the notion of untranslatability and different codes is not only the notion but the very possibility of individual personalities. Cf. also idem, "Primary and Secondary," 95-98. "A participant in communication is operative for me precisely because he is 'another person,' and the information obtained from him is valuable precisely insofar as it issues from another person and does not duplicate what is already known to me. To the extent that participants in communication are united by a common code, they are one person. Nevertheless, only that aspect of their involuntary signalization not deciphered by this common code--not deciphered automatically but demanding amplification, a conscious semiotic act of decipherment--constitutes the individuality of each of them and is of informational interest for the other." Ibid., 96.
249. Lotman, "Знаковый механизм," 199.
250. "Primary and Secondary," 97.

IV BAKHTIN AND LOTMAN: LITERATURE AS COMMUNICATION AND COGNITION

Ultimately, it is the question of language which separates the theories of Bakhtin and Lotman from so many other contemporary theories. While it may not be possible to prove that hypothesis logically or empirically, I believe I have demonstrated above that it does have considerable validity. Having thus set off Bakhtin and Lotman from competing trends, I would now like to highlight certain significant aspects of their theories which underlie important areas of similarity and compatibility. The thrust of this selective comparison and attendant analysis will be towards the contention that literature, seen as markedly distinct from the sphere of action of natural language, is for both Bakhtin and Lotman primarily characterized by its communicative and cognitive nature.

To avoid subsequent repetition, two points should be born in mind throughout. The first point is that the argument should be seen against the background of the Russian formalist-Prague school line and its emphasis on the aesthetic function of literature (and art). As a corrollary to this, one could include all or at least many other schools and trends which stress a similar aesthetic function or otherwise deny the cognitive and/or communicative nature of literature, whether by denying or negating to various degrees the author, the text, the reader, or reality itself.

Secondly, since in large measure the formulation "Literature is communication and cognition" has been taken from Lotman, the task at hand can be seen as one of attempting to measure Bakhtin up to Lotman, without effecting a simple reduction. There is, however, no intent to imply that Lotman sets the standard; it is simply an analytic position. One could conceivably formulate the question in terms of trying to argue that for Lotman, literature is dialogue. There is ample evidence to support this, but, first of all, the often nearly amorphous notion of dialogue is very difficult to deal with in such a context, and secondly, it would require a massive transformation of concepts and terms. It is much more straightforward to try to reveal communication and cognition in Bakhtin's dialogue than dialogue in Lotman's communication and cognition. The result will largely determine the validity of the procedure.

The danger of reduction is, unfortunately, very real, especially since I will concentrate more on similarities than on differences, and often I will be dealing with general notions. However, one important, determining reason for this particular analytic position is that the *Bakhtinomania* of the last two decades has led not only to a somewhat distorted picture of Bakhtin centered almost exclusively on the notions of carnival, dialogue, and the novel--in all their amorphousness--but also has, largely by process of denial, led to an impoverished view of Lotman's theoretical position,[1] which is not only technically sophisticated but full of a profound and passionate search for what Bakhtin has called "understanding" of human reality.

IV.1 Methodology

Before turning directly to the notions of communication and cognition, I will examine some aspects of methodological similarities in Bakhtin and Lotman, and illustrate them with references to some of their applied studies, i.e. theory in practice. It seems appropriate to take as a starting point what appears to be Bakhtin's last completed work, which contains his most carefully and fully elaborated references to Lotman, namely "Ответ на вопрос редакции Нового мира."[2] In this brief essay, Bakhtin both summarizes his view of how literature should be studied, how it interrelates with other dimensions of culture, and refers approvingly to Lotman's endeavors in the field up to that point.[3] The essay has been discussed in some detail above, so I will point out only that in it Bakhtin sets out to distinguish what he considers to be the two general tasks of literary scholarship, at least in reference to the literature of the past.[4] These can be viewed as the synchronic and diachronic approaches to the study of literature, as long as synchronic is not confused with the notion of a closed or strictly immanent approach.

The synchronic dimension is concerned with establishing literature's ties to other cultural series and to culture in general within the epoch in which a given work arose.[5] "Литература — — неотрывная часть культуры, ее нельзя понять вне целостного контекста всей культуры данной эпохи."[6] Literature, he says, must not be isolated within its so-called specificity, nor should external, for example, socio-economic, factors be seen to affect it directly when, in fact, their impact is mediated through the whole cultural system. Bakhtin stresses the need to allow not only the traditionally viewed cultural spheres or series but also the various levels of culture, including especially the often-neglected lower levels, to manifest their influences and role.[7] Bakhtin himself realized this program in his study of Rabelais. A major portion of that work was dedicated to demonstrating the close ties of Rablelais' work with other cultural series of the epoch and its complex relationship with both the upper and lower social strata, but in a special way emphasizing the latter.[8] That he may have idealized and even exaggerated the importance of certain aspects of the broad masses and the folk consciousness is beside the point in this respect. What matters here is the methodological principle he outlined and attempted to implement in his study of Rabelais, and which he presents again in more schematic form in "Ответ." Indeed, he clearly did succeed in opening up and analyzing literary and cultural processes which had previously been largely ignored or unknown to scholars.[9]

The second, diachronic dimension or perspective is related to the question of discovering and studying the roots and origins of literary works in the distant past and seeing a given work's ties not only with the past relative to the time of its composition, but also with its future.[10]

> Великие произведения литературы подготовляются веками, . . . Пытаясь понять и объяснить произведение только из условий его эпохи, только из условий ближайшего

времени, мы никогда не проникнем в его смысловые глубины.[11]

Works, especially great works,[12] reveal ever newer and deeper levels of meaning with the passage of time, meanings which were present but not accessible to earlier readers.[13] For Bakhtin, the question of genres is especially important in this respect, ("Особо важное значение имеют жанры."[14]) He gives special emphasis to this question in his studies of Rabelais and of Dostoevsky; and it can probably be said that its most lucid expression is to be found in his study of Dostoevsky's poetics.[15] It is essential to remember that these two questions, these two dimensions of the study of literature, the synchronic and the diachronic are not totally separable except for analysis; in actuality they work hand-in-hand. Bakhtin expressed it as follows in his book on Dostoevsky:

Нам кажется, что наш диахронический анализ подтверждает результаты синхронического. Точнее: результаты обоих анализов взаимно проверяют и подтверждают друг друга.[16]

Lotman has certainly not written one single, individual work on the scale or scope of of Bakhtin's study of Rabelais[17] although he has just as certainly done comparable work. Taken as a whole, his several articles and monographs on Pushkin's Евгений Онегин form an imposing body of scholarly achievement, and if one adds to it all he has written on Pushkin in general, it is possible to speak of a truly colossal corpus.[18] There are also numerous studies dedicated to the historical period in which Pushkin lived and wrote.[19] Indeed, Pushkin and his period have been the focus of a majority of Lotman's "applied" works, and their impact on the scholarship of that period both within and without the Soviet Union has yet to be investigated. A detailed comparison just of Lotman's work on Евгений Онегин with Bakhtin's study of Rabelais could be the subject of several dissertations, and certainly, even just by virtue of the "encyclopedic"[20] character of both literary texts, would be very fruitful.[21] (Recently some scholars have begun to confront Lotman's studies of Pushkin's novel in verse with Bakhtin's writings on the same subject.)[22] Here I will limit myself to references to two of Lotman's works on Pushkin in order to highlight the common features of the methodological approaches of both Bakhtin and Lotman in this context.

In his commentary to Pushkin's Евгений Онегин, Lotman systematically realizes the first part of Bakhtin's methodological diad, as well as aspects of the second, reflecting the limitations he explicitly placed before himself in preparing the commentary.[23] Lotman unfolds before his reader a detailed and profound description of many important aspects of life relevant to any adequate understanding of Евгений Онегин. The significance of the boundaries he puts on the scope of his purview--

> при этом мы, разумеется, не ставим перед собой цели характеризовать быт эпохи как таковой--внимание будет привлекаться лишь к тем его сторонам, которые прямо или косвенно отразились в тексте пушкинского романа[24]

--is substantially diminished by the "encyclopedic" character of the novel.

Lotman presents his view of how various aspects of the culture of Pushkin's era interact with the text of the novel. This he does in an introductory chapter entitled "Очерк дворянского быта онегинской поры"[25] and then in the detailed and specific ("построчные") commentaries to individual passages of the novel. The need for such a study as a pre-condition for a proper understanding of the novel he sets out in terms very similar to those used by Bakhtin in a corresponding section of his work on Rabelais.

> Знание бытовых реалий необходимо для понимания текста даже тогда, когда они непосредственно не упоминаются или лишь мелькают в виде кратких отсылок, намеков на то, что было с полуслова понятно и автору, и современному ему читателю.[26]
>
> Но, используя творчество Рабле для раскрытия сущности народной смеховой культуры, мы вовсе не превращаем его только в средство для достижения вне его лежащей цели. Напротив, мы глубоко убеждены, что только таким путем, то есть только в свете народной

культуры, можно раскрыть подлинного Рабле, показать Рабле в Рабле.²⁷

Of course, beyond the clearly identifiable similarities in the methodological approach to the linking of the various cultural series, there are equally clearly identifiable differences. I have already referred to some of them, but it is worth restating the primary ones. First of all, Bakhtin's study of Rabelais takes in much more of the diachronic perspective; Lotman excludes that from his study for practical reasons dictated largely by his intended readership. Elements of it are present, for example, in numerous references to past and future literary traditions, and to various languages and historical processes flowing into and through the text. That he is actively aware of the great importance of the diachronic dimension to the study of literature, I will demonstrate presently. He has also devoted studies to the "future" of <u>Евгений Онегин</u>.²⁸ Secondly, Bakhtin's *primary* aim is not to study Rabelais' masterpiece <u>Gargantua and Pantagruel</u>, but to study the nature and importance of the culture of folk laughter:

По отношению к ней наша задача чисто теоретическая—-раскрыть единство и смысл этой культуры, ее общеидеологическую—-миросозерцательную—-и эстетическую сущность. Разрешить эту задачу лучше всего можно там, то есть на таком конкретном материале, где народная смеховая культура собрана, сконцентрирована и художественно осознана на своем высшем ренессансном этапе—-именно в творчестве Рабле. Для проникновения в самую глубинную сущность народной смеховой культуры Рабле незаменим.²⁹

However, that aim is barely distinguishable or separable from its partner, i.e. to discover and demonstrate, through the analysis of the culture of folk laughter, the meaning and aesthetic vision contained in Rabelais' work, i.e. "Рабле в Рабле."³⁰

An example of a study in which Bakhtin's conception of the diachronic perspective takes the fore is Lotman's study of Pushkin's poem "Andzhelo."³¹ Lotman covers a large number of questions in this brief study, however, in relating the poem to the literary source which inspired it--Shakespeare's Measure for Measure, in which Pushkin had an abiding interest[32]--Lotman concentrates on

> Three structural levels . . . in the story organization of 'Andzhelo':
> 1. The level organized by the laws of novella construction.
> 2. The level organized by the principles of folk and mythological consciousness.
> 3. Episodes connected with the political conception of 'power' and 'mercy,' which make "Andzhelo" akin to the *The Captain's Daughter*, 'Peter the Great's Feast' and other late works of Pushkin's (sic).[33]

The first two "levels" correspond quite closely with Bakhtin's second question, i.e. the diachronic perspective, but, of course, they would be rather limited if not related to Lotman's third level, i.e. to questions concerning Pushkin's overall opus. Lotman provides a fascinating and detailed analysis of each of these structural levels, while noting that their separation is artificial: the unity of the poem is dependant on their integration and interrelationship.[34] Here he makes an interesting and suggestive reference to Bakhtin's concept of the polyphonic novel.[35] Furthermore, he considers the stylistic and ideational levels of the text to be united by one particular feature: "low popular style."[36] He goes on to state, based on his analysis that

> Coarse simplicity combined with gutter jokes . . . is the mark of the narrator's speech as of the characters' words. This had particular significance for Pushkin. As we have seen there are represented in the poem two conceptions of power, that of the people and that of the highest levels of culture. In spite of the whole social and intellectual gulf between them there was, in Pushkin's opinion, an area where the mind of the people and the mind of the cultural elite came together, and this was the area of common speech, bare and unaffected. Affectation is alien alike to the top and the bottom of society and comes into being when poetry is created by "the middle class." Pushkin saw here the cause of the affectation of the French classicists and of the Russian socially rootless journalists and seminarists of the 1830s. [. . .] If we recall the significance that a rapprochement between the cultural elite and the popular masses had for Pushkin's political consciousness . . . then it becomes clear that the problem of popular speech as the basis of authorial style, and of the spirit of the common people as "the author's point

of view," took on a character leading far beyond the framework of purely literary research.[37]

One of the questions this particular set of texts raises when compared in this manner concerns the question of actual influence. Certainly the texts by Lotman here discussed do not read as if they were written by Bakhtin, but the presence of isomorphic elements is unmistakable. There is no doubt that his study of "Andzhelo" was written in a period marked by heightened interest in Bakhtin's ideas and works.[38]

It is an important underlying thesis of the present study that the question of influence is a far less important consideration than mutual interests, methodological principles, and general ideological or philosophical orientation. Therefore it is important to point out that these studies, while clearly bearing the imprint of contact with Bakhtin's ideas, also display strong and equally unmistakable affinities with much of Lotman's work from the early sixties, i.e. from a time when he very likely had not yet encountered Bakhtin.[39] I have in mind such works as his early study of Pushkin's Капитанская дочка (1962), where he already shows an awareness of Pushkin's preoccupation with the question of the relationship between the upper classes and the peasant masses and their respective languages. In the following quotation, the terminology is obviously different, but the parallels are easily discerned:

> Крестьянский уклад жизни овеян *своей* поэзией: песни, сказки, легенды пронизывают всю атмосферу повествования о народе. Особое место занимают пословицы, в которых выкристаллизовалось своеобразие народной мысли. Исследователи неоднократно обращали внимание на роль пословиц и загадок в характеристике Пугачева. Но пословицами говорят и другие персонажи из народа. [. . .] Пушкин подчеркнул, что речь Пугачева, вобравшая все своеобразие народного языка, дворянину непонятна. . . . При этом показательно, что тайный 'воровской' язык, которым пользуются Пугачев и хозяин 'умета'--это не арго, специальная речь, доступная лишь членам шайки, а язык пословиц и загадок--—сгусток национально—

самобытной стихии языка. Смысль речи,
непонятной Гриневу, прекрасно понятен
читателю.[40]

In this relatively early work Lotman demonstrates an awareness of the presence of deep and broad historical and cultural processes both in society and in literature and their interrelationships.[41] In another context, Lotman notes that

Живая культура--это движение, связывающее
прошедшее с будущим, это, по выражению
одного из поэтов ХУИИИ века, радуга, которая
Половиной в древность наклонилась, /А
другой в потомстве оперлась.'[42]

Other early works in which such parallels can be discerned include the important study (1963) of the differences in the linguistic and literary conceptions of structure--perhaps his first "structural-semiotic" publication--in which he discusses the need to see both the importance of the individual character of speech (the emphasis on *parole*) and correlatively the importance of extra-textual considerations, especially the relationship between the speaker's use of the word and his world-view.[43] There is also a brief but interesting study (1964) of a problem concerning an eighteenth century polemic which Lotman relates to a conflict between two fundamentally opposed world views. He shows how the use of a certain pair of contrasting epithets, with a tradition in Russia reaching back several centuries, reflects the essence of a literary polemic which lasted from the time of Derzhavin at least to the time of N.A. Ostrovskii. An awareness of both the tradition and the dynamics of the interaction of various "languages" within the given epoch are shown to be necessary to understand the point and the functioning of the conflict.[44]

Finally, I would mention his analysis (1962) of the problem of the authenticity of the Igor tale. His somewhat unusual strategy is to consider not whether the tale could have been written in the twelfth century, but whether it could have been written in the eighteenth. He brings to bear on his analysis a vast array of literary-historical, stylistic, social, historical, political, mythological, and other cultural perspectives. He shows a deep cognizance of the significance, for the proper understanding of the problem at hand, of their interrelationships on both the synchronic and diachronic planes. His conclusion takes into account not only the past of the "Слово," but also its future, noting it appears as a total anomaly located on the border of the eighteenth and nineteenth centuries, having "ни одного предшественника и даже—— ни одного последователя."[45] It is interesting to note that he also considers the question of forgeries as a *genre*, and in reference to this he makes some very telling remarks.

> Подделки——бесспорно, труднейший жанр литературного творчества. В этом мог бы убедиться любой скептик, попытавшись совершить в середине XX в., будучи вооруженным всем арсеналом научных данных, то, что, по его мнению, так безукоризненно выполнили полулюбители-полуученые конца ХУИИИ столетия.[46]

Here he underlines the importance and the inherent difficulties of reconstructing the social and cultural context and actual worldview of the author of a given text, or of its contemporary readers, depending on the the problem at hand. Again, in this reconstructive effort, he does not seek to establish a constant set of one-to-one relationships, but complex "structural" relationships.[47] This is a key tenet of both his own and Bakhtin's methodology and entire theoretical perspective.[48]

IV.2 Text

Turning now from an examination of more strictly methodological matters, I will examine selected fundamental concepts in the theories of Lotman and Bakhtin which are directly tied to the idea of literature as communication and cognition. I propose to do this by focussing on the notion of text as it appears in their respective theories. I believe the problem of the text illuminates significant aspects of how both Bakhtin and Lotman view literature as communication and cognition.

As indicated in a preceding section, the notion of text is an essential component of Lotman's theory of literature and culture.[49] It is both one of the most important and most complex of Lotman's key concepts. Its centrality obviously arises from the fact that if there are no texts, there is no literature, and hence no discussion.[50] The complexity of the concept of text[51] seems to arise primarily from its shifting relationship with its relational partner, i.e. system (language, code), and their amalgam, i.e. the notion of 'work of art' (художественное произведение). It can be said with some certainty, however, that text corresponds to the spatially and/or temporally registered (graphically and/or accoustically represented) organization of signs.[52] It exists in a relationship with at least two systems or languages or codes by means of which it is decoded or translated (understood), in the process of aesthetic communication.

For Bakhtin, the concept of text is no less central and, not surprisingly, no less complex. Some dimensions of Bakhtin's notions of what is contained in the concept of text have been presented above in relation to the work-of-art concept, as set out in his article on content, material and form. Another important source for Bakhtin's concept of text is his later essay ostensibly dedicated to that very subject.[53] There are serious textological problems associated with using this "essay" as a systematic treatment of the problem of the text or of any other problem. In the first place, it is not an essay but a set of notes and jottings *loosely* centered around a philosophical analysis of the concept of the text in the human sciences, particularly, but not exclusively, in linguistics and literary studies. The problem of the text is central to all of these disciplines, yet it is necessary to point out that the title of the essay comes not from Bakhtin but from his editor, V. Kozhinov. As with other similar publications, most of which are contained in the volume Эстетика словесного творчества, caution, or at least prudence, is necessary in deriving conclusions on the basis of these occasionally very provisional notes. Frequently, thoughts are not connected to those preceding or following, or, again, occasionally Bakhtin will make notes to himself.[54] As much as possible, in using this essay I have ignored: ideas which do not receive subsequent development; ideas which are contradicted elsewhere in the text; ideas which are not closely related to the problem of the text. For all its stylistic and organizational shortcomings, it does serve, nevertheless, as a relatively focussed source of Bakhtin's reflections on the question of text.

The first point to note is that Bakhtin takes the text as the starting point in all areas of the humanities.

> Текст является той непосредственной
> действительностью (действительностью мысли и
> переживаний), из которой только и могут
> исходить эти дисциплины и это мышление.
> Где нет текста, там нет и объекта для
> исследования и мышления.[55]

This textual orientation is the distinguishing characteristic of the humanities as opposed to the natural sciences:

> Мысли о мыслях, переживания переживаний,
> слова о словах, тексты о текстах. В этом
> основное отличие наших (гуманитарных)
> дисциплин от естественных (о природе).[56]

The humanities operate essentially as thoughts about thoughts or other semiotic representations of human subjects, actual and potential.[57] The second point to consider is that within the concept of text two distinctions are of primary importance for the present discussion. The first is between the text as understood by linguistics and the text as understood by other humanistic disciplines, primarily literary studies, but in fact all those which study texts as dialogue.[58] Linguistics studies texts in isolation, it studies that which is repeatable, non-individual non-intentional, and axiologically neutral.

> Linguistic theory is concerned primarily with an ideal speaker-listener, in a completely homogeneous speech-community, who knows its language perfectly and is unaffected by such grammatically irrelevant conditions as memory limitations, distractions, shifts of attention and interest, and errors (random or characteristic) in applying his knowledge of the language in actual performance.[59]

The words are Chomsky's, but Bakhtin would be quite comfortable with them. I do not mean to imply that their respective understandings of linguistics are equivalent, only that Bakhtin is neither overstating his case nor dwelling anochronistically on De Saussurian notions from the 1920s. Linguistics, then, can explain sentence structure, phonology, morphology, and so on, but it can not deal with meaning or communication as Bakhtin understands it. That requires a different, dialogical approach.

The second fundamental distinction which he makes is far less clearly formulated. It concerns not two terms, but three: text, utterance, and dialogue. In reality, not only are these three terms not clearly distinguished, but they are often used inconsistently by Bakhtin as substitutes for one another. In addition, they carry in their wake other terms which also enter into similarly contradictory relations and usages, including, especially, subject and language. My understanding of the three terms in this context is as follows. Text *when opposed to utterance* is taken in isolation from its actual context, without regard to its actual sender or receiver, as when we speak of a novel or poem, for example, in regards to its physical location.[60] An utterance is completely relational. "Каждое большое и творческое словесное целое есть очень сложная и многопланная система отношений."[61] This refers not just to a given text's complex immanent structural relationships, but also to its being the result of one's activity as addresser or addressee, sender or receiver of the text; it is the dialogical event. All relevant trans-linguistic (внелингвистические) elements enter into the utterance.

> Высказывание в его целом оформлено как таковое внелингвистическими моментами (диалогическими), оно связано и с другими высказываниями. Эти внелингвистические (диалогические) моменты пронизывают высказывание и изнутри.[62]

Dialogue, thus understood, is the actual process, the living, dynamic, infinite process of intersubjective communication,[63] including all the contextual elements contributing to its individuality. (This kind of dialogue is not equivalent to the standard notion of dialogue as in a dramatic text, although the latter can, in principle, be dialogic in Bakhtin's sense.)[64] Accordingly, a genuine verbal exchange between two (or more) individuals is made up of utterances, or could be seen as a single utterance from a certain meta-perspective.[65] A literary work is an utterance when viewed not as an object on a shelf but in contact with its perceiver. Utterances are always inter-subjective, existing between two or more conciousnesses.[66]

It must be stressed that Bakhtin is far less systematic in his use of terms than even this presentation suggests. That is hardly praiseworthy, but on the other hand--and this bears repeating--we are working from his notebooks. These are not essays, not even drafts of essays, but rough notes. In imposing some measure of *terminological* system on Bakhtin's ideas, I do not intend to distort his meaning. Finally, when referring to passages in Bakhtin's text, it may be, for example, that he says "text" where I say "utterance," but presumably such superficial inconsistencies have now been explained. I have only hoped to provide an interpretive model for separating some of the elements or ideas he works with. Their relational nature together with this terminological imprecision makes their systematic organization in this manner doubly arbitrary but at the same time even more desirable.

Bakhtin's description of text and utterance immediately raises at least two important issues in the context of a comparison with Lotman's corresponding concepts. The *first* concerns the question of the communicative dimension of literature and other texts/utterances, and the *second* concerns the relation of literary texts/utterances to reality. To avoid tiresome repetition and possible further confusion, in the context of Bakhtin's theory, I will adopt the convention of referring to non-literary dialogic texts as utterances and to literary utterances as literary works. Note that the overlap in Bakhtin's terminology makes it veritably impossible to make such a terminological determination consistently and clearly. To use the term "speech act," for example, would seem to be a way out, but the closest equivalent Russian term is высказывание, i.e. utterance. I am, as indicated, left to impose my own arbitrary terms, however reluctantly.

IV.3 Communication

Bakhtin's concern with communication is preeminent and legendary. "Я же во всем слышу *голоса* и диалогические отношения между ними."[67] It is located most securely within his concept of dialogue. This concept would appear to have grown out of Bakhtin's early concerns with such problems as the limitations of linguistics, the relation of the text to speaker, i.e. language as worldview and the entry of the speaker and listener into the text, and the relation of the text to reality. As such it is clearly present in more than germinal form in his 1924 essay on general aesthetics. Its first developed presentation is found in his study of Dostoevsky, especially in the notion of polyphony. Of course, Bakhtin's unusual publishing history makes a chronological description of the evolution of his ideas problematic, but since that is not my problem here, let it be said that the second edition of his study of Dostoevsky contains a more complex and sophisticated presentation of dialogue or communication in literature based on ideas developed but not published between the two editions of the Dostoevsky work, i.e. between 1929 and 1963.[68]

Communication as dialogue remains, if not the dominant focus of his thinking, certainly the foremost of a small group of key concepts. The implications of Bakhtinian dialogue are that a text or utterance exists between (at least) two subjects, not between a text and receiver, or between an idealized sender and receiver, who could not, by virtue of their idealization, be subjects. To the extent that a language, a speech genre, or a 'style' is seen as representing a worldview or a system of values, they are capable of entering into dialogue as an utterance.

> Могут ли вступать в такие отношения, то есть говорить друг с другом, языки, диалекты (территориальные, социальные, жаргоны), языковые (функциональные) стили (скажем, фамильярно—бытовая речь и научный язык и т. п.) и др.? Только при условий нелингвистического подхода к ним, то есть при условий трансформаций их в 'мировоззрения' (или некие языковые или речевые мироощущения), в 'точки зрения,' в 'социальные голоса' и т. п.[69]

Bakhtin expresses this much more clearly and unambiguously in his study of Dostoevsky:

> Диалогические отношения возможны не только между целыми (относительно) высказываниями, но диалогический подход возможен и к любой значащей части высказывания, даже к отдельному слову, если оно воспринимается не как безличное слово языка, а как знак чужой смысловой позиции, как представитель чужого высказывания, то

есть, если мы слышим в нем чужой голос. Поэтому диалогические отношения могут проникать внутрь высказывания, даже внутрь отдельного слова, если в нем диалогически сталкиваются два голоса (микродиалог . . .)

С другой стороны, диалогические отношения возможны и между языковыми стилями, социальными диалектами и т. п., если только они воспринимаются как некие смысловые позиции, как своего рода языковые мировоззрения, то есть уже не при лингвистическом их рассмотрении.

Наконец, диалогические отношения возможны и к своему собственному высказыванию в целом, к отдельным его частям и к отдельному слову в нем, если мы как-то отделяем себя от них, говорим с внутренней оговоркой, занимаем дистанцию по отношению к ним, как бы ограничиваем или раздваиваем свое авторство.[70]

Dialogue and the utterances which make up its continual flow are strictly relational and contextual, i.e. meta-linguistic.[71] Literature, especially the novel,[72] the highest or most developed form of which is the so-called polyphonic novel, embodies this type of communication. Creativity and self-discovery[73] as part of the process of experiencing literature (as author and perceiver) inhere in and are characterized by dialogic communication.

If we accept Bakhtin's notion of dialogue, whether genuinely or simply hypothetically, it then becomes synonymous with the notion of communication in general, or at least human sign communication, i.e. communication associated with semiotic phenomena.[74] The very nature of human beings is such that they can only communicate meaningfully in this way. An utterance is sent with an addressee in mind, whether real, potential or imagined.[75] The notion of addressee/receiver must be viewed as also that of respondent. His response is anticipated (whether rightly or wrongly does not immediately matter), by the sender.[76] His reception involves a response because the act of understanding involves a valuation--true/false, good/bad, aesthetic/non-aesthetic, etc.--and for him to treat it as an utterance he must respond to it.[77] Otherwise it is just an object, a linguistic text deprived of its contextual value/meaning, of its singularity and uniqueness, which in the sphere of dialogue is all-important. Reception, then, is equal to response, or at the very least implies it. Even if my response is incorrect or misguided, it is still a response. A linguist may take an utterance, whether from everyday speech or from literature, and study it as a fact of language, i.e. without regard to its singularity or individuality, without regard to its sender as subject, but then it is no longer an utterance. It is simply a sentence or a phrase or whatever unit of language, infinitely repeatable, but devoid of any dialogic or axiological meaning.

> Несколько упрощая дело: чисто лингвистические отношения (то есть предмет лингвистики)--это отношения знака к знаку и знакам в пределах системы языка или текста (то есть системные или линейные отношения между знаками). Отношения высказываний к реальной действительности, к реальному говорящему субъекту и к реальным другим высказываниям, отношения, впервые делающие высказывания истинными или ложными, прекрасными и т. п., никогда не могут стать предметом лингвистики. Отдельные знаки, системы языка или текст (как знаковое единство) никогда не могут быть ни истинными, ни ложными, ни прекрасными и т. п.[78]

Bakhtin, as far as I know, never explicitly states what distinguishes literary works from non-literary utterances within his discussion of text-utterance-dialogue.[79] What emerges, however, is that such a distinction would be based on the internal organization of the utterance. My choice of terms is obviously derived from Lotman, and were I not comparing Bakhtin with him, I might have chosen another term. The principle is however objectively present. What is important is to recognize the *primary* emphasis on internal organization or structure, and not on an external principle such as function or normative activity, nor on traditional generic distinctions.

> Вторичные (сложные) речевые жанры — романы, драмы, научные исследования всякого рода, большие публицистические жанры и т. п. — возникают в условиях более сложного и относительно высокоразвитого и организованного культурного общения (преимущественно письменного, художественного, научного, общественно-политического и т. п.) В процессе своего формирования они вбирают в себя и перерабатывают различные первичные (простые) жанры, сложившиеся в условиях непосредственного речевого общения. Эти первичные жанры, входящие в состав сложных, трансформируются в них и приобретают особый характер: утрачивают непосредственное отношение к реальной действительности и к реальным чужим высказываниям. . . .[80]

Literature is primarily a heteroglossial system of genres which contains utterances consisting of utterances, or speech about speech. Consider the following passage in which Bakhtin is obviously referring to the novel, but which, with modifications could readily apply to other genres as well.

> Роман как целое — это многостильное, разноречивое, разноголосое явление. Исследователь сталкивается в нем с несколькими разнородными стилистическими единствами, лежащими иногда в разных языковых планах и подчиняющимися разным стилистическим закономерностям. [. . .]
>   *Эти разнородные стилистические единства, входя в роман, сочетаются в нем в стройную художественную систему и*

> подчиняются высшему стилистическому
> единству целого, которое нельзя отождествлять
> ни с одним из подчиненных единств.[81]

This occasionally occurs in non-literary genres, especially when they involve quotation, but they do not generally meet the requirements of being aesthetic activity. Aesthetic activity, as Bakhtin argued in "Проблема содержания" requires the externality of the author/perceiver providing form to a content. This content consists of ethical-cognitive axiological positions expressed in or through verbal material. In terms of his theory of utterance/dialogue, this is expressed by his theory of author, especially the image of the author (образ автора).[82]

Literature, or literary works, includes an author whose voice, whose valorizing activity--every voice represents a worldview, i.e. a system of values[83]--informs or organizes the other voices (worldviews, value systems) contained or represented in the utterance *qua genre*, be it a novel, a poem, a short story, or whatever. Bakhtin carefully distinguishes between the image of the author as one voice in the text--part of the content--and the author who provides form to the content.

> Отношение автора к изображенному всегда
> входит в состав образа. Авторское
> отношение--конститутивный момент образа.
> Это отношение чрезвычайно сложно. Его
> недопустимо сводить к прямолинейной оценке.
> Такие прямолинейные оценки разрушают
> художественный образ.[84]

At this point it is necessary to recall the very tenuous positioning of non-novelistic literary genres within Bakhtin's theory of dialogue, speech genres, and literature. Bakhtin's fascination--one could almost say obsession--with the novel, to the exclusion or at least demotion of other genres, especially lyrical poetry, is well-known. It can only be considered a serious deficiency of his theory. However, as suggested above, by introducing the criterion of internal organization as the criterion of what a literary utterance is, a criterion which I believe is implicit in his theory, especially given his own application of his theory of the image of the author to lyrical poetry,[85] lyrical poetry and other non-novelistic genres seem to be largely accommodated without violating any part of his theory. Speech genres as he understood them remain a continuum, and novelistic utterances remain the highest or most dialogic forms of utterance. Other literary genres can be seen then as having a more secure, if intermediary, position.

Bakhtin's concept of literature as dialogic utterance refers most clearly to Lotman's theory especially on two levels, namely to his model of communication, and secondly to his notion of literature as communication broadly viewed. There are also significant points of contact in reference to the closely related concepts of personality, creativity, subjectivity, the relation between text and system, etc.

Lotman's model of communication is obviously more "mechanical" than Bakhtin's, that is, not in a mechanistic sense, but in a schematic one. He strives to represent everything that enters into the process of communication graphically and technically.[86] This is especially so for what both he and Bakhtin refer to as the essential component of untranslatability or misunderstanding.

> Но текст . . . никогда не может быть переведен до конца.[87]

> . . . Понимание, передача информации в принципе требует усилия, поскольку, в частности, подразумевает обратный процесс реконструкции переданого сообщения. Непонимание, неполное понимание или переосмысление — не побочные продукты обмена информацией, а принадлежат самой ее сути.[88]

The entire thrust of Lotman's model is to bring into the picture those aspects of communication which are not accounted for by most other models,[89] and which make up the essence of Bakhtinian dialogue. I have in mind first of all the notion of context, as Bakhtin employs it, which includes various random, non-constant elements, i.e. extra-textual or non-systemic elements, or in other words, that which makes two lexically and syntactically identical statements different in two different instances. Secondly, there is the active involvement of both poles of the utterance, of sender and receiver, neither of which is idealized: each is actively involved in the process of communication (dialogue) and it is this active involvement which forces us to view the transmission of a message as a translation, but one which is fundamentally and by its very nature imperfect and open.

Lotman's model stresses the non-identity of the codes of the receiver and sender. The sender encodes the message and I, intuitively recognizing it as a text or message,[90] then decode it. However, except in extreme circumstances (at one end of a continuum) my code(s) and the code(s) of the sender do not coincide.

> The addresser encodes the message with the help of a set of codes, of which only a part are present in the decoding consciousness of the addressee. It is for this reason that all understanding, no matter how many developed semiotic systems are used is partial and approximative. But it is important to emphasize that a degree of non-understanding cannot be interpreted only as 'noise'--a harmful consequence of an imperfection of the system, which is not present in the idealized schema. The growth of non-understanding and/or inadequate understanding may bear witness to the technical defects in the system of communications, but it may also be an indicator of the increased complexity of this system, its capacity to fulfill ever more complex and important cultural functions.[91]

Coincidence of codes is essentially equal to coincidence of personalities or individualities. The presence of individual, i.e. non-coinciding personalities is a *sine qua non* of the existence of culture and, therefore, of humanity.

> Пользование одними и теми же кодами и циркулирование одних и тех же, не меняющихся в процессе передачи сообщений, привело бы к тому, что коллектив оказался бы состоящим из семиотически однородных индивидов, то есть к утрате одной из наиболее существенных сторон, отличающих одну личность от другой. Составленный таким образом коллектив крайне потерял бы в устойчивости и выживаемости.[92]

The humanly indispensable transcoding (перекодировка) or translating of messages depends on and ensures the individuality and creativity of the members of a socio-cultural collective. The presence of a different point of view, indicative of the presence of an "other" is the key to the process in which I discover myself and develop, i.e. it is this interaction which ensures both the growth of culture by virtue of the increase and transfer of messages/texts, and the process of individuation or individual becoming.

> В более сложных коммуникативных ситуациях 'я' заинтересован в том, чтобы контрагент был именно 'другим,' поскольку неполнота информации может полезно восполняться лишь стереоскопичностью точек зрения сообщения. В этом случае полезным свойством оказывается не легкость, а трудность взаимопонимания, поскольку именно она связывается с наличием в сообщении 'чужой' позиции. В этом случае акт коммуникации уподобляется не простой передаче константного сообщения, а переводу, влекущему за собой преодоление некоторых— —иногда весьма значительных——трудностей, определенные потери и, одновременно, обогащение 'меня' текстами, несущими 'чужую' точку зрения. В результате 'я' получаю возможность стать для себя 'другим.'[93]

The dialogic activity which this description characterizes is, as has been stated, dependent on the presence of different codes and points of view, or worldviews.[94] The process is relentlessly active and both poles of the communication process are involved. Their active involvement insures the integrity of both subjects, i.e. of "I" and of "you." It is, very much in the Bakhtinian sense, dialogical.

> It follows that the act of communication (in any sufficiently complex, and consequently culturally valuable, instance) should be seen not as a simple transmission of a message which remains adequate to itself from the consciousnes of the addresser to the consciousness of the addressee, but as a *translation* of a text from the language of my "I" to the language of your "you." The very possibility of such a translation is determined by the fact that the codes of both participants in the communication, although not identical, form intersecting sets. But since, in the given act of translation, a certain part of the message is always cut off, and "I" am submitted to a transformation in the course of translation into

language "you," what is lost is just the individuality of the addressee, that is, what, from the point of view of the whole, is the most valuable thing in the message.

The situation would be hopeless if the received part of the message did not contain indications as to how the addressee should transform his personality in order to understand the lost part of the message. In this way the nonidentity of the partners in the communication turns just this fact from a passive transmisssion into a game of conflict in the course of which each side aims to construct the semiotic world of his opponent according to his own model, and at the same time is interested in the preservation of his partner's individuality.[95]

Of course, Lotman does not speak of anticipation and response, nor does he develop explicit notions of the double-voiced word,[96] but much of this is implicit in his theory as can be seen in some of the passages cited above. Lotman does insist, meanwhile, that a speaker/sender always has an adressee in mind,[97] and in decoding or more properly transcoding the message/text, I am always aware of it having had a sender who initially encoded it, and the sender's intention is part of my perception of the text, without totally determining it.[98]

IV.4 Cognition

The difference between standard, every-day communication and literature is, as was discussed above, a matter (from a certain perspective) of the degree of organization. Literary texts are much more complex than non-literary texts. The major factor in determining this greater degree of complexity is that for both Bakhtin and Lotman, literary texts include in their structure the consciousness of the author/perceiver and, insofar as they are constructed on (над) the level of natural language,[99] they have the secondary modelling properties which form the leitmotif of Lotman's theory. Natural language, according to Lotman, as we have seen, is a model of the world. According to Bakhtin it is a world view.

Языки——это мировоззрения, притом не отвлеченные, а конкретные, социальные, пронизанные системой оценок, неотделимые от жизненной практики и классовой борьбы.[100]

A literary text, organized in the manner of language,[101] models the model.

Текст как субъективное отражение объективного мира, текст——выражение сознания, что-то отражающего. Когда текст становится объектом нашего познания, мы можем говорить об отражении отражения. Понимание текста и есть правильное отражение отражения. *Через чужое отражение к отраженному объекту.*[102]

Автора нельзя отделять от образов и персонажей, так как он входит в состав этих образов как их неотъемлемая часть (образы двуедины и иногда двуголосы). Но *образ* автора можно отделить от образов персонажей: но этот образ сам создан автором и потому также двуедин. [. . .] *Речь изображающего (реального) автора, . . . определяет последнее единство произведения . . .* [103]

Clearly, Bakhtin's theory of the informing presence of the author/perceiver (as opposed to the image of the author) is very close to Lotman's notion of the consciousness of the author/perceiver being an integral part of the secondary system. One of the main thrusts of Bakhtin's study of Rabelais is devoted to a demonstration of how conflicting systems of representation of reality (languages, systems of images)[104] are organized by Rabelais' artistic consciousness.

У Рабле эта система образов живет напряженной, актуальной и вполне сознательной жизнью, притом живет вся с начала и до конца, до мельчайших деталей,

Literature as Comunication and Cognition in Bakhtin and Lotman 155

> . . . В каждой детали присутствует ответственное и ясное (но конечно, не узкорассудочное) *художественное сознание* Рабле.[105]

A number of his works also include references to the role of the observer in the theory of quantum physics in which the observer partially determines the results of the experiment.[106] Bakhtin uses this analogy to illustrate the notion of the inclusion of the author's/perceiver's consciousness in the text, although I seriously doubt he would be willing to accept all the apparent metaphysical and ontological implications of quantum theory.

The level of primary modeling includes any number of intersecting languages, genres, models, codes, etc., which are transformed within the work of art.

> Все данное как бы создается заново в созданном, преображается в нем. Сведение к тому, что заранее дано и готово. Готов предмет, готовы языковые средства для его изображения, готов сам художник, готово его мировоззрение. И вот с помощью готовых средств, в свете готового мировоззрения готовый поэт отражает готовый предмет. На самом же деле и предмет создается в процессе творчества, создается и сам поэт, и его мировоззрение, и средства выражения.[107]

Literature as a whole and individual texts are complex semantic sign-systems modelling natural language and the consciousness/individuality of the artist resulting thereby in a new, complex, artistic model of the world. This, i.e. "model of the world," may not be Bakhtin's favorite or most customary expression, but it is certainly not alien to his vocabulary. In his final summarizing remarks at the very end of his study of Dostoevsky, probably his masterwork, he states:

> Необходимо отрешиться от монологических навыков, чтобы освоится в той новой художественной сфере, которую открыл Достоевский, и ориентироваться в той не

сравненно более *сложной художественной модели мира*, которую он создал.[108]

Although it may not be necessary, it must be noted that the notion of a model of the world is not at all the same as the notion of an artistic world which is ontologically, axiologically and/or cognitively distinct and separate from the world of everyday experience. Neither Lotman nor Bakhtin deal in detail with the ontology of the artistic text, but given its cognitive properties, their discussions clearly indicate that it is not to be understood as some sort of separate world, unrelated to "our" world.

It is this modelling property of literary texts, fundamentally different from the modelling property of ordinary language communication, which unites the two questions of communication and cognition. A literary message is so much more complex than a natural language message that it requires a greater degree of structuration, a more complex organization. The notion of literature as a form of cognition is perhaps the key to understanding what links Lotman and Bakhtin, and I suspect it is missed, ignored, or at least under-estimated by most commentators. Neither Lotman nor Bakhtin provides us with a clear and systematic theory of cognition despite its prominent position in their theories. For Lotman cognition in art has the properties of a model, the function of which is to be a representation of the world from a certain perspective.[109] Most sciences employ and actually depend on models, but Lotman obviously feels art, and in particular literature,[110] has exceptionally high powers for modelling reality: "в этом отношении с ним не может сравниться ничто, созданное руками человека."[111]

In my earlier discussion of Bakhtin's essay on the problem of content, material, and form, it was abundantly obvious that Bakhtin opposes any confusing of aesthetic activity and cognitive or practical activity. Like Lotman he also does not elaborate a viable theory of cognition, but he just as definitely distinguishes and separates it from aesthetic activity. How is it then possible to say that for Bakhtin literature is a form of cognition? First of all, when Bakhtin speaks of cognition in this context, he most definitely does not have in mind all possible manifestations of what is generally associated with knowing. His notion of cognition, just like his tri-une division of culture, is ultimately derived from a Kantian framework, although at the same time it is not nearly equivalent to it. Pure reason, practical reason, and aesthetic judgement--these are what Bakhtin bases his distinctions on. "Cognition" for Bakhtin refers, within his theory, broadly speaking, to abstract and/or scientific thought, conceptual thinking, even rational thought. That does not exclude all forms of cognition, broadly viewed, although for some epistemologists it most certainly would. In his theoretical works Bakhtin develops a distinction between cognition of objects or things and knowledge of subjects, "субъекты." This is expressed in various ways, and can be found in practically every one of his works.[112] This is also related to the question of the distinction between what he calls 'precision' and 'depth.'[113]

Access to this depth is not via the cognitive processes of abstract, conceptual, object- or thing-orientated cognition, but through "understanding."[114] There is no need to point out how hopelessly vague and unreliable such a term is considered by itself. This is particularly evident when Bakhtin must speak, for example, of understanding understanding.[115] However, it is primarily determined and substantially clarified when opposed to conceptual and abstract thought.[116] Moreover, Bakhtin associates it with dialogue.[117] True dialogue and true understanding are very nearly the same thing, and at the very least are intimately related.

Dialogue, as stated, is *intersubjective* communication by means of texts/utterances. Understanding, as a form of cognition, when referred to literary texts, is, then, another way of describing the aesthetic activity of the creator/perceiver of a literary text and/or the relationship between them. Aesthetic activity, going back to Bakhtin's early work and the distinctions as he used them there, is a way of organizing cognitively and ethically valued moments, the world of cognition and practical life, i.e. the content of a work of art. In this activity, by providing form to the content, a new view, a new understanding of the world is created. Bakhtin has called it "artistic cognition."[118] In his study of Rabelais he describes various aspects of this process, and gives several formulations of his views. Consider the following passage.

> Основная задача Рабле — — разрушить
> официальную картину эпохи и ее событий,
> взглянуть на них по—новому, осветить
> трагедию или комедию эпохи с точки зрения
> смеющегося народного хора на площади.
> Рабле мобилизует все средства трезвой
> народной образности, чтобы вытравить из всех
> представлений о современности и ее событиях

всякую официальную ложь и ограниченную серьезность, продиктованную интересами господствующих классов. Рабле не верит на слово своей эпохе 'в том, что она говорит о себе и что она воображает о себе,'——он хочет раскрыть ее подлиный смысл для народа, народа растущего и бессмертного.

Разрушая официальные представления об эпохе и ее событиях, Рабле не стремится, конечно, дать ее научный анализ. Ведь он говорить не на языке понятий, а на языке народно—смеховых образов.[119]

Some of his statements about the function of carnival and laughter in his study of Dostoevsky are highly illustrative of his views on this important question of cognition.

Карнавальные формы, транспонированные на язык литературы, стали мощными средствами художественного постижения жизни, стали особым языком, слова и формы которого обладают исключительной силой символического обобщения, то есть обобшения в глубину. Многие существенные стороны жизни, точнее, пласты ее, притом глубинные, могут быть найдены, осмыслены и выражены только с помощью этого языка.[120]

....

Смех——это определенное, но не поддающееся переводу на логический язык эстетическое отношение к действительности, то есть определенный способ ее художественного ви́дения и постижения, а следовательно, и определенный способ построения художественного образа, сюжета, жанра.[121]

Carnival and laughter are not simply artistic or stylistic devices, but part of the complex of systems or languages which establish the extra-textual relationships of a given work. Insofar as they inhere in the author's or artist's consciousness, his worldview, they are active in the process of providing form to the content of the literary work, to the ethically and cognitively valorised reality.

Both Bakhtin and Lotman have theories of literature and culture which are broad, provocative, complex, and occasionally inconsistent. Inevitably, however, their concerns are always directed at achieving a unified view of their subject. Literature is always viewed in relation to the rest of culture, and culture is viewed in as broad and inclusive a perspective as is possible. Not only are various cultural series seen to be interrelated, but they are viewed as integral phenomena. The key factors in developing this theoretical perspective are those of communication and cognition. Communication and cognition allow Bakhtin and Lotman to work toward a theory of literature which includes human cultural reality and human reality in general.

> Идея как предмет изображения занимает громадное место в творчестве Достоевского, но все же не она героиня его романов. Его героем был человек, и изображал он в конце концов не идею в человеке, а, говоря его собственными словами, 'человека в человеке.' Идея же была для него или пробным камнем для испытания человека в человеке, или формой его обнаружения, или, наконец,——и это главное——тем 'медиумом,' тою средою, в которой раскрывается человеческое сознание в своей глубочайшей сущности.[122]

This characterization of Dostoevsky as an artist[123] reveals a great deal not only about Dostoevsky, but also about Bakhtin and his views on literature. The important thing is to see, to understand man. Bakhtin's study of Dostoevsky

> . . . было сосредоточено на той новой художественной позиции, которая позволила расширить горизонт художественного видения,

позволила ему взглянуть на человека под другим углом художественного зрения.[124]

This new discovery of Dostoevsky's was, of course, the polyphonic novel, the full significance of which can only be understood in terms of Bakhtin's theory of dialogue. Finally, it is most important to point out that the significance of polyphony and the new view of man associated with it is not limited to the sphere of art. This would reduce the import of the discussion to the level of a sterile formalism. According to Bakhtin, the polyphonic view of the world, more so than previous genres, and in new ways, opens to artistic vision and representation new dimensions of human reality.

> *Мыслящее человеческое сознание и диалогическая сфера бытия этого сознания* во всей своей глубине и специфичности недоступны монологическому художественному подходу. Они стали предметом подлинно художественного изображения впервые в полифоническом романе Достоевского.[125]

As indicated above, Lotman has always asserted the very prominent or even definitive role played by communication and cognition in his theoretical position.[126] He has frequently expressed himself very forcefully and eloquently on this subject, but perhaps never more succinctly than in the following paragraph written in the early 1970s, and in which he sums up not only the great importance of understanding communication and cognition in literature, but of literature's integral relationship with all of culture:

> . . . поэтический мир——модель реального мира, но соотносится с ним чрезвычайно сложным образом. Поэтический текст мощный и глубоко диалектический механизм поиска истины, истолкования окружающего мира и ориентировки в нем.
> [. . .] Цель поэзии, конечно, не 'приемы,' а познание мира и общение между людьми, самопознание, самопостроение человеческой личности в процессе познания и общественных

коммуникаций. В конечном итоге цель поэзии совпадает с целью культуры в целом.[127]

In fact, the whole thrust of Lotman's literary theorizing, as I see it, has been to deal with the cognitive and communicative dimension of literature in a manner which avoids the inevitable shallowness of theories which seek to correlate literary works with "reality" in a simplistic fashion, whether as a mirroring of reality, or as a straightforward reflection of personal or collective ideologies.[128] At the same time, obviously, he has consciously avoided descending into a formalistic or mechanistic treatment of literature with *langue*-based theories. His unusual incorporation of information theory, his model of communication and his unique version of the semiotic-structuralist perspective and methodology have enabled him to do this with considerable success.

NOTES

1. Of course, Bakhtin himself had a hand--albeit an ambivalent one--in this process. The problem, however, is that his followers, disciples, and idolizers, for the most part, never seriously challenged, questioned or evaluated his remarks on and allusions to Lotman and his school, not to mention his editors' questionable reworking of texts. See above.
2. See the earlier references to this essay in Chapter II, above. It will hereinafter be referred to as "Ответ."
3. As mentioned above, he is ostensibly referring not only to Lotman, but also to Konrad, Likhachev, and to the Moscow-Tartu school in general. Of course, I would contend that Lotman comes closer than any of the others to realizing the desiderata which Bakhtin sets out.
4. He is rather vague on the question of why he declines to include "contemporary" literature and literary criticism ("Otvet," 329), but there are probably two factors. One is his ostensible lack of interest in contemporary literature--it is barely ever mentioned in his writings--and the other is that the essay contains some thinly veiled hostile references to the doctrine and practice of socialist realism. Ibid., e.g. 331:

    "Говоря несколько упрощенно и грубо: если значение какого—нибудь произведения сводить, например, к его роли в борьбе с крепостным правом (в средней школе это делают), то такое произведение должно полностью утратить свое значение, когда крепостное право и его пережитки уйдут из жизни, а оно часто еще увеличивает свое значение, то есть входит в *большое время*."

5. Ibid., esp. 329-331.
6. Ibid., 329.
7. Ibid., 330.
8. Bakhtin, Рабле, e.g. 4, 409 and passim. Of course, the synchronic and diachronic perspectives are actually very closely interwoven in any study of this sort. Cf. also Bakhtin's frequent references to the fact that the folk worldview evolved

and became established over thousands of years, e.g. 487 and passim; and Bakhtin, Проблемы, 208.

9. Cf. "Ответ," 330: "Могучие глубинные течения культуры (в особенности низовые, народные), действительно определяющие творчество писателей, остаются не раскрытыми, а иногда и вовсе не известными исследователям."

10. For his discussion of the future of literary works see esp. "Ответ," 331-333. Cf. also "Слово в романе," in ВЛЭ, 232-233.

11. Bakhtin, "Otvet," 331.

12. E.g., ibid.

13. Ibid., esp. 332, and 334-335, and compare Lotman, "Художественная структура Евгения Онегина," 32.

14. "Ответ," 332.

15. Cf. esp. Проблемы, chap. IV, "Жанровые и сюжетно-композиционные особенности произведений Достоевского." Bakhtin pays particular attention to the question of genres throughout his career, and--although it fits quite comfortably within his overall theoretical position--he has a somewhat idiosyncratic approach to the problem. Cf. e.g. "Проблема речевых жанров," in ЭСТ, 237-280; "Слово в романе" and "Формы времени и хронотопа в романе: Очерки по исторической поэтике," in ВЛЭ, 72-233, 234-407.

16. Проблемы, 208.

17. That is, of course, if one restricts from the discussion his main theoretical monographs which, of course, belong to a different "genre."

18. Some of the major texts are: *"К эволюции построения характеров в романе Евгений Онегин," in Пушкин: Исследования и материалы, Vol. III, (Moscow, Leningrad: Izdatel'stvo AN SSSR, 1960), 131-173; "Идейная структура Капитанской дочки," in Пушкинский сборник,

(Pskov: np, 1962), 3-20; "О проблеме значений," 1965; "Художественная структура Евгения Онегина,"1966; *Роман в стихах Пушкина 'Евгений Онегин': Спецкурс. Вводные лекции в изучение текста, (Tartu: n.p., 1975); Роман А.С. Пушкина. 'Евгений Онегин': Комментарий. Пособие для учителя, (Leningrad: Prosveshchenie, 1980); Александр Сергеевич Пушкин: Биография писателя. Пособие для учащихся, 2nd ed., (Leningrad: Prosveshchenie, 1983). Those marked with an asterisk (*) have not been extensively consulted and therefore do not appear in the attached bibliography. For a complete list of Lotman's works on Евгений Онегин and on Pushkin in general, see "Список печатных трудов."

19. Cf. e.g. "Поэзия 1790--1810-х годов," in Поэты 1790--1810-х годов, ed. comp. and with an introduction by Iu.M. Lotman, (Leningrad: Sovetskii pisatel', 1971), 5-62; and several articles in part II of Ju.M. Lotman, B.A. Uspenskij, The Semiotics of Russian Culture, ed. Ann Shukman, Michigan Slavic Contributions No. 11, (Ann Arbor: Department of Slavic Languages and Literatures, University of Michigan, 1984).

20. Cf. Lotman, Комментарий, 35, and Bakhtin, Рабле, 495.

21. E.g., both Pushkin and Rabelais had an incomparable impact on the development of the literary language of their respective native languages, (cf. Bakhtin, Рабле, e.g. 497: "Рабле рядом с Кальвином был создателем французского литературного прозаического языка.") There is also the question of their respective ties with the lower levels of society (see below), as well as their critical view of authority, etc.

22. E.g. J. Douglas Clayton, Ice and Flame: Aleksandr Pushkin's Eugene Onegin, (Toronto, Buffalo, London: University of Toronto Press, 1985), and Russian Views of Pushkin's Eugene Onegin, tr. with an Introduction and notes by Sona Stephan

Hoisington, (Bloomington and Indianapolis: Indiana University Press, 1988). Bakhtin's discussions of Евгений Онегин are to be found primarily in "Слово в романе," 136, 142, 160-61, and "Из предыстории романного слова," esp. 410-417.

23. Cf. Lotman, Комментарий, 5-12. It is worth noting that the commentary was intended to bring this type of scholarship to a much wider audience--in particular, to teachers of Russian literature in the Soviet Union--than standard scholarly publications normally reach. It had a press run of 150,000, much larger than one could expect for a more theoretically oriented work.

24. Ibid., 36.
25. Ibid., 35-110.
26. Ibid., 35.
27. Bakhtin, Рабле, 67, and also Ibid., e.g. 474: "Эта раблезианская система образов, столь универсальная и мирообъемлющая, в то же время допускает и даже требует исключительной конкретности, полноты, детальности, точности, актуальности и злободневности в изображении современной исторической действительности. Каждый образ здесь сочетает в себе предельную широту и космичность с исключительной жизненной конкретностью, индивидуальностью и злободневной публицистичностью. Этой замечательной особенности раблезианского реализма посвящена последняя глава нашей книги."

28. E.g. Y. Lotman, "The Transformation of the Tradition Generated by Onegin in the Subsequent History of the Russian Novel," in Hoisington, Russian Views, 169-177. His closing remarks are worth citing both for their own sake and, given the present context, for their close parallels with the statement quoted in the following section below by Bakhtin concerning the relation between Rabelais and his cultural context. "To conclude: In the case of Onegin the opposition between

intrinsic textual analysis and historical analysis proves illusory. When we analyze the historical relationship of Eugene Onegin to the preceding and following traditions, we find ourselves inevitably analyzing the text as such, and when we do a textual analysis we inevitably find ourselves investigating extratextual historical ties. Only where these two perspectives intersect can we find the gates to the artistic world of Eugene Onegin." 177. And compare "Художественая структура Евгения Онегина," 32.

29. Ibid., 66. Incidentally, someone working from the English translation of Рабле would likely arrive at a significantly different understanding of this passage due to the exceptional liberties (translational and editorial) taken by the translator. Actually, this is true of practically the entire translation right from the very title. Творчество Франсуа Рабле и народная культура средневоковья и ренессанса, becomes Mikhail Bakhtin, Rabelais and His World, tr. Hélène Iswolsky, (Bloomington: Indiana University Press, 1984). The passage corresponding (approximately) to the one quoted above is on p. 58. She omits Bakhtin's last eight lines (not cited by me) entirely.

30. Bakhtin, Рабле, 67, and compare idem, Проблемы, "Задача всей нашей работы--раскрыть неповторимое своеобразие поэтики Достоевского, 'показать в Достоевском Достоевского,'" 208.

31. Yu.M. Lotman, "The Structure of Ideas in Pushkin's Poem 'Andzhelo'," tr. Ann Shukman, in Poetry and Prose, Russian Poetics in Translation II, 1976, 66-84.

32. Ibid., 66-67, 70-72.

33. Ibid., 72-73.

34. Ibid., 79.

35. Ibid., 84 n. 22. "It is not stretching a point to compare the structure of the poem (i.e. "Andzhelo," A.R.) with the polyphonic novel of the nineteenth century, on which see the works of M. M. Bakhtin."

36. Ibid., 80.

37. Ibid., 80. Lotman's penultimate paragraph in which he states his overall conclusion is also worth citing: "The

Shakespearean model of culture, or in wider terms, the Renaissance model, placed at Pushkin's disposition (sic) a type of text in which he could express both his own thoughts and opinions, as well as popular superstitions, and fuse them into a contradictory and yet at the same time harmonious whole." 81.

38. Cf. e.g. the following works by Lotman clearly showing evidence of interest in Bakhtin: "О содержании и структуре," (1973), which was published in the Bakhtin *Festschrift*, and in which Lotman suggests Bakhtin has dealt with the question of the diachronic movement of literature far more successfully than anyone else, including Tynianov with his over-simplified scheme, 30; "Художественная природа русских народных картинок," (1976), in which he cites Bakhtin's authority on certain aspects of carnival, 250; "О Хлестакове," Ученые записки тартуского государственного университета, 369, Труды по русской и славянской филологии, XXVI, Литературоведение, 19-53, in which he does not mention Bakhtin but--as can be seen from the following passage--he is very close to Bakhtin in formulating his objectives: "Цель настоящей работы——не изучение образа Хлестакова как части художественного целого комедии Гоголя, а реконструкция, на основании этого глубокого создания синтезирующей мысли художника, некоторых типов поведения, образующих тот большой культурно—исторический контекст, отношение к которому приоткрывает двери в проблему прагматики гоголевского текста," 36; and many others.

39. Lotman's interests and ideas actually show a clear line of development and interest right from the time of his earliest work. This reflects the traditions of the Leningrad school of literary history, associated with such names as Eikhenbaum, Tynianov, and Lotman's teachers Gukovskii and Mordovchenko. Cf. Shukman, Literature and Semiotics, 6. Cf.

also Egorov, "К 60-летию": "Уже содержание и метод студенчиских трудов Ю.М. Лотмана (тем более, проецируемые на известный нам последующий путь ученого) позволяют сделать выводы о его интересах, склонностях, о своеобразии его творческого мышления. . . . ." 6.

Of course, his studies are generally much more sophisticated than even the best works of this school. This is primarily accounted for by his more sophisticated notion of how "worldviews" are reflected in literature, i.e. in secondary modelling systems, and by his understanding--unfettered by the restrictions of socialist realism and primitive historicism--of the *complexity* of the interrelationships of various systems on both the synchronic and diachronic perspectives. For an example of passages where he polemicizes with such a position, see Lotman, "О содержании и структуре," 29, and idem, "Идейная структура Капитанской дочки," 16-17.

40. Ibid., 7. Cf. also idem, "Andzhelo," 83 n. 20.
41. Ibid., e.g. 8, 19-20.
42. Iu. Lotman, "Поэзия Карамзина" in N.M. Karamzin, Полное собрание стихотворений, ed. Iu. Lotman, (Moscow, Leningrad: Sovetskii pisatel', 1966), 5. (He does not identify the poet.)
43. Lotman, "О разграничении'.
44. Iu. Lotman, "С кем же полемизировал Пнин в оде 'человек?'" Русская литература, год VII, #2, 1964, 166-7.
45. Iu. Lotman, "Слово о полку Игореве и литературная традиция ХУИИИ-начала ХИХ в," in D.S. Likhachev, ed. *Слово о полку Игореве--Памятник ХИИ века*, (Moscow, Leningrad: Izdatel'stvo AN SSSR, 1962), 404.
46. Ibid.
47. Cf. Lotman, "О содержании и структуре," esp. 30.

48. Cf. e.g. Bakhtin, Рабле, 243, 300, and Lotman, e.g., Анализ, 89-90. Cf. also the passage from Segal, "О некоторых проблемах," 94, cited above.
49. Refer to Chapter III, part 5 above, for a more detailed discussion of text in Lotman and for source references.
50. Besides large sections of his three major theoretical monographs, Lotman has devoted numerous shorter studies to the problem of text. Each of these looks at the problem from a slightly different perspective, and should be read with that perspective in mind. Cf. e.g. Iu.M. Lotman, "К проблеме типологии текстов," in Тезисы докладов во Второй летней школе по вторичным моделирующим системам. 16–26 августа, 1966, (Tartu: Tartuskii gosudarstvennyi universitet, 1966), 83-91; Yu.M. Lotman and A.M. Piatigorsky, "Text and Function," tr. Ann Shukman, New Literary History, IX, 2, 1978, 233-44; Iu.M. Lotman, "О некоторых принципиальных трудностях в структурном описании текста," TZS, IV, 1969, 478-482; idem, "Семиотика культуры и понятие текста," TZS, XII, 1981, 3-7; idem, "Текст в тексте," TZS, XIV, 1981, 3-18.
51. To get a sense of how complex the notion of text is and to what extent it is interrelated with other systems, cf. Lotman and Piatigorsky, "Text and Function," and Lotman, "Семиотика культуры и понятие текста."
52. Лекции, 154-5.
53. M.M. Bakhtin, "Проблема текста в лингвистике, филологии и других гуманитарных науках. Опыт философского анализа," in ЭСТ, 281-307. According to the editors of the volume, these notes were recorded in the period 1959-1961. Ibid., 401.
54. E.g., "(придумать убедительный пример)," ibid., 296.
55. Bakhtin, "Проблема текста," 281. Cf. also 282: "Каковы бы ни были цели исследования,

исходным пунктом может быть только текст." 292-293.
56. Ibid., 281.
57. Ibid., 281, 282. He also considers human behaviour or action (поступок) to be a potential text. Ibid., 286, 292. This is a popular subject of many semioticians.
58. E.g. Ibid., 283.
59. N. Chomsky, "Methodological Preliminaries," in Jerrold J. Katz, ed., The Philosophy of Linguistics, (London, New York, Toronto, etc.: Oxford University Press, 1985), 80-125. Cf. also Bakhtin "Проблема, текста," e.g. 286, 297, and passim.
60. Cf. Ibid., 284, where he compares the mechanical reproduction of a text and a fingerprint and opposes it to a reading of a text or other personal, aesthetic interaction with it.
61. Ibid., 303. The quote could just as easily be from Lotman.
62. Ibid., 287.
63. On the question of the infinity of dialogue as opposed to the limited participation of any given participants in it, cf. e.g. ibid., 306.
64. Ibid., 304.
65. The problem of the limits of texts and utterances remains largely unresolved in Bakhtin, although he does raise it several times and notes its importance. Cf. e.g., ibid., 282, 290.
66. Ibid., e.g. 282, 285, 300.
67. М.М. Bakhtin, "К методологии гуманитарных наук," in ЭСТ, 372.
68. In this context it is interesting that Bakhtin appears to have had at least one predecessor in developing his theory of dialogue, namely the formalist L.P. Iakubinskii. "On Verbal Dialogue," Dispositio IV, 11-12 (June-October, 1979), 321-336. Cf. Jane Knox, "Lev Jakubinskij as a Precursor to Modern Soviet Semiotics," Dispositio IV, 11-12 (June-October, 1979), 317-320; and idem, "The Dialogic Mode: Lev Jakubinskij and Mixail Baxtin," in Mikhail Mikhailovich Bakhtin: His Circle, His Influence, 78-88.
69. Bakhtin, "Проблема текста," 298. Of course, no dialogue is possible between languages or elements of a language linguistically understood. Ibid., 304. Note that if we compare the passage cited here with Bakhtin's criticism of

Lotman's use of "code" in reference to Евгений Онегин, it is abundantly obvious that Bakhtin is "shortchanging" Lotman's position.

70. Bakhtin, Проблемы, 213-214.
71. Cf. Ibid., 210-212.
72. Cf. "Слово в романе,"75.
73. Cf. "Проблема содержания": "я нахожу себя," 57; and 59, 69, 70, etc.; "Автор и герой," 174-175.
74. Bakhtin restricts dialogic communication to semiotic phenomena (cf. Проблема, 214) and never really addresses any other forms of communication. Lotman, on the other hand, having derived or at least based his fundamental understanding of communication on information theory, considers all potential forms of communication. He considers semiotic communication as a special case--obviously a very important one. Структура, 77.
75. Bakhtin's position on dialogic auto-communication is somewhat inconsistent, but his theory itself clearly does not oppose or exclude it. Compare Проблемы, 214, where it is clearly affirmed, and "Автор и герой," 174, where he apparently denies its possibility. The former represents both a later and completed authorial statement, but that does not necessarily override the latter.
76. E.g. "Проблема текста," 292-293.
77. Ibid., e.g. 283-305, and "Проблема речевых жанров," e.g. 247.
78. Ibid., 303.
79. Note that the discussion in "Проблема содержания" operates on a different level. While Bakhtin remains largely true to the ideas in that essay (cf. e.g. the emphasis on the axiological dimension, as evidenced in the last quotation above, of which there are many more), his later period is characterized by a greater fluidity among divisions on the continuum of all speech genres. Both perspectives must be born in mind.
80. Bakhtin, "Проблема речевых жанров," 239.
81. Bakhtin, "Слово в романе," 75. Cf. also Проблемы, 311, and "Проблема текста," 294: "Автор литературного произведения (романа)

создает единое и целое речевое произведение (высказывание). Но он создает его из разнородных, как бы чужих высказываний. И даже прямая авторская речь полна осознанных чужих слов."

82. Cf. "Проблема текста," 295, and idem. "Автор и герой в эстетической деятельности (фрагмент первой главы)," 13ff, where the context, unusually for Bakhtin, refers primarily to lyrical poetry.
83. E.g. "Проблема текста," 283.
84. Ibid., 294.
85. See fn. 82 above.
86. For his model see e.g. Iu.M. Lotman, "Знаковый механизм культуры," in <u>Сборник статей по вторичным моделирующим системам</u>, (Tartu: Tartuskii gosudarstvennyi universitet, 1973), 1955-199; idem "Culture as Collective Intellect and Problems of Artificial Intellegence," tr. Ann Shukman, <u>Dramatic Structure, Poetic and Cognitive Semantics</u>, <u>Russian Poetics in Translation</u> VI, 1979, 84-96.
87. Bakhtin, "Проблем текста," 284. "Текст" here is roughly equivalent to utterance.
88. Lotman, "Знаковый механизм," 196.
89. It would seem that both Bakhtin and Lotman are concerned with basically the same type of idealized model. "В курсах общей лингвистики (даже и в таких серьезных, как де Соссюра) часто даются наглядно-схематические изображения двух партнеров речевого общения——говорящего и слушающего (воспринимающего речь), дается схема активных процессов речи у говорящего и соответствующих пассивных процессов восприятия и понимания речи у слушающего. Нельзя сказать, чтобы эти схемы были ложными и не соответствовали определенным моментам действительности, но, когда они выдаются за реальное целое

речевого общения, они становятся научной фикцией." Bakhtin, "Проблема речевых жанров," 246.

90. Cf. e.g. Iu.M. Lotman, "К проблеме типологии текстов."

91. Lotman, "Culture as Collective Intellect," 90. Note that he considers the most complex semiotic systems to be the semiotic systems of art, with literature occupying the first place.

92. Lotman, "Знаковый механизм," 197-198.

93. Lotman, "Динамическая модель семиотической системы," in <u>Readings in Soviet Semiotics</u>, 90. He expands on some of the points in this passage from a slightly different perspective a little further on in his text: "Чем интенсивнее язык ориентирован на сообщение о другом и других говорящих и на специфическую трансформацию ими уже имеющихся у 'меня' сообщений (то есть на объемное восприятие мира), тем быстрее должно протекать его структурное обновление. Язык искусства является предельной реализацей этой тенденции." Ibid., 92.

94. Ibid.

95. Lotman, "Culture as Collective Intellect," 91, and cf. Bakhtin, "Проблема текста": "Увидеть и понять автора произведения--значит увидеть и понять другое, чужое сознание и его мир, то есть другой субъект." 289.

96. Cf. Bakhtin, <u>Проблемы</u>, esp. chap. 5.

97. "Автор, . . . не может не учитывать отношения воспринимающего." Lotman, "К проблеме типологии текстов," 88.

98. E.g., Lotman, "Динамическая модель," 91.

99. Bakhtin, like Lotman, recognizes that a literary work can be seen as a single sign, but also recognizes, like Lotman, that it is made of other signs. This is implicit in the notion of it

being speech about speech, an utterance about other utterances. He also recognizes that all semiotic systems, (languages) are organized according to similar principles, which are in principle capable of being translated into one another. "Следовательно, есть общая логика знаковых систем, потенциальный единый язык языков." He stresses very strongly that this applies to languages, not to texts/utterances.

100. Bakhtin, Рабле, 513, and cf. also 458, 507, 508-510.
101. Bakhtin, "Проблема текста," 307.
102. Bakhtin, Ibid., 292. (My emphasis, A.R.)
103. Ibid., 295. (My emphasis, A.R.) Bakhtin has the following to say concerning what is actually represented in Dostoevsky's writings: "Ведь главным предметом его изображения является само слово, притом именно полнозначное слово. Произведения Достоевского--это слово о слове, обращенное к слову. *Изображаемое слово сходится со словом изображающим на одном уровне и на равных правах. Они проникают друг в друга, накладываются друг на друга под разными диалогическими углами.*" Ibid., Проблемы, 311.
104. Cf. Bakhtin, Рабле, 507ff but also passim.
105. Ibid., 229-230. There are a great number of passages in the text which echo and reaffirm the thought contained in this one.
106. Ibid., "Проблема текста," e.g. 283, 302, 305.
107. Ibid., 299.
108. Bakhtin, Проблемы, 314.
109. "Существенным свойством художественного текста является то, что он находится в отношении двойного подобия: он подобен определенному изображаемому им куску жизни--части всемирного универсума,--и он подобен всему этому универсуму." Lotman, Структура, 302.
110. Lotman, Анализ, 22.

111. Ibid., 131. In another place, after extensively comparing art and play, Lotman makes the following conclusion: "Игра представляет собой овладение умением, тренировку в условной ситуации, искусство--овладение миром (моделирование мира) в условной ситуации. Игра--'как бы деятельность,' а искусство--'как бы жизнь.' Из этого следует, что соблюдение правил в игре является целью. Целью искусства является истина, выраженная на языке условных правил. Поэтому игра не может быть средством хранения информации и средством выработки новых знаний (она лишь путь к овладену уже добытыми навыками). Между тем именно это составляет сущность искусства." <u>Структура</u>, 91.

112. Cf. e.g. Bakhtin, "К методологии," 372; idem, "Из записей 1970-1971 годов," in <u>ЭСТ</u>, 342-343.

113. Cf. e.g. Bakhtin, "К методологии," 371, 372; and "Проблема текста," 307.

114. Cf. e.g. Bakhtin, "К методологии," 364; "Проблема текста," 305.

115. Bakhtin, "Из записей," 346.

116. Cf. e.g. Bakhtin, <u>Рабле</u>, 439-443.

117. Cf. e.g. Bakhtin, "Проблема текста," 305.

118. Bakhtin, <u>Проблемы</u>, 314. Note that a major, but not absolute, distinction between artistic cognition and abstract cognition involves the function of representation in the former. "Характеризуемая нами особенность Достоевского не есть, конечно, особенность его мировоззрения в обычном смысле слова,--это особенность его художественного восприятия мира: только в категории сосуществования он умел его

	видеть и изображать. Но, конечно, эта особенность должна была отразиться и на его отвлеченном мировоззрении." Ibid., 35.
119.	Bakhtin, Рабле, 477. In the next paragraph he continues: "Проследим теперь на ряде примеров, как отражена в романе Рабле современная ему действительность от ближайшего жизненного окружения автора до больших событий эпохи." Ibid. Cf. also e.g. idem, 492-493, 494-495,
120.	Bakhtin, Проблемы, 182.
121.	Ibid., 191.
122.	Ibid., 37.
123.	And, indeed, as a man.
124.	Ibid., 312.
125.	Ibid., 313.
126.	See Lotman, Лекции, 14, and Chapter III, part 5, above.
127.	Lotman, Анализ, 131.
128.	See e.g. the brief discussion above of his study of Khlestakov, and the article itself. Similarily, in his commentary to Евгений Онегин, he chastises those (including everyone from Tynianov to those of Pushkin's contemporaries who dealt with the problem in their memoirs) who spend their time searching for authoritative prototypes. For Lotman, that is first of all, not a primary consideration, but insofar as it does have bearing, he notes, just as he did in his study of Khlestakov, that the ties are complicated and go not only from reality to the novel but *vice versa* and back again in a spiral. Lotman, Комментарий, 23-31. Bakhtin treats the question of prototypes in Dostoevsky's works, and describes the artistic transformation of them in his novels, such that for him they also do not have a one-to-one correspondence. Bakhtin, Проблемы, 104-106.

V CONCLUSION

There should be no doubt that Bakhtin and Lotman have effectively distanced themselves and their theories from any and all theories which are oriented towards the centrality of the so-called aesthetic function and which are based on the notion that poetics is a part of linguistics. They have sought to strengthen the ties of literature: with external reality, including other cultural systems; and with the individual personality of author and reader. At the same time they affirm the centrality of the text without fetishizing it.

Just as there is no single explanation why Bakhtin's essay on content, material and form has received so little attention even though it has been familiar at least in name to practically all Bakhtin scholars so there is no single explanation why Bakhtin and Lotman have not previously been studied together. Part of the explanation inheres in the character of the dominant trends in literary scholarship. Bakhtin tends to be seen as an "anti-systematist" theorist, the guru of carnival and dialogue, while Lotman is seen as a formalistic, rigorously systematic thinker, and the camps line up behind those two poles. I have, I believe, demonstrated that despite differences in their positions and styles, no such genuine polarity separates them. Indeed, the notion of literature as communication and cognition underlies a bond between them which is much stronger than any points separating them. This was also demonstrated in the context of Bakhtin's conflicting and seemingly problematic comments on Lotman.

A great many commentators have found and no doubt will continue to find fault, often justifiably, with various details in the theories of both Bakhtin and Lotman. Still others take issue with all or some of Bakhtin and Lotman's applications of their theories to specific literary or cultural texts. Again, these criticisms are often justified. It seems to me, however, that many of these critics and commentators are missing the point. While it is incontestable that Bakhtin and Lotman have made significant contributions in their studies of various works of literature and of extra-literary texts, and while the ultimate test of a theory of literature must be in its applicability, there is another important dimension to the question of their theories and their theoretical orientations. By striving to maximize their embrace of human reality, they have adopted a significantly different approach than the vast majority of their colleagues who endeavor to radically restrict their purview. Even though it has nothing immediately to do with literature, the following quotation illustrates quite clearly what I have in mind.

> Aristotle's system includes himself. The phenomena of thought and consciousness, the looks of colours and the ringings of sounds *as we experience them*, our thoughts *in the way that we think them*, are an integral part of our world and must figure in any explanation of it. That means, in effect, that our general account of the world must be one in which the basic modes of explaining physical reality are, from the beginning, such that our own knowledge of our lives as we live them could be integrated with them. It is this inclusion of the scientist, as he knows himself and as he lives his life, within the scope of his most basic explanations, that modern science renounced; and when it was reintroduced into physics at the beginning of this century it was only in the form of making the observer and his observation factors in what was observed, the "observer" being a depersonalized locus for inspection and intervention and not a human being. . . . It is precisely to this renunciation of comprehensiveness that our science owes its continuously astonishing success. But it is because of that renunciation that Aristotle's way of going about things may still strike us as a more serious attempt to explain *our* world than anyone has come up with since. He got everything wrong, his system is obsolete in principle and in detail; but he saw what an explanation of the world would have to attempt.[1]

It seems to me that much of what Sparshott says about science could also be referred to the study of literature as it has developed over the last 75 years or so. The trend has been to concentrate on the 'specificity' of literature, or in various other ways to restrict the focus of attention to a smaller and more limited field. Bakhtin and Lotman go against this trend.

Their theories of literature attempt valiantly to achieve the sort of comprehensiveness Sparshott so eloquently describes. Whether they are as wrong in detail as Aristotle remains to be seen, but I think they have gone a long way to indicate at least in outline what a theory of literature must strive for. It is my contention that it is precisely by focussing, each in his own way (but in ways strikingly similar to those of each other) on the communicative and cognitive dimensions of literature that they have accomplished this.

NOTES

1. Francis Sparshott, "Aristotle's World and Mine," in Mohan Matthen, ed. <u>Aristotle Today</u>, (Edmonton: Academic Printing and Publishing, forthcoming), 32-33.

VI BIBLIOGRAPHY

VI.1 Works by Bakhtin and the Bakhtin Circle

VI.1.1 WORKS BY BAKHTIN

MIKHAIL MIKHAILOVICH BAKHTIN. "Arkhitektonika postupka." Ed. S.G. Bocharov. Sotsiologicheskie issledovania 2, (April-June, 1986). 157-169.

———. The Dialogic Imagination: Four Essays. Ed. Michael Holquist. Tr. Caryl Emerson and Michael Holquist. University of Texas Press Slavic Series, No. 1. Austin: University of Texas Press, 1981.

———. `Estetika slovesnogo tvorchestva. Moscow: Iskusstvo, 1979.

———. "Iskusstvo slova i narodnaia smekhovaia kul'tura." Kontekst--1972: Literaturno-teoreticheskie issledovaniia. Moscow: Izdatel'stvo "Nauka," 1973. 248-259.

———. "K èstetike slova." Kontekst--1973: Literaturno-teoreticheskie issledovaniia. Moscow: Izdatel'stvo "Nauka," 1974. 258-280.

———. "K filosofii postupka." Ed. S.G. Bocharov. In Filosofiia i sotsiologiia nauki i tekhniki. Moscow: Nauka, 1986. 80-160.

———. "K metodologii literaturovedeniia." Kontekst--1974: Literaturno-teoreticheskie issledovaniia. Moscow: Izdatel'stvo "Nauka," 1975. 203-212.

———. Literaturno-kriticheskie stat'i. Moscow: "Khudozhestvennaia literatura," 1986.

———. Problems of Dostoevsky's Poetics. Ed. and tr. Caryl Emerson. Introduction by Wayne C. Booth. Theory and History of Literature, Vol. 8. Minneapolis: University of Minnesota Press, 1984.

———. Problemy poètiki Dostoevskogo. Fourth edition. Moscow: "Sovetskaia Rossiia," 1979.

———. Problemy tvorchestva Dostoevskogo. Leningrad: Priboi, 1929.

———. Tvorchestvo Fransua Rable i narodnaia kul'tura srednevekov'ia i renessansa. Moscow: Izdatel'stvo "Khudozhestvennaia literatura," 1965.

———. Voprosy literatury i èstetiki: Issledovaniia raznykh let. Moscow: "Khudozhestvennaia literatura," 1975.

VI.1.2 WORKS BY THE BAKHTIN CIRCLE

BAKHTIN SCHOOL PAPERS. Russian Poetics in Translation X, 1983.

MEDVEDEV, PAVEL N. Formal'nyi metod v literaturovedenii: Kriticheskoe vvedenie v sotsiologicheskuiu poètiku. Leningrad: Priboi, 1928. Reprinted by Documentica Semiotica, Serie 2: Litteraria. Hildesheim, New York: Georg Olms Verlag, 1974.

VOLOSHINOV, V. N. Freudianism: A Marxist Critique. Tr. I.R. Titunik. Ed. I.R. Titunik and Neal H. Bruss. New York: Academic Press, 1976.

———. Marksizm i filosofiia iazyka: Osnovnye problemy sotsiologicheskogo metoda v nauke o iazyke. Second edition. Leningrad: n.p., 1930. Reprinted The Hague, Paris: Mouton, 1972.

VI.2 Works by Lotman and the Moscow-Tartu School

VI.2.1 ANTHOLOGIES, JOURNALS, FESTSCHRIFTEN, ETC.

JU.M. LOTMAN AND B.A. USPENSKIJ. The Semiotics of Russian Culture. Ed. Ann Shukman. Michigan Slavic Contributions, No. 11. Ann Arbor: Department of Slavic Languages and Literatures, The University of Michigan, 1984.

READINGS IN SOVIET SEMIOTICS (RUSSIAN TEXTS). Ed. with foreword and commentaries by L. Matejka, S. Shishkoff, M.E. Suino, and I.R. Titunik. Michigan Slavic Materials, No. 15. Ann Arbor: Michigan Slavic Publications, 1977.

SBORNIK STATEI PO VTORICHNYM MODELIRUIUSHCHIM SISTEMAM. Tartu: Tartuskogo gosudarstvennogo universiteta, 1974.

SEMIOTICS AND STRUCTURALISM: READINGS FROM THE SOVIET UNION. Ed. and with an introduction by Henryk Baran. White Plains, N.Y.: International Arts and Sciences Press, 1976.

THE SEMIOTICS OF RUSSIAN CULTURAL HISTORY: Essays by Iurii M. Lotman, Lidiia Ia. Ginsburg, Boris A. Uspenskii. Introduction by Boris Gasparov. Ed. A.D. Nakhimovsky and A. Stone Nakhimovsky. Ithaca and London: Cornell University Press, 1985.

SOVIET SEMIOTICS: AN ANTHOLOGY. Ed., tr. and with an Introduction by Daniel P. Lucid. Baltimore and London: The Johns Hopkins Press, 1977.

STRUKTURNO-TIPOLOGICHESKIE ISSLEDOVANIIA: SBORNIK STATEI. Ed. T.N. Moloshnaia. Moscow: Izdatel'stvo AN SSSR, 1962.

TEKSTY SOVETSKOGO LITERATUROVEDCHESKOGO strukturalizma. (Texte des Sowjetischen Literaturwissenschaftlichen Strukturalismus). Herausgegeben und eingeleitet von Karl Eimermacher. Centrifuga, Russian Reprintings and Printings, Vol. 5. Munich: Wilhelm Fink Verlag, 1971.

TEZISY DOKLADOV IV LETNEI SHKOLY PO VTORICHNYM
 Modeliruiushchim sistemam, 17-24 avgusta 1970 g. Ed. Iu.M.
 Lotman. Tartu: Tartuskogo gosudarstvennogo universiteta, 1970.
TEZISY DOKLADOV VO VTOROI LETNEI SHKOLE PO
 VTORICHNYM modeliruiushchim sistemam, (16-26 avgusta,
 1966). Tartu: Tartuskogo gosudarstvennogo universiteta, 1966.

VI.2.2 WORKS BY LOTMAN

LOTMAN, IURII MIKHAILOVICH. Aleksandr Sergeevich Pushkin:
 Biografiia pisatelia. Posobie dlia uchashchikhsia. Second edition.
 Leningrad: "Prosveshchenie," 1983.
———. Analiz poèticheskogo teksta: Struktura Stikha. Leningrad:
 Izdatel'stvo "Prosveshchenie," 1972.
———. "Asimmetriia i dialog." Trudy po znakovym sistemam XVI,
 1983. 15-30.
———. "Culture and Information." Tr. S. White. Dispositio I, 3 (1976),
 213-215.
———. "Culture as Collective Intellect and the Problems of Artificial
 Intelligence." Tr. Ann Shukman. Semantic Structure, Poetic and
 Cognitive Semantics. Russian Poetics in Translation 6, 1976.
 84-96.
———. "The Decembrist in Everyday Life: Everyday Behaviour as a
 Historical-Psychological Category." In The Semiotics of
 Russian Culture, q.v. 71-123.
———. "Dinamicheskaia model' semioticheskoi sistemy." Trudy po
 znakovym sistemam X, 1978. 18-33.
———. "Eshche raz o poniatiiakh "slava" i "chest'" v tekstakh kievskogo
 perioda." Trudy po znakovym sistemam V, 1971. 469-475.
———. "Fenomen kul'tury." Trudy po znakovym sistemam X, 1978. 3-
 17.
———. "Gogol' and the Correlation of 'The Culture of Humor' with the
 Comic and Serious in the Russian National Tradition." In
 Semiotics and Structuralism, q.v. 297-300.

———. "Ideinaia struktura Kapitanskoi dochki." In Pushkinskii sbornik. Pskov: n.p., 1962. 3-20.

———. "Khudozhestvennaia priroda russkikh narodnykh kartinok." In Materialy nauchnoi konferentsii (1975): Narodnaia graviura i folklor v rossii XVII-XIX vv. (K 150-letiiu so dnia rozhdeniia D.A. Rovinskogo). Moscow: Sovetskii khudozhnik, 1976. 247-267.

———. "Khudozhestvennaia struktura Evgeniia Onegina." Uchenye zapiski tartuskogo universiteta, 184. Trudy po russkoi i sliavianskoi filologii IX. 1966. 5-32.

———. "K probleme tipologii kul'tury." Trudy po znakovym sistemam III, 1967. 30-38.

———. "K probleme tipologii tekstov." In Tezisy dokladov II, q.v. 83-91.

———. Lektsii po struktural'noi poètike: Vvedenie, teoriia stikha. Brown University Slavic Reprint V. Providence, Rhode Island: Brown University Press, 1968.

———. "Literaturovedenie dolzhno byt' naukoi." Voprosy literatury 11, No. 1 (1967). 90-100.

———. "Neskol'ko slov po povodu retsenzii Ia.M. Meiera 'Literatura kak informatsiia.'" Russian Literature 9, (1975) 111-118.

———. "Neskol'ko zamechanii po povodu stat'i prof. Marii R. Maienovoi, 'Poètika v rabotakh tartuskogo universiteta.'" Russian Literature 6, (1974). 83-89.

———. "Ob oppozitsii 'chest''-'slava' v svetskikh tekstakh kievskogo perioda." Trudy po znakovym sistemam III, 1967. 100-112.

———. "O dvukh modeliakh kommunikatsii i ikh sootnoshenii v obshchei sisteme kul'ture." In Tezisy dokladov IV, q.v. 163-165.

———. "O Khlestakove." Uchenye zapiski tartuskogo gosudarstvennogo universiteta, 369. Trudy po russkoi i slavianskoi filologii XXVI, 1975. 19-53.

———. "O mifologicheskom kode siuzhetnykh tekstov." In Sbornik statei, q.v. 86-90.

———. "O. M. Freidenberg as a Student of Culture." In Semiotics and Structuralism, q.v. 257-268.

———. "O modeliruiushchem znachenii poniatii 'kontsa' i 'nachala' v khudozhestvennykh tekstakh." In Tezisy dokladov II, q.v. 69-74.

———. "On the Reduction and Unfolding of Sign Systems. (The Problem of 'Freudianism and Semiotic Culturology.') In Semiotics and Structuralism, q.v. 301-309.

———. "O postroenii tipologii kul'tury." In Tezisy dokladov II, q.v. 82-83.

———. "O probleme znachenii vo vtorichnykh modeliruiushchikh sistemakh." Trudy po znakovym sistemam II, 1965. 22-37.

———. "O razgranichenii lingvisticheskogo i literaturovedcheskogo poniatiia struktury." Voprosy iazykoznaniia 3, (1963). 44-52.

———. "O semiosfere." Trudy po znakovym sistemam XVII, 1984. 5-23.

———. "O semiotike poniatii 'styd' i 'strakh' v mekhanizme kul'tury." In Tezisy dokladov IV, q.v. 98-101.

———. "O soderzhanii i strukture poniatiia 'khudozhestvennaia literatura.'" In Problemy poètiki i istorii literatury, q.v. 20-36.

———. "O sootnoshenii poèticheskoi leksiki russkogo romantizma i tserkovno-slavianskoi traditsii." In Tezisy dokladov IV, q.v. 85-87.

———. "Ot redaktsii." Trudy po znakovym sistemam II, 1965. 5-8.

———. "Ot redaktsii." Trudy po znakovym sistemam III, 1967. 5-6.

———. "Ot redaktsii." Trudy po znakovym sistemam XV, 1982. 3-9.

———. "Ot redaktsii: K probleme prostranstvennoi semiotiki." Trudy po znakovym sistemam XIX. 3-6.

———. "O zadachakh razdela obzorov i publikatsii." Trudy po znakovym sistemam 3 (1967). 363-66.

———. "Poèziia Karamzina." In N. M. Karamzin. Polnoe sobranie stikhotvorenii. Ed. and introduction by Iu.M. Lotman. Moscow, Leningrad: Sovetskii pisatel', 1966.

———. "Poèziia 1790--1810-kh godov." In idem, Poèty 1790--1810-kh godov. Introduction and comp. Iu.M. Lotman. Leningrad: Sovetskii pisatel', 1971. 5-62.

———. Roman A.S. Pushkina "Evgenii Onegin": Kommentarii. Posobie dlia uchitelia. Leningrad: "Prosveshchenie," 1980.

———. "Semiotika kul'tury i poniatie teksta," Trudy po znakovym sistemam XII, 1981. 3-7.

———. "S kem zhe polemiziroval Pnin v ode 'Chelovek'?" Russkaia Literatura, year 7, 2 (1964). 166-167.

———. "Slovo o polku Igoreve i literaturnaia traditsiia XVIII--nachala XIX v." In "Slovu o polku Igoreve:" Pamiatnik XII veka. Ed. D.S. Likhachev. Moscow, Leningrad: Izdatel'stvo AN SSSR, 1962. 330-405.

———. "The Structure of Ideas in Pushkin's Poem 'Andzhelo.'" Tr. Ann Shukman. Poetry and Prose. Russian Poetics in Translation II, 1976. 66-84.

———. Struktura khudozhestvenngo teksta. Introduction by Thomas G. Winner. Brown University Slavic Reprint IX. Providence: Brown University Press, 1971.

———. "Tekst kak dinamicheskaia sistema." In Struktura teksta: Tezisy simpoziuma. Ed. Viach. Vs. Ivanov, T.M. Sudnik, T.V Tsiv'ian. Moscow: Institut slavianovedeniia i balkanistiki, AN SSSR, 1981. 104-105.

———. "Tekst v tekste." Trudy po znakovym sistemam XIV, 1981. 3-18.

———. "Tema kart i kartochnoi igry v russkoi literature nachalo XIX veka." Trudy po znakovym sistemam VII, 1975. 120-142.

———. "Tezisy k probleme 'iskusstvo v riadu modeliruiushchikh sistem.'" Trudy po znakovym sistemam III, 1967. 130-145.

———. "Theatre and Theatricalness in the Order of Early Nineteenth-Century Culture." In The Semiotics of Russian Culture, q.v. 141-164.

———. "Zametki o khudozhestvennom prostranstve." Trudy po znakovym sistemam XIX, 25-43.

———. "Znakovyi mekhanizm kul'tury." In Sbornik statei, q.v. 195-199.

LOTMAN, IU. MIKHAILOVICH AND A.M. PIATIGORSKII. "Text and Function." New Literary History IX, 2 (1978). 233-244.

LOTMAN, IU. MIKHAILOVICH AND BORIS A. USPENSKII. "Authors' Introduction" to The Semiotics of Russian Culture, q.v. ix-xiv.

———. "'Izgoi' i 'izgoinichestvo' kak sotsial'no-psikhologicheskaia pozitsiia v russkoi kul'ture preimushchestvenno dopetrovskogo perioda. ('Svoe' i chuzhoe' v istorii russkoi kul'tury)." Trudy po znakovym sistemam XV, 1982. 110-121.

———. "Myth--Name--Culture." In Semiotics and Structuralism, q.v. 3-32.

VI.2.3 WORKS BY OTHER MEMBERS OF THE MOSCOW-TARTU SCHOOL

IVANOV, VIACHESLAV VSEVOLODOVICH. "Iz zametok o stroenii i funktsiiakh karnaval'nogo obraza." In Problemy poètiki i istorii literatury, q.v. 37-53.

———. "Kategoriia 'vidimogo' i 'nevidimogo' v tekste: Eshche raz o vostochno-slavianskikh fol'klornykh paralleliakh k gogolevskomu Viiu." In Structure of Texts and Semiotics of Culture. Eds. Jan van der Eng and Mojmir Grygar. The Hague, Paris: Mouton, 1973. 151-76.

———. "O Bakhtine i o semiotike." Rossija/Russia. 2 (Torino, 1976). 284-97.

———. Ocherki po istorii semiotiki v SSSR. Moscow: Nauka, 1976.

———. "O primenenii tochnykh metodov v literaturovedenii." Voprosy literatury 11, No. 10 (1967). 115-26.

———. "Roman Jakobson: The Future." In A Tribute to Roman Jakobson, 1896-1982. Berlin, New York, Amsterdam: Mouton, 1983. 47-57.

———. "The Semiotic Theory of Carnival as the Inversion of Bipolar Opposites." In Carnival, q.v. 11-35.

———. "The Significance of Mikhail Mikhailovich Bakhtin's Ideas on Sign, Utterance, and Dialogue for Modern Semiotics." In Semiotics and Structuralism, q.v. 310-367.

MELETINSKIJ, E.M., AND DMITRI SEGAL. "Structuralism and Semiotics in the USSR." Diogenes 73, (1971). 88-125.

PIATIGORSKY, ALEXANDER M. "On Some Theoretical Presuppositions of Semiotics." Tr. A. Shukman. Semiotica 12, (1974). 185-88.

REVZINA, O.G. Untitled report under section "Nauchnaia zhizn'." Voprosy iazykoznaniia, year 20, 2 (1971). 160-162.

SEGAL, DMITRI. Aspects of Structuralism in Soviet Philology. Papers on Poetics and Semiotics, 2. Tel-Aviv: Tel-Aviv University, 1974.

———. "O nekotorykh problemakh semioticheskogo izuchenii mifologii." In Simpozium po strukturnomu izucheniiu znakovykh sistem: Tezisy dokladov. Moscow: Izdatel'stvo AN SSSR, 1962. 92-99.

USPENSKII, BORIS A. "The Language of Ancient Painting." Dispositio
I, 3 (1976). 219-246.
——. "On the Poetics of Chlebnikov: Problems of Composition."
Russian Literature 9, (1975). 81-85.
——. Poètika kompozitsii: Struktura khudozhestvennogo teksta i
tipologiia kompozitsionnoi formy. Moscow: Izdatel'stvo
"Iskusstvo," 1970.
ZHOLKOVSKII, ALEKSANDER K., AND IURII K. SHCHEGLOV. "Iz
predystorii sovetskikh rabot po strukturnoi poètike." Trudy po
znakovym sistemam 3 (1967). 367-77.
——. "O vozmozhnostiakh postroeniia strukturnoi poètiki." In
Strukturno-tipologicheskie issledovaniia, q.v. 138-141.
——. "Strukturnaia poètika--porozhdaiushchaia poètika." Voprosy
literatury XI, 1 (1967). 74-89.

VI.3 General Works

AUCOUTURIER, Michal. "Mikhail Bakhtine, philosophe et théoricien
du roman." Preface to Mikhail Bakhtine, Esthétique et théorie du
roman. Tr. Daria Olivier. N.p.: Gallimard, 1978. 9-19.
——. "The Theory of the Novel in Russia in the 1930'S: Lukacs and
Bakhtin." In The Russian Novel from Pushkin to Pasternak. Ed.
John Garrard. New York and London: Yale University Press,
1983. 227-240.
BAKHTIN: ESSAYS AND DIALOGUES ON HIS WORK. Ed. Gary
Saul Morson. Chicago and London: University of Chicago
Press, 1986.
BAILEY, R.W. "Maxwell's Demon and the Muse." Dispositio I, 3
(1976). 293-301.
BARAN, HENRYK. Introduction to Semiotics and Structuralism, q.v.
vii-xvi.
BARTHES, ROLAND. The Semiotic Challenge. Tr. Richard Howard.
New York: Hill and Wang, 1988.

BELLERT, IRENA. "The Sign and Its Object in Everyday Language, Literature, and Theatre." Semiosis, q.v. 39-52.
BENNETT, TONY. Formalism and Marxism. London and New York: Methuen and Co., Ltd., 1979.
BOVÉ, CAROL MASTRANGELO. "The Text as Dialogue in Bakhtin and Kristeva." University of Ottawa Quarterly, q.v. 117-124.
CARNIVAL. Ed. Thomas A. Sebeok. Approaches to Semiotics, 64. Berlin, New York, Amsterdam: Mouton. 1984.
CERVENKA, Miroslav. "A Contribution to the Semantics of the Literary Work." Papers in Slavic Philology, I, q.v. 27-35.
———. "New Perspectives on Czech Structuralism." Review of Sound, Sign and Meaning: Quinquagenario of the Prague Linguistic Circle, ed. Ladislav Matejka. In PTL, 4 (1976). 359-370.
CHAMPAGNE, P.A. "A Grammar of the Languages of Culture: Literature and Jury M. Lotman's Semiotics." New Literary History IX, 2 (1978). 205-210.
CHERNOV, IGOR. "A Contextual Glossary of Formalist Terminology." Tr. Ann Shukman and L.M. O'Toole. Formalist Theory. Russian Poetics in Translation IV, 1977. 13-48.
CHOMSKY, NOAM. "Human Language and Other Semiotic Systems." Semiotica 25, 1/2 (1979). 31-44.
———. "Methodological Preliminaries." In The Philosophy of Language. Ed. Jerrold J. Katz. London: Oxford University Press, 1985. 80-125.
CLARK, KATERINA, AND MICHAL HOLQUIST. "A Continuing Dialogue." "Forum." Slavic and East European Journal XXX, 1 (Spring 1986). 96-102.
———. Mikhail Bakhtin. Cambridge, Mass. and London, England: Harvard University Press, 1984.
CLAYTON, J. DOUGLAS. Ice and Flame: Aleksandr Pushkin's "Eugene Onegin." Totonto: University of Toronto Press, 1985
CORTI, MARIA. "Culture as Text in the Thirteenth Century." Semiosis, q.v. 53-64.
———. An Introduction to Literary Semiotics. Translated by M. Bogat and A. Mandelbaum. Bloomington and London: Indiana University Press, 1978.
CULLER, JONATHON. Ferdinand de Saussure. Revised edition. Ithaca, New York: Cornell University Press, 1986 (1976).
DANOW, DAVID K. "Mikhail Mikhailovitch Bakhtin's Concept of the Word." American Journal of Semiotics III, 1 (1984). 79-97.

———. "Mikhail Mikhailovitch Bakhtin in Life and Art." Review of Mikhail Bakhtin by Clark and Holquist and The Dialogic Principle by T. Todorov. In American Journal of Semiotics III, 1 (1984). 131-141.
DEJEAN, JOAN. "Bakhtin and/in History." In Language and Literary Theory, q.v. 225-40.
DEELY, JOHN N. "Cognition from a Semiotic Point of View." Semiotics, 1981. New York and London: Plenum Press, 1983. 21-29.
DOLEZEL, LUBOMIR. "A Framework for the Statistical Analysis of Style." In Statistics and Style, q.v. 10-25.
———. "Literary Transduction: Prague School Approach." In The Prague School and Its Legacy, q.v. 165-176.
———. "Mukarovsky and the Idea of Poetic Truth." Russian Literature XII (1982). 283-298.
———. "Narrative Semantics." PTL I (1976). 129-151.
———. "Narrative Worlds.' In Sound, Sign and Meaning, q.v. 542-552.
———. "A Pragmatic Typology of Dialogue." In Papers in Slavic Philology I, q.v. 62-68.
———. "Truth and Authenticity in Narrative," Poetics Today, I, 3 (1980). 7-25.
EAGLE, HERBERT. "The Semiotics of Cinema: Lotman and Metz." Dispositio I, 3 (1976). 303-313.
ECO, UMBERTO. "The Frames of Comic Freedom." In Carnival!, q.v. 1-9.
EGOROV, B.F. "K 60-letiiu Iuriia Mikhailovicha Lotmana." In Finitis Duodecim Lustris, q.v. 3-20.
EIKHENBAUM, BORIS. "Kak sdelana 'Shinel'' Gogolia." In Texte I. 122-158.
———. "Teoriia 'formal'nogo metoda.'" In O literature: Raboty raznykh let. Moscow. Sovetskii pisatel', 1982. 375-408.
EIMERMACHER, KARL. "Some Aspects of Semiotic Studies of the Moscow and Tartu Schools." In Subject Bibliography of Soviet Semiotics, q.v. vii-xii.
EMERSON, CARYL. "The Outer Word and Inner Speech." In Bakhtin: Essays and Dialogues, q.v. 21-40.
———. "Problems with Baxtin's Poetics." Slavic and East European Journal XXXII, 4 (1988). 503-525.

———. "Translating Bakhtin: Does his Theory of Discourse Contain a Theory of Translation?" University of Ottawa Quarterly 53, 1 (January-March, 1983). 23-33.

ERLICH, VICTOR. "The Concept of the Poet as a Problem of Poetics." Poetics--Poetyka--Poetika. Warsaw: PWN, 1961. 707-718.

———. Russian Formalism: History-Doctrine. Third Edition. Slavistic Printings and Reprintings, IV. The Hague, Paris: Mouton, 1969.

FINITIS DUODECIM LUSTRIS: Sbornik statei k 60-letiiu profesora Iu.M. Lotmana. Comp. S. Isakov. Tallin: Eesti Raamat, 1982.

FISH, STANLEY, E. "What is Stylistics and Why are They Saying Such Terrible Things About It." In Approaches to Poetics, q.v. 109-32.

FOKKEMA D.W. "Continuity and Change in Russian Formalism, Czech Structuralism, and Soviet Semiotics." PTL 1, (1976). 153-96.

FORMALIST THEORY. Russian Poetics in Translation IV, 1977.

GARVIN, PETER. A Prague School Reader on Esthetics, Literary Structure, and Style. Washington: 1964.

GASPAROV, M. L. "Quantitative Methods in Russian Metrics: Achievements and Prospects." Metre, Rhythm, Stanza, Rhyme. Russian Poetics in Translation VII. 1980. 1-19.

GODZICH, WLAD. "The Construction of Meaning." New Literary History IX, 2 (1978). 389-97.

GOPNIK, MYRNA. "Language, Cognition and the Theory of Signs." Recherches Sémiotique/Semiotic Inquiry I, 4 (1981). 310-327.

GRYGAR, MOJMIR. "A Contribution to the Theory of Literature." Review of Narrative Modes in Czech Literature by Lubomir Dolezel. In PTL I, (1976). 569-578.

HAMMARBERG, GITTA. "A Reinterpretation of Tynyanov and Jakobson on Prose (With Some Thoughts on the Baxtin and Lotman Connection)." In Language and Literary Theory, q.v. 379-401.

HANDBOOK OF RUSSIAN LITERATURE. Ed. Victor Terras. New Haven and London: Yale University Press, 1985. S.v. "Bakhtin, Mikhail Mikhailovich," by James Michael Holquist; s.v. Lotman, Yury Mikhailovich," by Victor Terras; s.v. "Structuralism and Semiotics," by Henryk Baran.

HANSEN-LOVE, AAGE. "Russian Formalism." Tr. Alison Herford. Essays in Poetics VI, 2 (1981). 54-62.

HAVRANAK, BOHUSLAV. "The Functional Differentiation of the Standard Language." In A Prague School Reader. 3-16.

HAVRANAK, BOHUSLAV *ET AL.* "By Way of Introduction." In Recycling the Prague Linguistic Circle. Ed. Mark Johnston. Ann Arbor: Karoma Publishers, 1978. 32-46.

HIRSCHKOP, KEN. "A Response to the Forum on Mikhail Bakhtin." In Bakhtin: Essays and Dialogues, q.v. 73-79.

HOLENSTEIN, E. "Jakobson and Husserl: A Contribution to the Genealogy of Structuralism." The Human Context VIII, 1 (1975). 61-83.

HOLQUIST, JAMES MICHAEL. "'Bad Faith' Squared: The Case of Mikhail Mikhailovich Bakhtin." In Russian Literature and Criticism, q.v. 214-234.

———. "The Carnival of Discourse: Baxtin and Simultaneity." Canadian Review of Comparative Literature XII, 2 (June, 1985). 220-234.

———. Introduction to M.M. Bakhtin. "Speech Genres" and Other Late Essays. Tr. Vern W. McGee. Ed. Caryl Emerson and Michael Holquist. University of Texas Press Slavic Series, No. 8. Austin: University of Texas Press, 1986. ix-xxiii.

———. "The Politics of Representation." In Allegory and Representation: Selected Papers from the English Institute, 1979-1980, N.s. 5. Ed. Stephen J. Greenblatt. Baltimore and London: The Johns Hopkins University Press, 1981.

IAKUBINSKII, L.P. "On Verbal Dialogue." Trans. Jane E. Knox and Luba Barna. Dispositio IV, 11-12 (June-October, 1979). 321-336.

———. "O poèticheskom glossemosochetanii." In Poètika: Sborniki, q.v. 7-12.

———. "O zvukakh stikhotvornogo iazyka." In Poètika: Sborniki, q.v. 37-49.

IGETA, SAGAYESI. "Ivanov--Pumpianskii--Bakhtin." In Comparative and Contrastive Studies in Slavic Languages and Literatures: Japanese Contributions to the Tenth International Congress of Slavists, Sofia, September 14-21, 1988. Ed. Japanese Association of Slavists. Tokyo: College of Arts and Sciences, University of Tokyo, 1988. 81-91.

JAKOBSON, ROMAN. "The Dominant." In Readings in Russian Poetics: Formalist and Structuralist Views. Ed. L. Matejka, K. Pomorska. Cambridge, Mass.: MIT Press, 1971. 82-87.

———. "Linguistics and Communication Theory." In idem, Selected Writings, II. The Hague: Mouton, 1971. 570-579.

———. "Linguistics and Poetics." In T.A. Sebeok, ed. Style in Language. New York: John Wiley, 1960.
———. Noveishaia russkaia poèziia: Nabrosok pervyi, Velimir Khlebnikov. In Texte II, q.v. 18-134.
———. "Poèziia grammatiki i grammatika poèzii." In Poetics--Poetyka--Poètika. Warsaw: PWN, 1961. 397-418.
———. "Quest for the Essence of Language." Diogenes 51 (Fall 1965). 21-37.
———. "Sign and System of Language." In Verbal Art, Verbal Sign, Verbal Time, q.v. 28-33.
———. Verbal Art, Verbal Sign, Verbal Time. Ed. K. Pomorska, S. Rudy. Minnesota: University of Minnesota Press, 1985.
———. "What is Poetry." In Semiotics of Art, q.v. 164-175.
JAKOBSON, ROMAN AND IURII TYNIANOV. "Problemy izucheniia literatury i iazyka." In Texte II, q.v. 386-390.
JEFFERSON, ANN. "Intertextuality and the Poetics of Fiction." In Comparative Criticism: A Yearbook, 2. Ed. Elinor Shaffer. Cambridge, England: Cambridge University Press, 1980. 235-50.
KAISER, MARK. "P.N. Medvedev's The Collapse of Formalism." In Language and Literary Theory, q.v. 405-41.
KNOX, JANE E. "The Dialogic Mode: Lev Jakubinskij and Mixail Baxtin." In Mikhail Mikhailovich Bakhtin: His Circle, His Influence, q.v. 78-88.
———"Lev Jakubinskij as a Precursor to Modern Soviet Semiotics." Dispositio IV, 11-12 (June-October, 1979). 317-20.
KOZHINOV, V. "Nauchnost--èto sviaz' s zhizn'iu," Voprosy literatury VI, 3 (March 1962). 83-95.
———. "Vozmozhna li strukturnaia poètika?" Voprosy literatury 9, No. 6 (1965). 88-107.
KOZHINOV, V. AND S. KONKIN. "Mikhail Mikhailovich Bakhtin: Kratkii ocherk zhizni i deiatel'nosti." In Problemy poètiki i istorii literatury, q.v. 5-19.
LANGUAGE AND LITERARY THEORY; IN HONOR OF LADISLAV MATEJKA. Ed. Benjamin A. Stolz, I.R. Titunik, Lubomir Dolezel. Papers in Slavic Philology, 5. Ann Arbor: Department of Slavic Languages and Literature, University of Michigan, 1984.

LEFEVRE, ANDRE. "The Growth of Literary Knowledge." PTL 2 (1977). 33-64.
LEONT'EV, A.A. Psikholingvistika. Leningrad: n.p., 1967.
LOCK, CHARLES L. Review of Speech Genres and Other Late Essays by M.M. Bakhtin, tr. Vern W. McGee, ed. Caryl Emerson and Michal James Holquist, and Bakhtin: Essays and Dialogues on His Work, ed. Gary Saul Morson. In Canadian Slavonic Papers XXIX, 2/3 (June-Sept. 1987). 344-5.
LOWRIE, WALTER. A Short Life of Kierkegaard. Princeton, N.J.: Princeton University Press, 1942.
LUCID, DANIEL P. Introduction to Soviet Semiotics, q.v. 1-23.
MAIAKOVSKII, VLADIMIR V. "Kak delat' stikhi?" In Sobranie sochinenii v 8-i tomakh, vol. 5. Moscow: Biblioteka "Ogonek," Izdatel'stvo "Pravda," 1968. 466-500.
MAJENOWA, MARIA R. "Lotman as a Historian of Literature." Russian Literature I, (January 1977). 81-90.

———. "Poètika v rabotakh tartuskogo universiteta," Russian Literature 2, (1972). 152-165.

"MANIFESTO PRESENTED TO THE FIRST CONGRESS OF SLAVIC Philologists in Prague." In Recycling the Prague Linguistic Circle, q.v. 1-31.
MARGOLIN, URI. "The (In)dependence of Poetics Today: PTL IV, (1980). 545-586.

———. "Juri Lotman on the Creation of Meaning in Literature." Canadian Review of Comparative Literature II, 3 (Fall 1975). 243-261.

———. Review of Soviet Literary Structuralism: Background - Debate - Issues, by Peter Seyffert. In Canadian Slavonic Papers XXIX, (March 1987). 112-113.

MATEJKA, LADISLAV. "Languages of Art in Soviet Semiotics." Dispositio I, 13 (1976). 207-212.

———. "The Roots of Russian Semiotics of Art." In The Sign, q.v. 146-172.

———. "The Sociological Concerns of the Prague School." In The Prague School and its Legacy, q.v. 219-226.

MATEJKA, L., S. SHISHKOFF, M.E. SUINO, AND I.R. TITUNIK. Foreword to Readings in Soviet Semiotics, q.v. ix-xvii.

MEIJER, JAN M. "Literature as Information: Some Notes on Lotman's Book Struktura khudozhestvennogo teksta." In Structure of Texts and Semiotics of Culture, q.v. 209-23.
MIKHAIL MIKHAILOVICH BAKHTIN: HIS CIRCLE, HIS INFLUENCE. Papers Presented at the International Colloquium, Queens University, October 7-9, 1983.
"M.M. BAKKHTIN i M.I. KAGAN. (Po materialam semeinogo arkhiva.) Publikatsiia K. Nevel'skoi." Pamiat' 4, (Moscow, 1979, Paris, 1981). 249-281.
MONAS, SIDNEY. "Introductory: Russian Literary Criticism in the Twentieth Century." In Russian Literature and Criticism, q.v. 209-213.
MORGAN, THAIS E. "Is There an Intertext in this Text?: Literary and Interdisciplinary Approaches to Intertextuality." American Journal of Semiotics III, 4 (1985). 1-40.
MORSON, GARY SAUL. "The Baxtin Industry." "Forum." Slavic and East European Journal XXX, 1 (Spring 1986). 81-90.
———. "Dialogue, Monologue, and the Social: A reply to Ken Hirschkop." In Bakhtin: Essays and Dialogues, q.v. 181-188.
———. "The Heresiarch of Meta." PTL 3, (1978). 407-436.
———. "Preface: Perhaps Bakhtin." In Bakhtin: Essays and Dialogues, q.v. vii-xii.
———. "Who Speaks for Bakhtin." In Bakhtin: Essays and Dialogues, q.v. 1-19.
MORTON, A.Q. "Authorship: The Nature of the Habit." The Times Literary Supplement No. 4, 481 (February 17-23, 1989). 164, 174.
MUKAROVSKY, JAN. Aesthetic Function, Norm and Value as Social Facts. Tr. Mark E. Suino with notes and afterword. Michigan Slavic Contributions, No. 3. Ann Arbor: University of Michigan, Department of Slavic Languages and Literatures, 1979.
———. "Art as Semiotic Fact." In Semiotics of Art, q.v. 3-9.
———. On Poetic Language. Ed. and tr. J. Burbank, P. Steiner. Lisse: The Peter de Ridder Press, 1976.
———. "Poetic Reference." In Semiotics of Art, q.v. 155-163.
———. "Standard Language and Poetic Language." In A Prague School Reader. 17-30.

MYASNIKOV, GEORGY. "Yury Mikhailovich Lotman: An Essay-Tribute on the Fiftieth Anniversary of His Birth." Tr. R.J. Rosengrant. Russian Literature Tri-Quarterly 6, (Spring 1973). 575-578.
NATOV, NADINE. "Structural and Typological Ambivalence of Bulgakov's Novels Interpreted Against the Background of Baxtin's Theory of 'Grotesque Realism' and Carnivalization." In American Contributions to the VIII Annual International Congress of Slavists (Zagreb and Ljubljana, September 3-9, 1978). Volume 2: Literature. Ed. Victor Terras. Columbus, Ohio: Slavica Publishers, Inc., 1978. 536-549.
NEUMANN, GRETE. "Signs on Signs on Signs on Signs." Review of Ocherki po istorii semiotiki v SSSR by V.V. Ivanov. In Semiotica 21: 3/4 (1977). 339-56.
OGUIBENINE, BORIS. "Linguistic Models of Culture in Russian Semiotics: A Retrospective View." PTL 4 (1979). 91-118.
PAPERS IN SLAVIC PHILOLOGY, I: IN HONOR OF JAMES FERRELL. Ed. Benjamin A. Stolz. Ann Arbor: Michigan Slavic Publications, 1977.
PARROTT, RAY. "(Re)capitulation, Parody, or Polemic?" In Language and Literary Theory, q.v. 463-88.
PELC, JERZY. "Poetics and Logical Semantics." PTL 4, (1979). 77-89.
PERLINA, NINA. "Bakhtin - Medvedev - Voloshinov: An Apple of Discourse." University of Ottawa Quarterly 53, 1 (January-March, 1983). 35-47.
———. "Funny things are Happening on the Way to the Bakhtin Forum." Kennan Institute For Advanced Russian Studies. Occasional Paper #231. (March 1989).
———. Review of Speech Genres and Other Late Essays by Mikhail M. Bakhtin. In Slavic and East European Journal XXXII, 3 (Fall, 1988). 461-62.
PHILLIPS, K.H. Language Theories of the Early Soviet Period. Exeter LInguistics Series, X. Exeter: University of Exeter, 1986.
PIATIGORSKY, ALEXANDER M. "Philosophy or Literary Criticism." In Russian Literature and Criticism, q.v. 235-44.
PO`ETIKA: SBORNIKI PO TEORII PO`ETICHESKOGO IAZYKA. St. Petersburg: n.p., 1919. Reprint, Bibliotheca Slavica, No. 1, reprint series. Zug, Switz.: Intra Documentation Company Ag., 1967.

POMORSKA, KRYSTYNA. "Mikhail Bakhtin and and His Verbal Universe." PTL 3, (1978). 384-395
———. "Poetics of Prose." In Verbal Art, Verbal Sign, Verbal Time, q.v. 169-177.
———. Russian Formalist Theory and its Poetic Ambiance. Slavistic Printings and Reprintings, 82. Ed. C.H. van Schoonevald. The Hague, Paris: Mouton, 1968.
PONZIO, AUGUSTO. "Semiotics Between Pierce and Bakhtin." Recherches Sémiotique/Semiotic Inquiry IV, 3/4 (September-December 1984). 273-92.
POSNER, R. "Poetic Communication vs Literary Language or: The Linguistic Fallacy in Poetics." PTL I (1976). 1-10.
THE PRAGUE SCHOOL AND ITS LEGACY IN LINGUISTICS, LITERATURE, SEMIOTICS, FOLKLORE, AND THE ARTS: Containing the Contributions to a Colloquium on the Prague School and Its Legacy held at the Ben-Gurion University of the Negev, Be'er Sheva, Israel, May 1984. Ed. Yishai Tobin. Amsterdam, Philadelphia: John Benjamins Publishing Company, 1988.
THE PRAGUE SCHOOL: SELECTED WRITINGS, 1929-1946. Ed. Peter Steiner. Tr. John Burbank, Olga Hasty, Manfred Jacobson, Bruce Kochis, and Wendy Steiner. University of Texas Press Slavic Series, No. 6. Austin: University of Texas Press, 1982.
PRAGUIANA: SOME BASIC AND LESS KNOWN ASPECTS OF THE PRAGUE LINGUISTIC SCHOOL. Ed. and tr. Josef Vachek and Libuse Dusková, with an introduction by Phillip A. Luelsdorff. Amsterdam and Philadelphia: John Benjamins Publishing Company, 1982.
PRINCE, GERALD. Review of Structuralist Poetics, Structuralism, Linguistics and the Study of Literature by Jonathan Culller. In PTL I (1976). 197-202.
PROBLEMY PO`ETIKI I ISTORII LITERATURY. (Sbornik stat'ei): K 75-letiiu so dnia rozhdeniia i 50-letiiu nauchno-pedagogicheskoi deiatel'nosti Mikhaila Mikhailovicha Bakhtina. Ed. S.S. Konkin. Saransk: Kafedra russkoi i zarubezhnoi literatury, Mordovskii gosudarstvennyi universitet im. N.P. Ogareva, 1973.
QUINQUAGENARIO: Sbornik statei molodykh filologov k 50-letiiu profesora Iu.M. Lotmana. Tartu: Tartusskii gosudarstvennyi universitet, 1972.

READINGS IN RUSSIAN POETICS: RUSSIAN TEXTS. Comp. L.
Matejka. Second revised edition. Michigan Slavic Materials, No.
2. Ann Arbor: University of Michigan, Department of Slavic
Languages and Literatures, 1971.
RECYCLING THE PRAGUE LINGUISTIC CIRCLE. Ed. M.K.
Johnston. Ann Arbor: Karoma Publishers Inc., 1978.
RETHINKING BAKHTIN: EXTENSIONS AND CHALLENGES. Ed.
Gary Saul Morson and Caryl Emerson. Evanston, Illinois:
Northwestern University Presss, 1989.
REWAR, WALTER. "Cybernetics and Poetics: The Semiotic
Information of Poetry." Review of Analiz poèticheskogo teksta
by Iu.M. Lotman. In Semiotica 25 3/4, (1979). 273-305.
_____. "Tartu Semiotics." Bulletin of Literary Semiotics 3, (1976).
1-16.
ROSENGRANT, S.F. "The Antecedents of Soviet Structuralism."
Dispositio IV, 11-12 (June-October, 1979). 283-88.
RUDY, STEPHEN. "Semiotics in the USSR." In The Semiotic Sphere.
Ed. T.A. Sebeok and J. Umiker-Sebeok. New York and London:
Plenum Press, 1986. 555-582.
RUSINKO, ELAINE. "Intertextuality: The Soviet Approach to Subtext."
Dispositio IV, 11-12 (June-October, 1979). 213-35.
RUSSIAN FORMALIST CRITICISM: FOUR ESSAYS. Tr. and with
an introduction by Lee T. Lemon and Marion J. Reis. Lincoln
and London: University of Nebraska Press, 1965.
RUSSIAN LITERATURE AND CRITICISM: Selected Papers From the
Second World Congress for Soviet and East European Studies,
Garmisch-Partenkirchen, September 30-October 4, 1980. Ed.
Evelyn Bristol. Berkeley, Calif: Berkeley Slavic Specialties,
1982.
RUSSIAN VIEWS OF PUSHKIN'S "EUGENE ONEGIN". Tr. with an
introduction and notes by Sona Stephan Hoisington.
Bloomington and Indianapolis: Indiana University Press, 1988.
SALVAGGIO, J. "Between Formalism and Semiotics: Eisenstein's Film
Language." Dispositio IV, 11-12 (June-October, 1979). 289-297.
SALVESTRONI, SIMONETTA. "Bachtin in Soviet and West European
Semiotic Research." In Mikhail Mikhailovich Bakhtin: His
Circle, His Influence, q.v. 197-221.
DE SAUSSURE, FERDINAND. Course in General Linguistics. Ed.
Charles Balley, Albert Sechehaye, with Albert Reidlinger. Tr.
Wade Baskins. New York: Philosophical Library, 1959.

SAVAN, DAVID. "Toward a Refutation of Semiotic Idealism." Recherches Sémiotique/Semiotic Inquiry III, (1983). 1-7.
SCHNAIDERMAN, B. "Semiotics in the U.S.S.R.: A Search for Missing Links." Dispositio VI, 17-18 (Summer-Fall, 1981). 93-107.
SEBEOK, THOMAS A. "Vital Signs," American Journal of Semiotics. III, 3 (1985). 1-27.
SEGRE´, CESARE. "Culture et texte dans la pensée de Jurij M. Lotman." In Semiosis, q.v. 3-15.
―――. "Space and Time of the Text." Twentieth-Century Studies. (December 1974). The Limits of Comprehension. 12. 37-41.
SELECTED PAPERS FROM THE ENGLISH INSTITUTE: Approaches to Poetics. Ed. Seymour Chatman. New York and London: Columbia University Press, 1973.
SEMIOSIS: SEMIOTICS AND THE HISTORY OF CULTURE: *IN HONOREM Georgii Lotman*. Ed. Morris Halle, Krystyna Pomorska, Ladislav Matejka, and Boris Uspenskij. Michigan Slavic Contributions, No. 10. N.p.: The University of Michigan, 1984.
SEMIOTICS OF ART: PRAGUE SCHOOL CONTRIBUTIONS. Ed. Ladislav Matejka and I.R. Titunik. Cambridge, Mass. and London: The MIT Press, 1976.
SEYFFERT, PETER. Soviet Literary Structuralism: Background--Debate--Issues. Columbus, Ohio: Slavica Publishers, Inc., 1983.
SHISHKOFF, SERGE. "Note." In Subject Bibliography of Soviet Semiotics, q.v. xi-xii.
SHKLOVSKII, VIKTOR. "Iskusstvo kak priem." In Poètika: Sborniki, q.v. 101-114.
―――. "Parodiinyi roman Tristram Shandi Sterna." In Texte I. 244-298.
―――. "Potebnia." In Poètika: Sborniki. 3-6.
―――. "Voskreshenie slova." In Texte I. 2-16.
SHUKMAN, ANN. "Between Marxism and Formalism: The Stylistics of Mikhail Bakhtin." In Comparative Criticism: A Yearbook, 2. Ed. Elinor Shaeffer. Cambridge, England: Cambridge University Press, 1980. 221-234.
―――. "The Canonization of the Real: Jurij Lotman's Theory of Literature and Analysis of Poetry." PTL I, (1976). 317-338.
―――. "Introduction." Bakhtin School Papers. Russian Poetics in Translation X, (1983). 1-4.

———. "Jurij Lotman and the Semiotics of Culture." Russian Literature V-I (January 1977). Special Issue: Jurij M. Lotman. 41-53.

———. Literature and Semiotics: A Study of the Writings of Yu.M. Lotman. Meaning and Art, Vol. I. Amsterdam, New York, Oxford: North-Holland Publishing Company, 1977.

———. "Lotman: The Dialectic of a Semiotician." In The Sign, q.v. 194-206.

———. "Soviet Semiotics and Literary Criticism." New Literary History IX, 2 (1978). 189-97.

THE SIGN: SEMIOTICS AROUND THE WORLD. Ed. R.W. Bailey, L. Matejka, and P. Steiner. Michigan Slavic Contributions, No. 9. Ann Arbor: The University of Michigan, 1978.

SOSNOSKI, P. "The Study of Diachronicity in Literature: Ralph Cohen and Jurij Lotman." Dispositio IV, 11-12 (June-October, 1979). 273-282.

SOUND, SIGN AND MEANING: Quinquagenary of the Prague Linguistic Circle. Ed. Ladislas Matejka. Michigan Slavic Contributions, No. 6. Ann Arbor: University of Michigan, 1976.

SPARSHOTT, FRANCIS. "Aristotle's World and Mine." In Mohan Matthen, ed. Aristotle Today. Edmonton: Academic Printing and Publishing, forthcoming. 25-50.

STANKIEWICZ, EDWARD. Baudouin de Courtenay and the Foundations of Structural Linguistics. PdR Press Publications in The History of Linguistics, 3. Lisse: Peter de Ridder Press, 1976.

STAROBINSKI, J. "Considerations on the State of Literary Criticism." Diogenes 74, (Summer 1971). 57-88.

STATISTICS AND STYLE. Ed. Lubomir Dolezel and Richard W. Bailey. New York: American Elsevier Publishing Company, Inc., 1969.

STEINER, PETER. "On Semantic Poetics: O. Mandelshtam in the Discussions of the Soviet Structuralists." Dispositio I, 3 (1976). 339-48.

———. "The Roots of Structuralist Esthetics." In The Prague School: Selected Writings, q.v. 174-219.

———. "To Enter the Circle: The Functional Structuralism of the Prague School." In The Prague School: Selected Writings, q.v. ix-xii.

STEINER, WENDY. "Point of View from the Russian Point of View." Dispositio I, 3 (1976). 315-26.

STEINER, PETER, AND WENDY STEINER. "Postscript: The Relational Axes of Poetic Language." In J. Mukarovsky, On Poetic Language, q.v. 71-86.
STRIEDTER, JURIJ. "The Russian Formalist Theory of Prose." PTL 13, (1977). 429-470.
STRUCTURE OF TEXTS AND SEMIOTICS OF CULTURE. Ed. J. van der Eng, Mojmir Grygar. The Hague and Paris: Mouton, 1973.
SUINO, MARK. "Communication and Culture.: Dispositio I, 3 (1976). 349-52.
———. "Poetic closure." In Papers in Slavic Philology I, q.v. 271-75.
TEXTE DER RUSSISCHE FORMALISTEN, Band I. Texte zur allgemeine Literaturtheorie und zur Theorie der Prosa. Mit einer einleitenden Abhandlung herausgegeben von Jurij Streidter. Ed. Witold Kosny. Munich: Wilhelm Fink Verlag, 1969.
TEXTE DER RUSSISCHE FORMALISTEN, Band II. Texte zur Theorie des Verses und der poetischer Sprache. Eingeleitet und herausgegeben von Wolf-Dieter Stempel. Ed. Inge Paulman. Munich: Wilhelm Fink Verlag, 1972
THOMAS, JEAN-JACQUES. "Metasemantics." Dispositio IV, 10 (February 1979). 91-97.
THOMPSON, CLIVE. "The Semiotics of Mikhail Mikhailovich Bakhtin." University of Ottawa Quarterly 53, q.v. 11-22.
THOMPSON, EWA M. "D.S. Likhachev and the Study of Old Russian Literature." In Russian Literature and Criticism, q.v. 245-254.
TITUNIK, IRWIN R. "Bachtin &/or Voloshinov &/or Medvedev: Dialogue &/or Doubletalk." In Language and Literary Theory, q.v. 535-64.
———. "Bakhtin and Soviet Semiotics. (A Case Study: Boris Uspenskij's Poètika kompozitsii)." Russian Literature X-1, (July 1981). 1-16.
———. "The Baxtin Problem: Concerning Katerina Clark and Michael Holquist's Mikhail Bakhtin." "Forum." Slavic and East European Journal XXX, 1 (Spring 1986). 91-95.
———. "M.M. Baxtin (the Baxtin School) and Soviet Semiotics." Dispositio I, 3 (1976). 327-338.
———. "The Problem of 'Skaz' (Critique and Theory)." In Papers in Slavic Philology I, q.v. 276-301.

———. Review of <u>Speech Genres and Other Late Essays</u> by Mikhail Mikhailovich Bakhtin. In <u>Slavic Review</u> 47, 1 (Spring 1988), 171-172.
TODOROV, TZVETAN. "The Fantastic in Fiction." <u>20th Century Studies</u>, 3 (May 1970). <u>Structuralism</u>. 76-92.
———. <u>Introduction to Poetics</u>. Tr. Richard Howard. Theory and History of Literature, Vol. 1. Minneapolis: University of Minnesota Press, 1981. (Originally published 1968.)
———. <u>Mikhail Bakhtin: The Dialogical Principle</u>. Tr. Wlad Godzich. Theory and History of Literature, Vol. 13. Minneapolis: University of Minnesota Press, 1984.
———. "La Poétique en URSS." <u>Poétique</u> 9 (1972). 102-115.
TOMASHEVSKII, BORIS. <u>Kratkii kurs poètiki</u>. Moscow, Leningrad: Gosudarstvennyi izdatel'stvo, 1928. Second edition (reprint) Russian Study Series, No. 70. Chicago: Russian Language Specialties, 1969.
———. "Tematika." In <u>Teoriia literatury: Poètika</u>. Fourth edition. Moscow, Leningrad: Gosudarstvennoe izdatel'stvo, 1928. Reprint, The Slavic Series, No. 6, New York, London: Johnson Reprint Corporation, 1967.
TYNIANOV, IURII. "O literaturnoi èvoliutsii." In <u>Readings: Russian Texts</u>, q.v. 99-114.
UNIVERSITY OF OTTAWA QUARTERLY 53, 1 (1983). <u>Special Bakhtin Edition</u>.
VAN SCHOONEVELD, C.H. "By Way of Introduction: Roman Jakobson's Tenets and Their Potential." In <u>Roman Jakobson: Echoes of His Scholarship</u>. Ed. Daniel Armstrong and C.H. van Schooneveld. Lisse: The Peter de Ridder Press, 1977.
VENCLOVA, TOMAS. <u>Neustoichivoe ravnovesie: Vosem' russkikh poèticheskikh tekstov</u>. New Haven: Yale Center for International and Area Studies, 1986.
VROON, R., AND G. VROON. "V.V. Ivanov's <u>Essays on the History of Semiotics in the USSR</u>, Moscow: Nauka, 1976." <u>Dispositio</u> I, 3 (October 1976). 356-360.
WAUGH, LINDA R. "The Poetic Function and the Nature of Language." In <u>Verbal Art, Verbal Sign, Verbal Time</u>, q.v. 143-168.
WEHRLE, ALBERT J. "Introduction: M.M. Bakhtin/P.N. Medvedev." In P.N. Medvedev/M.M. Bakhtin. <u>The Formal Method in Literary Scholarship: A Critical Introduction to Sociological Poetics</u>. Tr.

Albert J. Wehrle. Baltimore and London: The Johns Hopkins University Press, 1978. ix-xxiii.

WELLEK, RENE. Review of Semiotics of Art: Prague School Contributions, ed L. Matejka and I.R. Titunik. In Dispositio I, 3 (1976). 361-63.

———. The Literary Theory and Aesthetics of the Prague School. Michigan Slavic Contributions. Ann Arbor: Department of Slavic Languages and Literature, The University of Michigan, 1969.

WINNER, THOMAS G. "Jan Mukarovsky: The Beginnings of Structural and Semiotic Aesthetics." In Sound, Sign and Meaning, q.v. 433-455

———. "Russian Theories of the Twenties and Thirties." Les littératures de langues européennes au tournant du siècle: Lectures d'aujourd'hui. Série D: La perspective critique soviétique. Cahier I. 1984. (Travaux du groupe de recherches international "1900"). Carleton University. 81-91.

———. "The Semiotics of Texts and its Application to Contemporary Poetics." In Papers in Slavic Philology, I, q.v. 304-13.

WINTER, WERNER. "Styles as Dialects." In Statistics and Style, q.v. 3-9.

ZERMACH, EDDY M. "Farewell to the Aesthetic Experience." PTL 2 (1977). 65-72.

VI.4 Works on Cybernetics, Information Theory, and Philosophy of Science

ARISTOTLE. "Nicomachean Ethics." In The Basic Works of Aristotle. Ed. and with an introduction by Richard Mckeon. New York: Random House, 1941. 935-1112.

CAMPBELL, JEREMY. Grammatical Man: Information, Entropy, Language, and Life. New York: Simon and Schuster, 1982.

COPERNICUS, NICHOLAS. Complete Works II: On the Revolutions. Ed. Jerzy Dobrzycki. Tr. and commentary by Edward Rosen. Warsaw-Cracow: Polish Scientific Publishers, 1978.

CREASE, ROBERT P. AND CHARLES C. MANN. "How the Universe Works." The Atlantic. August 1984. 66-93.
ENCYCLOPAEDIA OF CYBERNETICS. Tr. G. Gilbertson. New York and Manchester: Manchester University Press, Barnes and Noble, Inc., 1968. (1964)
FUCHS, WALTER R. Cybernetics for the Modern Mind. Tr. K. Kellner. New York: The MacMillan Co., 1971.
GARDNER, HOWARD. The Mind's New Science: A History of the Cognitive Revolution. New York: Basic Books, Inc., Publishers, 1985.
GARDNER, MARTIN. "Of Crackpots and Clear Thinkers." Review of Dismantling the Universe: The Nature of Scientific Discovery, in Science 84, (March), 110-12.
GLEICK, JAMES. Chaos: Making a New Science. New York: Viking Penguin Inc., 1987.
LE LIONNAIS, FRANCOIS. "Bases and Lines of Force in Cybernetics." Diogenes 9, (1955). 55-81.
POPPER, KARL R. Conjectures and Refutations: The Growth of Scientific Knowledge. New York: Harper Torchbooks, Harper and Row, Publishers, 1965.
PORTER, ARTHUR. Cybernetics Simplified. London: The English Universities Press, Ltd., 1969.
WEAVER, WARREN. "Recent Contributions to the Mathematical Theory of Communication." In Claude E. Shannon and Warren Weaver, The Mathematical Theory of Communication. Urbana: University of Illinois Press, 1949. 94-117.

VI.5 Bibliographical Works

LE BULLETIN BAKHTINE/THE BAKHTIN NEWSLETTER. #1, 1983.
LE BULLETIN BAKHTINE/THE BAKHTIN NEWSLETTER. #2, 1986.
CHERNOV, IGOR. "Brief Biographical and Bibliographical Notes on Leading Formalists." Tr. Ann Shukman. Russian Poetics in Translation 4. 1-12.

EIMERMACHER, KARL, AND SERGE SHISHKOFF. <u>Subject Bibliography of Soviet Semiotics: The Moscow-Tartu School</u>. Ann Arbor: Michigan Slavic Publications, 1977.

———. "Selected Bibliography of Soviet Semiotics." <u>Dispositio</u> I, 3 (1976). 364-370.

KOZHINOV, VLADIMIR, AND SERGEI KONKIN. "Mikhail Mikhailovich Bakhtin: Kratkii ocherk zhizni i deiatel'nosti." In <u>Problemy poètiki i istorii literatury</u>, q.v. 5-19.

SHUKMAN, ANN. "The Moscow-Tartu School: A Bibliography of Works and Comments in English." <u>PTL</u> 3, 1978. 393-401.

"SPISOK PECHATNYKH TRUDOV IU.M. LOTMANA: (MATERIALY K BIBLIOGRAFII)." Comp. L.N. Kiseleva, G.M. Ponomareva, I.A. Chern'. In <u>Finitis Duodecim Lustris</u>, q.v. 20-53.

For Product Safety Concerns and Information please contact our EU representative GPSR@taylorandfrancis.com
Taylor & Francis Verlag GmbH, Kaufingerstraße 24, 80331 München, Germany

www.ingramcontent.com/pod-product-compliance
Lightning Source LLC
Chambersburg PA
CBHW070400240426
43661CB00056B/2484